Analyze and Understand SAP Processes with Knowledge Maps

SAP Process Library:

Analyze and Understand SAP Processes with Knowledge Maps

**Jürgen Röhricht, Thomas Teufel,
Birgit Teufel-Weiss and Peter Willems**

ADDISON-WESLEY

An imprint of Pearson Education

London   Boston   Indianapolis   New York   Mexico City   Toronto   Sydney   Tokyo   Singapore
Hong Kong   Cape Town   New Delhi   Madrid   Paris   Amsterdam   Munich   Milan   Stockholm

PEARSON EDUCATION LIMITED

Head Office:
Edinburgh Gate
Harlow CM20 2JE
Tel: +44 (0)1279 623623
Fax: +44 (0)1279 431059

London Office:
128 Long Acre
London WC2E 9AN
Tel: +44 (0)20 7447 2000
Fax: +44 (0)20 7240 5771

Website: *www.aw.com/cseng/*
www.it-minds.com

First published in Germany in 2000 as *SAP R13-Prozeßanalyze mit Knowledge-Maps*

© Pearson Education 2002

ISBN 0-201-71512-0

British Library Cataloguing in Publication Data
A CIP catalogue record for this book can be obtained from the British Library

Library of Congress Cataloging-in-Publication Data
   [SAP R/3 Prozebanalyse mit Knowledge Maps. English]
SAP process library : analyse and understand SAP processes with knowledge maps /
Jürgen Röhricht, Thomas Teufel, Birgit Teufel-Weiss and Peter Willems.
      p. cm.
   Includes bibliographical references and index.
   ISBN 0-201-71512-0
   1. Computer integrated manufacturing systems. 2. Client/server computing. 3.
   Reengineering (Management) I. Röhricht, Jürgen.

   TS155.63 .S2813 2002
   670'.285--dc21

                                                                         2001056121

10 9 8 7 6 5 4 3 2

Translated by Mirja Nissan, Siedlungstraße 11a, 67378 Zeiskam, Germany and Naomi Wilson, Friedrich-Ebert-
Anlage 47, 69117 Heidelberg, Germany.
Typeset by Mathematical Composition Setters Ltd, Salisbury, Wiltshire.
Printed and bound in Great Britain by Biddles Ltd of Guildford and King's Lynn.

The Publisher's policy is to use paper manufactured from sustainable forests.

D
621·78
SAP

Contents

Foreword

The continuous improvement of knowledge management is an important process in view of the unfortunate fact that our society does not always function as it should. We must all learn to be careful of how we deal with this precious asset, knowledge. Only companies which can implement and direct their organizational knowledge effectively will be successful in the future. This is the message of the knowledge society.

The key for companies to enter the knowledge society is knowledge management. Individual knowledge stored in the minds of employees must be 'gathered' and made accessible to the entire company as organizational knowledge. This is particularly important in high-tech companies; knowledge circulates much faster in the software industry than in traditional markets. We can assume that in our high-tech industry, half of the knowledge we have today will be out of date in only 18 months. Knowledge is a crucial production factor and a scarce and valuable resource that has to be managed with precision and care throughout its life cycle.

This book will explain specific practical ways to speed up business engineering and realize standardized process knowledge management with the help of knowledge maps. It also provides a wide variety of concrete process and organizational knowledge maps of the most important process areas of the SAP system.

The knowledge maps created by the authors use the conventional MindMapping method and apply it to SAP process modules. Each process module contains a structured combination of typical consultant questions for implementing the SAP system, the ASAP method (Q&Adb), SAP documentation, SAP system transactions, process models, and tips and tricks from consultants.

I hope you enjoy reading this book and I am sure that it will help you to deal more efficiently with your knowledge management.

Gerhard Oswald, Member of the Board of Directors of SAP AG, March 1999.

Process management is essential for a company to be successful. Information technology enables the optimization of processes both within and across enterprises. This dramatically changes competition and business structures. Information technology forms the basis of new products and services, new types of customer relations, and management instruments. This development boosts effectiveness and efficiency immensely but can also make processes a great deal more complex. A multitude of business engineers are busy developing structures and processes for the companies of the information age. The cost of training employees to carry out these processes is rocketing.

Business engineering tools are urgently needed to ensure that the enormous investment a company makes in reorganizing its structures and processes will produce the expected benefits; the company will continue to develop and the costs of processes will fall. Companies increasingly see this transformation as an organizational development process.

Business engineering tools help people to understand a company. They make processes, results, and management structures easy to visualize. The descriptions made with business engineering tools give the business engineer or process employee different views – such as the organizational structure, business objectives, or the supply chain strategy. The business engineering tools present information about the company in graphic, tabular, or text form. They combine elements to create a comprehensive picture focussed on specific uses and goals. Computer-aided tools help to edit images and to search for and link information.

The result is business engineering knowledge management. The material it represents is the entire organizational knowledge of a company. The target group includes process employees, management, business engineers, auditors, and financial analysts. Evolving from software engineering, the new discipline of business engineering offers a wide range of tools for developing and implementing a company's knowledge. The authors of this book present a new semi-structured approach based on the knowledge map technique which reflects the thinking processes of the human brain and makes use of hyperlinks to form an integrated network. This approach is an excellent method of structuring, and navigating through, knowledge.

The success of new approaches in business engineering is hard to predict because it depends on a highly complex range of factors. However, the authors' experience and the use of proven concepts show excellent promise. The basic theoretical concepts represent an innovative and pragmatic approach to knowledge management.

Prof. Dr. Hubert Österle, St. Gallen, Switzerland, March 1999.

Preface

The SAP Process Library is a standard reference work for analyzing and describing the basic processes of the SAP product *mySAP.com*, the new SAP internet strategy.

The Process Library comprises the following books:

Book 1. Analyze and Understand SAP Processes with Knowledge Maps

This book forms the basis of the SAP Process Library and is a 'must' for those who want to understand the general methods of process analysis, knowledge management, and working with knowledge maps. The book explains what knowledge maps are, how they were derived from the MindMapping method, and how they can be used to reflect real-life situations. It describes in detail the theoretical background of process analysis within the framework of business engineering and knowledge management. An overview of *mySAP.com* is also included.

Book 2. SAP Processes: Finance and Controlling

A short theoretical introduction gives an overview of the *mySAP.com* product and the basics for working with processes and knowledge maps. The book describes the most important controlling philosophies and procedures, and deals with possible value flows (for different cost objects) through the SAP system. Finally, the financial accounting, and controlling organizational units and processes are explained, from overhead cost controlling and product cost controlling to profitability analysis. These are subsequently visually displayed in the form of EnjoySAP screens.

Book 3. SAP Processes: Planning, Procurement, and Production

A short theoretical introduction gives an overview of the *mySAP.com* product and the basics of working with processes and knowledge maps. The book explains the organizational units and SAP processes of logistics planning, beginning with the processes of demand management (independent requirements) and material requirements planning (independent and dependent requirements). It then describes procurement from purchase orders and goods receipt to invoice verification. Finally, production processes are explained in a logical sequence including, amongst others, production order processing and confirmation processes. Knowledge maps and EnjoySAP screens are used as visual aids.

Book 4. SAP Processes: Sales and Distribution, and Customer Service

A short theoretical introduction gives an overview of the *mySAP.com* product and the basics for working with processes and knowledge maps. The book explains the wide range of sales and distribution processes from quotation processing to billing. In the customer service section, it describes all the processes from notification processing to order settlement with the help of EnjoySAP. Knowledge maps are used to explain organizational units.

An important feature of *mySAP.com* is the business scenarios which show a process-oriented view of the *mySAP.com* components. These are the standard SAP products such as the SAP system (R/3), the Advanced Planner and Optimizer, the Business Information Warehouse, Business-to-Business Procurement, etc. All these separate software solutions are part of the overall concept of *mySAP.com*. The core functionality, however, will remain the same. The SAP system in particular retains its importance because, as a back-end system, it integrates central processes such as financial accounting, logistics, and human resources. With the new components, these integrated internal processes will be based on cooperation and lead to collaborative process integration across enterprises. The first book of this SAP Process Library deals primarily with structured process analysis within the framework of business engineering and organizational knowledge management. This method can be applied to the complete *mySAP.com* product. Books 2, 3, and 4 discuss in detail the analysis of the process flows in the *mySAP.com* SAP back-end system and provide the knowledge required in the form of knowledge maps.

The MindMapping method and the EnjoySAP user interface have been used to enable structured and simple explanations of these SAP processes. Specific ways are also shown for expanding the knowledge gained within the framework of business engineering to achieve process-oriented knowledge management. The authors also include over 200 knowledge maps in the complete Process Library. They combine general documentation, questions about process analysis, tips and tricks, and consultant experience. This enables faster process analysis and more independence for the customer. The books in this series are interconnected but each one can also be useful on its own.

Process analysis is a central task in the implementation of business software. We, the authors, have jointly dealt with this topic in SAP implementation projects during our long experience as SAP consultants. The experience gained led us to rethink the process analysis procedure. New potential in the area of knowledge management directed us to a fresh approach. In particular the reference-based implementation of the SAP system calls for software knowledge, and other knowledge from both external and internal project team members, to be used more productively. Organizational knowledge within a company is considered as an additional production factor today. It is all the more important, therefore, that knowledge management be put to good use during SAP implementation.

This series of books is intended for the following groups:

- decision makers in different departments

- project managers

- process owners

- management consultants, particularly SAP consultants

- SAP project teams

- SAP users

- students

- anyone interested in knowing more about the SAP system.

Our roles as management consultants and our work with the target groups listed above have shown us again and again that, despite the high level of complexity shown by integrated processes, a simple form of representation must be found. The idea of using the well-known MindMapping method developed by Tony Buzan to describe standard business software inspired us to write this Process Library.

Our aims were to:

- explain the SAP back-end system in simple terms,

- provide exclusive consultant expertise for business engineering,

- show innovative ways to structure knowledge management.

We refer to this comprehensive SAP knowledge, represented using the MindMapping method, as knowledge maps. This is a pragmatic and visual method of presentation and is used to build up a company's knowledge pool during SAP implementation.

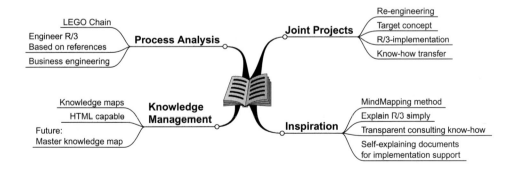

A whole range of information becomes evident when structured in a knowledge map, and we have tried to include our consultant experience in the form of notes (see light bulbs on the branches of the knowledge maps [section 4.2.4 of this book]). Before we discuss the process area of knowledge maps in the second part of the book, the reader can learn about the theory behind process analysis. In Chapter 5 we describe the procedure behind a process analysis workshop. Every project is different of course, and the process analysis steps described here should be seen as suggestions. We welcome your feedback and invite you to visit us on the internet at www.knowledge-map.de. Each of the process knowledge maps included in the series of books is shown as a LEGO brick. This is another method of simplifying the visual display of business processes. They can be joined together as LEGO chains. In *Sophie's World*, Jostein Gaarder refers to LEGO as "the greatest toy in the world." We decided to use this method for business (re)engineering and have been given permission by LEGO GmbH to use this graphic symbol.

Acknowledgements

For their support in putting together this series we would like to thank our colleagues Hans-Peter Thomas, Ümit Özdurmus, Dzenita Medusalec, Maren Vaterrodt (for the LEGO bricks design), Melanie Machold (graphics), and Susanne Lencinas (marketing). Our thanks also go to Anja Holzwarth and Christian Schneider from Addison-Wesley for editing this book. For his support throughout the entire project, we would like to express our sincere appreciation to Christian Rauscher, manager of Addison-Wesley. Thanks also to Miho Birimisa and Robert Viehmann of ASAP, as well as to Michael Jetter for supplying the *MindManager* tool, and to Michael Louis for his work on the CD-ROM that accompanies the series. For marketing support, we would like to thank Maithri Samaradivakara of Hardlight Multimedia, London.

For their support in creating and reviewing the knowledge maps, we give special thanks to our consultant colleagues Markus Hauser (Controlling), Ralf Brechter (Controlling), Angela Wahl-Knoblauch (Controlling), Mathias Weber (Sales and Distribution), Liane Richter (Sales and Distribution), Jörg Minge (Service Management), Helmut Bartsch (Procurement, Production), Dragan Grujic (Production), and Arvind Prasad (Production).

As promoters, we would like to thank our friends Mr. Gerhard Oswald, member of the Board of Directors of SAP AG; Prof. Dr. Hubert Oesterle, IWI-HSG University of St. Gallen; and Prof. Dr. Walter Brenner, Economics and Informatics, University Gesamthochschule Essen.

For her contribution to the area of financial accounting (Book 2), very special thanks goes to Birgit Teufel-Weiss. Our thanks also go to Dr. Christiane Prange for the inspiring discussions about process-oriented knowledge management. We would also like to give a special mention to Martin Boll, Managing Director of Steeb Anwendungssysteme GmbH, for his contribution to the evaluation and implementation tests.

Thomas Teufel, Jürgen Röhricht, and Peter Willems,
Walldorf, March, 1999.

This Process Library is dedicated to our parents:
Tina
Eva
Lalanthi
Benjamin

1 Motivation

1.1 Current issues in the life cycle of an R/3 system

As part of the implementation and operation of the R/3 system, a whole range of issues, particularly management concepts, comes to the fore. Depending on the enterprise goals and what is expected of a productive R/3 system, these factors can have an essential role in the design of the system and its effects on the enterprise. The most important of these issues are introduced here. Please refer to the relevant literature for more detailed information.

1.1.1 Business process re-engineering

The buzzword and most widely discussed management concept in the business world of the nineties has been business (process) re-engineering (BPR). This term refers to the complete redesigning of business processes and thus the reorganization of an enterprise. The aim of this concept is to achieve a lasting increase in the value and growth of the enterprise. The emphasis is placed on the complete reorganization of processes, as if the enterprise were to be founded from scratch all over again. Hammer and Champy, in particular, support this approach: "Business re-engineering isn't about fixing anything. Business re-engineering means starting all over, starting from scratch" (Hammer and Champy, p. 2).

Davenport's approach, *Process Innovation*, is based on a similar concept, moving away from gradual improvement within the framework of the continuous improvement process towards the " … fundamental redesign of work" (Davenport, 1993, p. 1). The focus of these concepts is not on functions, industries, or series of products, but on processes. Ever since Adam Smith had the idea of dividing work into the smallest possible workable units to achieve the highest possible level of efficiency, almost every enterprise has been structured based on this concept – regardless of whether we look at production or administration tasks. In our post-industrial age, these fragmented tasks now have to be brought together again to form a coherent process. This approach of fundamental rethinking and radical redesigning of processes aims to achieve substantial improvement and is based on four keywords (Hammer and Champy, p. 32):

- *Fundamental:* Fundamental questions need to be raised such as: "Why are we doing what we are doing?"; "Why are we doing it in the way we are doing it?"

- *Radical:* Radical redesign means getting down to the roots and not just making superficial improvements. It means beginning from scratch all over again, with no regard for what already exists.

- *Drastic:* The overall aim of the approach is to achieve drastic improvements; to make quantum leaps, not merely gradual improvements, with regard to cost, quality, and time.

- *Processes:* As the name suggests, BPR is about processes and not individual functions, tasks, roles, structures, etc. In Smith's approach of breaking work down into small individual parts, the focus shifts away from the total process to which these tasks and activities belong. The business process is defined as a series of activities, for which different incoming bits of information, materials, or other aids are required, and which create a value for the customer.

Most well-known authors regard data processing in BPR purely as an **enabler** (Hammer and Champy, p. 83), which means that re-engineering occurs with absolutely no consideration of available software programs. Business processes determined in this way can only be realized, if at all, with complicated workaround solutions within the implementation of an enterprise resource planning (ERP) system. This causes unnecessary extra work (Servatius, 1998, p. 326). Thome and Hufgard express this in a more radical way: " ... the optimization we aim at by means of BPR does not exist" (Thome and Hufgard, p. 61).

The truth is that most enterprises find themselves in a situation in which BPR is first mentioned when new ERP software is implemented. Therefore, an approach is generally favored today which combines business re-engineering with the implementation of ERP software. The R/3 system particularly, due to its consequent process orientation, forces the enterprise to think in terms of processes. In this regard R/3 software may also be described as an **enabler**, but it plays a much more important role in business re-engineering than in the approaches described by Hammer and Champy or Davenport. The R/3 system can actually be seen as a **driver** of re-engineering and is thus closer to the Business Process Improvement approach, suggested by Harrington, which focuses more on the optimization of business processes than on creating something new. "Business Process Improvement ... will aid you in simplifying and streamlining your operations" (Harrington, p. 20). Other, mostly European, authors also tend to advocate the evolutionary process of change combined with organizational learning processes and the rather more cautious change or optimization process as its result (Servatius, 1994). Even Hammer eventually revised the approach he so dogmatically held with regard to its radicalism for practical reasons, "I have now realized that I was wrong then. Radical change is not the most important aspect of business re-engineering ... the keyword in the definition is 'process' ... " (Hammer, 1996, p. 12). Where BPR is mentioned in the following, it refers to the focus on processes and their optimization within the field of business engineering.

1.1.2   Business engineering

The terms and theories behind business engineering and BPR (see Chapter 1.1.1) cannot be considered separately; in fact they are directly linked. They ultimately handle the same task – redesigning the organization and processes of an enterprise – and there are only a few small differences. The main difference between the Hammer/Champy and the Davenport approaches of BPR and the business engineering approach supported by Österle is most obvious in the role assigned to information technology. The first authors mentioned see the role of information technology (as described in Chapter 1.1.1) purely as a means to an end, as an **enabler** of BPR, " ... information technology is part of a re-engineering effort, an essential enabler ... but, ... merely throwing computers at an existing business problem does not cause it to be re-engineered" (Hammer and Champy, p. 83). Österle, on the other hand, sees the transformation of the industrial society into an information society and the potential of information technology which goes along with it, fundamentally enabling new business solutions, services, and more efficient internal and external processes, as the basis of business (re)engineering: "Business (re)engineering ... is based on the evolution of the information society" (Österle, p. 7, p. 14). He claims that information technology (IT) creates the potential essential for optimization within the framework of a revolution or evolution, and that business (re)engineering uses it.

Here again, the process is the key linking a series of tasks which may be distributed across a number of organizational units, consuming input and producing output, and

Figure 1.1.2-1:   *Process development/analysis as a link between strategy and IS development*
(Österle, p. 21)

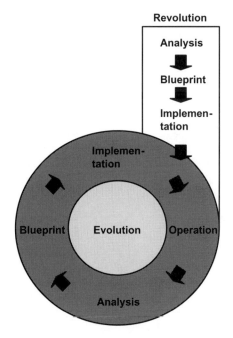

Figure 1.1.2-2:   *Revolution and evolution business engineering*
(Österle, p. 21)

which is supported by IT applications. Business engineering only has an effect by linking strategy development and information system development through process development or process analysis if a process clearly defines a business strategy and combines it with the information system (Figure 1.1.2-1).

Within the framework of business (re)engineering, the controversial discussion often arises as to whether this term refers to one-time radical changes to business (i.e. revolution) as Davenport and Hammer/Champy claim, or to the step-by-step development and optimization of what already exists (i.e. evolution) as maintained by Harrington. Österle sees business engineering as a combination of both approaches because, generally, a project is the starting point (revolution) making fundamental change possible which is then followed by ongoing further development and gradual improvement (evolution) (Figure 1.1.2-2). For more information on the subject of revolution, refer to the conclusions drawn at the end of Chapter 1.1.1.

If business engineering is to fulfil these tasks and requirements, decisions made in its course must affect all levels of the enterprise – business strategy, processes, and the information system (Figure 1.1.2-3).

1.1.3   Process-oriented implementation

There are many reasons for implementing R/3 software in an enterprise and these are usually documented in the project charter. The aim of implementation is to realize these

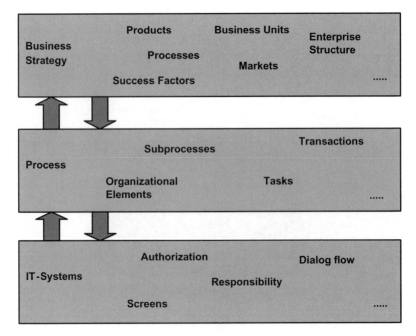

Figure 1.1.2-3:   Levels of business engineering
(Österle, p. 21)

goals in the best possible way. A range of procedure models, developed specifically for general project management, serves this purpose. The AcceleratedSAP (ASAP) concept, which is now the standard procedure of SAP and consulting partners for implementing R/3 and which replaces or complements the previous procedure model, is discussed in Chapter 3.3. All procedures aim to break down the total implementation process into small, manageable (and thus easier to handle) steps or phases, which additionally enable milestone monitoring. Regardless of which general project management method is preferred, there are two fundamentally different concepts for adapting the enterprise to the R/3 system:

- function-oriented

- process-oriented.

In order to explain both concepts, it is first necessary to take a brief look at the structure of the R/3 system. It is characterized by the extensive range of business services it offers, and its applications are divided up according to functions within the enterprise (for instance, controlling, financial accounting, human resources, materials management, production planning and controlling, etc). At the same time, there is a high level of integration between them (Buck-Emden and Galimow, pp. 109). This vertical structure of the applications is linked by horizontal and integrated processes.

The **functional procedure** for the implementation of the R/3 system proceeds in line with the structures which already exist within the enterprise. Most enterprises today are function-oriented (Wöhe, p. 178), that is split up into functions such as human resources, development, materials management, marketing/sales, and remain that way after the implementation of R/3. The implementation project is therefore divided into corresponding functions (Figure 1.1.3-1). However, this procedure does not use the huge potential of the R/3 system to support processes throughout the enterprise. As in Smith's division of labour, only small sub-units or functions are implemented and optimized,

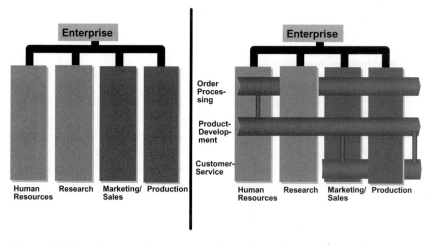

Figure 1.1.3-1:   Functional vs. process-oriented procedure in R/3 implementation
SAP AG

while the full picture of the process as a whole is lost. For these reasons, and the demand for business (re)engineering linked to the implementation of the R/3 system, the **process-oriented implementation strategy** is becoming more and more popular.

For this, R/3 implementation is linked to the core process across individual applications. This means that all process modules or functions of the individual applications required for the core process are implemented. This procedure meets the demand, from a process and organizational point of view, for ongoing and complete support and optimization of business processes. The implementation process is thus organized in a process-oriented way (Figure 1.1.3-1) and is usually supported by a **matrix project organization** consisting of a process-oriented and a functional dimension. Another important (side) effect of this concept is that time-consuming interface programming can be avoided.

In addition, the process-oriented implementation strategy can be limited to certain core processes, or at least to functionality which is absolutely necessary in the first step. This avoids problems stemming from the complexity of the solution, such as the lack of internal or external resources, or expensive adaptation and coordination.

1.1.4   Continuous (system) engineering

Unlike the – at least partially – revolutionary procedure of BPR, continuous system engineering (CSE) considers the continuous adaptation of business information processing and organization with regard to processes and organizational structures as the key to success (Thome and Hufgard, p. 78). The reason behind this approach is that today an enterprise has to adapt to constantly changing market requirements to remain competitive. This is even more true in the light of increasingly shorter cycles to improve existing products and to develop new information processing technologies. All these factors have the effect that nothing is more constant in today's world than change. This change also affects the organizational processes of an enterprise. Kommo Paavola, project manager of R/3 implementation at Nokia, stresses this:

> "We had to implement quickly. Had we spent a long time creating and redesigning processes to start with, the framework conditions would have changed drastically again by the time of R/3 implementation, and our work [the re-engineering] would have been in vain." (IWI-HSG).

CSE is based on the assumption that the challenges listed above may only be met by a continuous adaptation process (Thome and Hufgard, p. 78).

In the same way as business (re)engineering, CSE aims to simplify the business processes happening within an enterprise, and also to ensure ongoing adaptation to changing framework conditions. An essential factor is the integration of business management in the form of organizational requirements and information technology. Here, the emphasis is more on an evolutionary than a revolutionary procedure. The main goal is to achieve a functioning information system in the shortest possible time, which can then be optimized step by step when using CSE.

A central component of CSE is the **software library**. This is a repository of software modules which automatically supports business processes and functionality primarily within the enterprise. It is important to identify the prevailing business disciplines to be supported by the software. The relevant library components must then be selected and assigned to ensure an integrated and functioning information system. To achieve this, the software library must, as far as possible, provide all the software solutions needed for the changes to the enterprise organization. To enable navigation in the software library within the framework of a business nomenclature, a navigation requirement system must adopt the formulated goals, select the corresponding software components, and define the relevant settings.

CSE can realistically be achieved only if both of the following basic requirements are met:

- organizational change should not trigger any expensive and time-consuming software development or modification of standard application software;

- the description of organizational requirements must be in a form which is quickly applicable to the software implementation process.

Thome and Hufgard point out that the business flow realized in this way is similar to improvements achieved with BPR. Classifying the process flows eases the identification and definition of the main processes for supporting essential enterprise activities. Furthermore, the authors point out that the process structures implemented in enterprises which use a standard software library are not the same in all enterprises. Rather, the wide range of configuration options offered by the software library enables an enterprise-specific layout of the process organization and structure. According to Thome and Hufgard, CSE offers the following advantages compared to normal software development procedures, and also BPR (Thome and Hufgard, p. 84).

- The information system is up and running after a short adaptation and installation phase and is therefore able to support business procedures quickly.

- The software library ensures that the enterprise is able to change or add to existing processes at any time.

- There is a consistent, and at all times up-to-date, description of the latest settings concerning the level of IT, i.e. which processes and organizational structures are represented in what form within the information system – this is a good basis for further consideration of the enterprise procedure.

1.1.5   Change management

Organizational change management is a comprehensive term covering a wide range of aspects. In the last few years, it has been established as a discipline of general management. Change management can be broadly described as a strategy for the management of continuous or rapid change, and the changes connected with it in relation to the enterprise as a whole (Hammer and Champy, p. 99). It refers, therefore, to the enterprise as a changing object both internally and externally. However, change management is not an entirely new management strategy; it has been known for some time in the form of classical **organizational development**. The object of organizational development as a strategy for planned and systematic change is to manage the development by influencing the organizational structure, enterprise culture, and individual behavior, with as much participation as possible by the employees concerned (Gabler Wirtschaftslexikon, p. 751). The organizational development strategy described here is characterized by socio-psychological approaches and procedures, which constituted the dominant paradigm of change management over a period of several years. Recently, this paradigm has been joined by others such as radical business transformation, business (re)engineering, continuous engineering, and the Kaizen process (Reiß, 1997, p. 6). Change management is essential, particularly in today's rapidly changing world. Change can be either endogenous (change necessary as a result of internal requirements) or exogenous (changing external conditions relating to the enterprise). The following could make change necessary (Tushman and O'Reilly, p. 30; Krebsbach-Gnath, 1992, p. 8; Reiß, 1998, p. 264):

- new technologies

- change in political climate

- increasing competition

- change in social values

- legal requirements

- demographic changes

- new economic situations (e.g. changes in the sales and procurement, equity, and human resource markets).

The change requirements triggered by these factors could be continuous or discontinuous. The implementation of process-oriented and integrated R/3 standard software, and with it business (re)engineering, represents a discontinuous type of change. The corresponding changes to the technical and social or organizational environment or structure due to changing processes (process organization) must be accompanied by extensive change management. "Process innovation [and BPR] requires large-scale organizational change" (Davenport, 1993, p. 167). However, these changes, and therefore change management tasks, are not completed with the realization of the actual implementation project. As the R/3 system may be considered not only as an **enabler** (Chapter 1.1.1 and 1.1.2) but also as a driver of continuous business engineering, changes in this phase must be supported by change management. This management of change, however, belongs to the continuous change category. In both cases the social (organizational) and the technical change in the sense of change management must be dealt with and carried out together (Davenport, 1993, p. 112). The concrete change management tasks are:

- *Management participation*
  As is the case with any far-reaching project, the implementation of the R/3 system and the business engineering connected with it, as well as the resulting changes, requires the active participation and a certain level of prioritization and identification from (top)

management. In particular, those responsible for the successful execution of the R/3 project should be included in performing change management tasks.

- *Communication*
  Within the framework of an extensive two-way communication strategy, it is important to define **what** is to be communicated, depending on the target group requirements, and then **how** communication should take place. For a project to be accepted and become successful it is vital that there is early, consistent, and ongoing dissemination of the vision and aims of the measures taken (i.e. the R/3 implementation provoking the change).

- *Structure and understanding of roles*
  Business (re)engineering particularly, triggered by the implementation of R/3, will lead to changes in organizational structure and, as a result, the fields of activity of employees. Even if the aim is not to downsize, new fields of activity will arise while others are abolished or changed considerably. The willingness and ability of employees have to be evaluated in preparation for these changes. The structure and content must be examined in addition to the skills needed for the roles, i.e. the fields of activity up to now. These roles will then have to be reconciled with the changed or new roles which have already been defined.

- *Training*
  Another important part of change management is the early training of employees. After all, employees are an enterprise's most important asset and largely determine the success of the enterprise. Role assignment must be analyzed to determine **what** training is necessary and **how** it should be carried out.

- *Management practices*
  The new business process structure, or new process flows, must also be reflected in the management structure. It is therefore necessary to introduce "process owners" (Striening, 1988, p. 40) who, within the framework of a matrix organization, are solely, or in addition to their regular activities, responsible for the effectiveness and efficiency of a business process as a whole.

- *Performance monitoring*
  It is also important for change management to evaluate whether goals set before implementing the project or measures have been achieved. In order to do so, there has to be a direct link between the employees' fields of activity and payment or incentives, and the perception and appreciation of these activities. It is a good idea to use key performance indicators (KPI) here, as in other areas of the enterprise. For instance, the KPIs **inventory** or **sales** could be used for the process team responsible for sales and production planning.

Many enterprises have employees known as **change agents**, specially trained for the tasks of change management (Reiß, 1998, p. 268). From the description above, it is apparent that the elements training and learning in particular are important for continuous change. This calls for an enterprise which is able to learn, as does knowledge management (see Chapter 1.1.6). **Organizational learning** is therefore essential to the success of change management (Krebsbach-Gnath, 1992, p. 7).

1.1.6   Knowledge management

In addition to a chief financial officer and chief executive officer, does your enterprise already have a **chief knowledge officer** (Davenport, 1996), responsible for the management of the resource **knowledge**, and have you considered **return on knowledge** (ROK)? This question, regardless of your answer, shows the importance that the topic of knowledge management has assumed recently.

Before expanding on this, let us look first at what we generally understand as **knowledge**. Kant sees it as not only an objective but also a subjective adequate notion of reality. We differentiate between **individual knowledge** (Albrecht, p. 34) and **organizational knowledge** (Schüppel, p. 83). Individual knowledge is described as the processing of information by an individual's consciousness. It affects the actions of the individual and is thus closely connected to the context of that person. If we talk about organizational knowledge, on the other hand, we are referring to the knowledge of an organization, in this case that of an enterprise. However, we have to break it down even further because organizational knowledge can be either explicit or implicit. **Explicit knowledge** has a concrete form and is clearly documented in the organization. **Implicit knowledge**, on the other hand, is in the heads of individual employees and is not accessible to all other employees in an enterprise. Both forms of organizational knowledge can be broken down into further categories, such as the knowledge of products (product designs, recipes, etc), patents (patent registrations, descriptions), customers (customer databases), processes (task instructions, process descriptions, job descriptions), etc. (Figure 1.1.6-1).

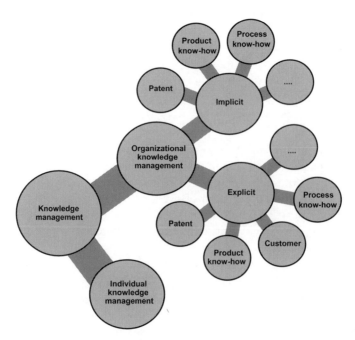

Figure 1.1.6-1:   Components of knowledge management

Now that we have looked at the basic terms of knowledge management, let us return to what we were discussing at the beginning of this chapter – the increasing importance of knowledge management for an enterprise in today's business environment. In an age in which knowledge as a resource represents an increasingly important component for the successful growth and value of an enterprise (Servatius, 1998, p. 324), the use of this commodity is ever more important. To meet this challenge, it is essential to secure targetted development, monitoring and improvement of strategies, processes, organizational structures, and technologies for processing knowledge within the enterprise (Probst et al.). This task is made more difficult by the fact that the half-life of knowledge is decreasing rapidly:

> "The drastic increase of knowledge available to humankind since the middle of the 20th century defies all comparison. The time necessary to double this knowledge has shrunk from formerly one hundred years to only six years." (Warnecke, p. 97, Figure 1.1.6-2).

This shows how knowledge is becoming an ever more decisive competitive production factor (Neumann et al., p. 194). Cohen backs up this statement:

> "In a complex, changing world, understanding is at a premium. Companies need to manage their knowledge assets well, in part because knowledge has become their most important 'product'." (Cohen et al., p. 5).

If we consider the historical economic production factors of work, land, and capital (Baßeler et al., p. 42), knowledge is already seen today as the fourth production factor (Neumann et al., p. 195). Even though the population and enterprises in developed

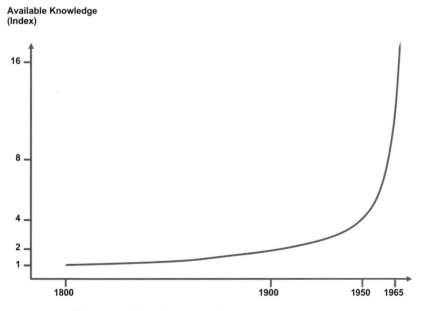

Figure 1.1.6-2:   Knowledge development in recent years
Warnecke, p. 97

countries have long been aware that **knowledge** is the key (Drucker, p. 9), this whole development announces the changeover from an industrial to a knowledge society (Figure 1.1.6-3; Bell; Gibbons et al.).

It appears that a knowledge management wave is following the re-engineering wave of the nineties (Davenport, 1999). However, the management of knowledge alone is not enough to make knowledge management a competitive factor. Rather, this goal is achieved by the efficient organization and application of acquiring and using knowledge. This task, which is influenced particularly by **soft components** (Neumann et al., p. 194), i.e. the willingness of the enterprise and its individuals to learn, is often referred to as organizational learning and can no longer be excluded from relevant up-to-date management literature. The development leading to this learning organization (Nachreiner, p. 57) is accompanied by recognition and development of the employees' potential and its initial and ongoing training (Antal, p. 85).

Knowledge management and organizational learning are thus closely linked and mutually dependent. Both management concepts have one goal: to stay or become successful in the market (Krebsbach-Gnath, 1992, p. 14; Servatius, p. 328). A picture cited by Benjamin Britten illustrates this point: "Learning is like rowing against the current – as soon as you stop, you will drift backwards."

However, knowledge management must be considered not only for monetary reasons but also for business and existential reasons. The enterprise must protect itself from the loss of knowledge which, in turn, has an effect on the financial situation of the enterprise. Imagine what would happen if, for example, the entire research and development group, or the whole organization department, were to leave the company suddenly. This would

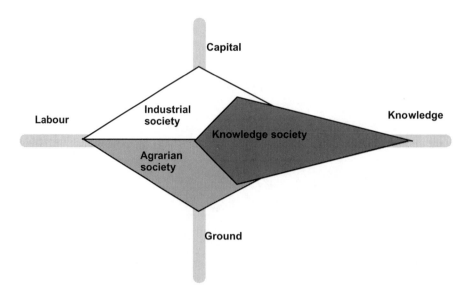

Figure 1.1.6-3:   Production factors in changing times: from the agricultural society to the knowledge society
(Neumann et al., p. 195)

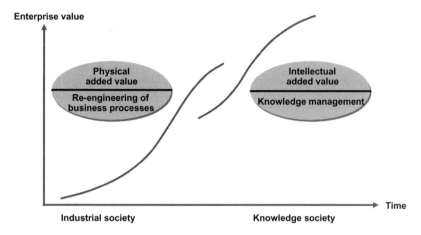

Figure 1.1.6-4:   From re-engineering to knowledge management
Servatius, 1998, p. 324

almost certainly mean the economic end of the enterprise. This example may be slightly exaggerated, but it goes to show that the loss of each employee incurs a loss of knowledge (Spek and de Hoog). This problem can be at least partially solved by consistent knowledge management. It becomes evident that knowledge management not only serves to protect against the loss of an enterprise's knowledge but is also vital for the development of an intellectual surplus which can be converted to market success.

What is the connection between knowledge management and business (re)engineering, and hence process analysis, as well as the implementation and operation of R/3 software?

Knowledge management can be considered as an extension of business re-engineering, as both concepts aim for a long-lasting increase in the value of the enterprise. The goal of re-engineering is to combat Taylorism in the physical creation of surplus value, while knowledge management is aimed at creating intellectual surplus value (Figure 1.1.6-4).

For information on how to realize the organizational knowledge management of process knowledge within the framework of the life cycle of the R/3 project, see Chapter 6.

1.1.7   Total cost of ownership

Many enterprises consider information technology and related components purely as cost factors, while others consider it an elementary competitive factor. One thing is sure, the aim of every enterprise is to maximize its competitiveness. The IT department has a decisive part to play in this, both now and even more so in the future. Competitiveness is very much affected by the costs within the enterprise in addition to the turnover; it is also affected by the benefit brought by capital investment. Generally, but particularly in IT, the question often arises, "how are the costs and benefits of IT evaluated?" This was often estimated only roughly in the past (Groh and Fähnrich). However, this is no longer good enough, and the total cost of ownership (TCO) method was developed and first coined by the Gartner Group (Wolf and Holm, p. 19). This is a procedure for identifying the overall costs of an information system over a long period of time, generally over its entire life cycle (Figure 1.1.7-1).

What has to be considered in relation to an ERP system, such as R/3, are the total or overall costs for purchase, licenses, hardware, IT infrastructure, implementation, use, maintenance, management, and end users, such as training, internal helpdesk, etc. (Kidler, p. 20).

TCO is not an entirely new procedure. In other areas, for instance the manufacturing industry, it has long been postulated that all direct and indirect operating and management cost factors must be included in the overall cost of a complex, technical, organizational system over and above investment costs. However, "TCO" is not always TCO as we can distinguish different TCO objectives (Bullinger et al., p. 15).

- TCO investigations which aim to determine a status quo and, from the results, form concrete recommendations on how to improve the IT structure. The result is a structured cost analysis with identification of the essential cost drivers.

- Evaluation of alternatives on how to act (e.g. decision for or against using an ERP system, or the upgrade of a system, the selection of a platform, etc.) which requires a detailed cost/benefit analysis. The results of the evaluation are several different scenarios which must be compared. The decision is then made for variant X, or against variants Y and Z, or to do nothing at all (Kidler, p. 20).

- Evaluation of products or concepts which are examined for the effect of TCO in different application scenarios. From test environments, several characteristics can be evaluated which enable assumptions to be made about TCO-relevant aspects.

- Formulation of customer-specific services and products which adapt the procedure and methods to fit a concrete application framework and are designed for business use by the customer, such as the lowest cost of ownership initiative created by SAP (Kidler, p. 22).

Groh and Fähnrich describe an adaptive procedure for executing the TCO. A rough analysis is carried out as a first step using a standard cost model with available material which enables preliminary results. This first analysis provides essential information about the areas requiring further examination. In the second step a specific cost model is used for the areas highlighted for further examination in the first step. To this end, additional data is collected from questionnaires, workshops, and surveys or other information sources. The additional effort involved is rewarded with more precise results, particularly regarding the sensitive points of each object examined. There are also other procedure

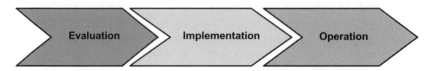

Figure 1.1.7-1:   Main phases of the R/3 life cycle

models and tools: e.g. Co$tmark by Strategy Partners, TCO-Wizard or Caseview, both by HMC, or TCO Manager by Gartner Group.

How can TCO help? In portraying the potential benefits described, the observation of TCO was limited to ERP software, such as the R/3 system:

- in determining the cost of an integrated solution,

- and thus transparency of costs which occur in connection with the ERP system,

- in providing a clearer overview of the multi-layered IT infrastructure,

- by comparing effort and benefits, conclusions can be drawn about the efficiency of the solution within the framework of a cost/benefit balance.

TCO can, for instance, be used as a benchmark for TCO-based SAP R/3 business management, which can help to provide answers to questions such as (Hüsken, p. 29):

- how much demand is there for SAP services, now and in the future?

- which SAP services are to be provided internally and which externally, e.g. outsourcing, suppliers?

- what information processing resources and infrastructure are necessary?

- what is the demand for human resources and what qualifications do employees need?

- which SAP services are to be provided centrally and which decentrally?

- which activity allocation modalities of data processing (DP) services must be conformed with?

- what is the overall cost efficiency that results from DP concept variants if TCO is taken into consideration?

- what kind of organizational concept evolves?

The following formula, where *TCAmax* = total competitive advantage and *TBPmax* = total business payback (Kidler, p. 22), can be used to achieve the objective of maximizing competitiveness, using IT and TCO to evaluate cost/benefit:

$$TCA_{max} = TBP_{max} - TCO_{min}$$

However, a certain level of doubt has arisen about the reliability of TCO. Some of the points criticized are listed at the end of the next section where TCO is compared with return on investment (ROI).

1.1.8 Return on investment

The ROI approach, related to the information processing (IP) investment, developed from the same motives as TCO – to carry out a cost/benefit comparison of investment in corporate electronic data processing (EDP) (Chapter 1.1.7). In the classical pre-investment analysis, the ROI represents a monetary evaluation method which is based on the assumption that revenue is returned on invested capital. Unlike TCO, profitability (i.e. the benefit of investment) plays a more important role. The following formula is generally used to calculate ROI (Wöhe, p. 775):

$$ROI = \frac{profit}{turnover} \times \frac{turnover}{equity} \times 100$$

As the formula shows, ROI has three main factors: profit, turnover, and capital. The ROI increases if the invested capital sinks with turnover and profits static, or if turnover increases with static profit margins. If ROI is used to refer to the implementation and operation of the R/3 system, we perceive that it is a very large and important investment for the viable economic existence of the company. If such an investment is made, then it must be for carefully considered business reasons. The management of the investing enterprise will then, depending on the reasons for the investment, expect a corresponding business payback from the investment. This may include qualitative factors (e.g. a higher level of working motivation) or quantitative factors (e.g. lower costs, increase in value and profitability). Selected strategic and concrete examples of such expected business benefits, and thus of ROI, are:

- reduced stock level

- lower procurement time or costs

- personnel reduction, e.g. in financial accounting

- reduced lead times

- reduced IT costs

- shorter sales order processing times

- higher level of flexibility and efficiency in a constantly changing competitive environment

- improved customer service, and thus a higher level of customer satisfaction

- better access to information in the DP system

- ability to adapt to new and rapid growth in a dynamic market.

Whether we aim for reduced costs or increased profitability, the main goal is to achieve the highest possible ROI. If, for instance, stock levels are reduced by 10 percent using the R/3 system over an implementation time span of one year, this may amount to a cost reduction of $1 million, which can be determined by ROI (higher profits). If, however, a reduction of 20 per cent is achieved, the ROI is naturally even higher. Another important factor is not just the level of ROI but also the time at which ROI is realized, i.e. the sooner the enterprise can profit from the business benefits of an investment, and the sooner this yields a ROI, the better. In the example above, this means that if the R/3 system was implemented in just six months, the ROI would have been achieved six months earlier.

In an enterprise, it is not easy to determine whether or not to make an investment. It has to make sense from a business perspective because the investment in the R/3 system, for instance, and the business engineering involved in its implementation is costly and time-consuming. **Business cases**, which are often also established in the project charter, are generally created in support of the argument. The business case, presented here using the example of R/3 implementation, can have several dimensions.

- *Strategic:* identification of the general business goals and strategies which can be achieved with R/3 implementation.

- *Operational:* identification and quantification of the potential for optimizing business processes as a result of business engineering and R/3 integration.

- *Technical:* identification of how the technical environment (client/server) offered by R/3 supports the overall business strategy with regard to the technological environment of the enterprise in view of IT costs and performance.

- *Financial:* determination and quantification of costs and benefits or profitability of an investment.

The ROI is then compared to the business case, particularly from a financial perspective, and examined as to whether the goal set before making the investment has been achieved. **Benchmarks** are often used for this, reflecting the best business practice which is predominant in the industry.

ROI is often preferred to TCO to evaluate an investment in IT. One reason for this could be that the TCO program often considers only the costs, which can lead to the wrong conclusions. On the one hand, the purely cost-related approach could result in a false strategy aimed only at minimizing costs, which is inconsistent with the benefits achievable by investment. On the other hand, the purely cost-related approach tends to generalize the status quo, as every investment incurs costs at the beginning, but also helps to minimize other costs in the future (Riepl, p. 10). Another criticism of TCO as the only key figure is that it is open to considerable theoretical and practical interpretation and does not have a high statement value. Another aspect mentioned, particularly, is the fact that TCO is industry-specific and does not consider the overall productivity of a job, as is possible with ROI analysis (Wolf and Holm, p. 22).

1.1.9 Business processes on the internet

"This is the vision of the digital future: if there is an increased demand for woolen pullovers in Benetton shops, a farmer in New Zealand receives an order via the web to shear his sheep" (Information Week, p. 10). Even though this scenario is likely to be viewed as material for science fiction for the next few years, e-commerce has already changed the face of business processes within enterprises and value chains beyond the boundaries of individual enterprises. Producers and suppliers are moving closer together and accelerating processes. The world-wide presence of the internet is breaking down the walls between companies and encouraging the tendency to globalize.

More and more enterprises are joining forces to organize inter-enterprise business processes by setting up a universal supply chain (Figure 1.1.9-1). This integrated supply chain forms an end-to-end process, from the procurement of raw materials (shearing the sheep), via increasingly specialized producers and distribution systems to the end user, the sale to consumers in the Benetton store. At the same time globalization is intensifying,

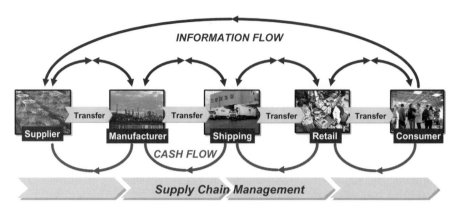

Figure 1.1.9-1:   Intercompany logistics chain
Perez et al., p. 18

and this requires us to act quickly if we do not want to miss out. IT dealing with intercompany business processes and the efficiency of physical logistics systems are becoming increasingly important competitive factors. The use of the internet for business processes between independent companies, connected only by IT and sharing the same business models, opens up a new dimension. Business management is also entering new waters by abandoning its previous focus, centered on one enterprise, and adopting a new intercompany perspective. In a very short period of time, the new internet technology has produced a number of business scenarios with a range of multimedia which reaches new users – anonymous end users and sporadic information users in a company (Perez et al., p. 18).

Electronic business-to-business (B2B) commerce has become a major international project. Industrial goods and services worth $43 billion were sold through the internet in 1998. According to Forrester Research, this total will have increased to $1,000 billion by 2003 (cf Wildemann, 1999).

A model for this type of intercompany business management is the PC "outfitter" Dell. Dell has shown that a team can sell products faster, and at lower prices, than individuals while cutting out storage costs and avoiding over-production at the same time, and still maintaining a constant level of quality. IT for intercompany business processes on the internet coupled with efficient physical logistics systems represents an increasingly important competitive factor. The king of re-engineering, Michael Hammer, points again and again to the money and human resources that enterprises waste in using a large number of communication methods (such as telephone, fax, and electronic data interchange, EDI) instead of the web, their lack of willingness to share information with other companies, and their insistence on controlling hundreds of downstream processes that would be better in the hands of specialists (cf Gfaller).

End-to-end electronic processing of value chains using internet technology not only ensures that transfer errors are eliminated but that processes are also accelerated and costs reduced. For example, partners in an intercompany value chain who have a good customer/supplier relationship exchange their planning data to synchronize planning.

This can prevent delivery bottlenecks and the need for large volumes of backup stock. Delivery times between the levels of the supply chain can also be reduced.

Internet-based business processing can be exploited further. Complete integration of internet sales and internet buying is based on the design of new internet transactions that synchronize two application systems simultaneously with a purchase order in the customer system and a sales order in the vendor system. The documents are generated simultaneously in both systems using **one-step business** (Figure 1.1.9-2). Redundant processes usually associated with interbusiness cooperation are eliminated. Compared to today's asynchronous EDI integration of customer and supplier systems, these new internet transactions represent a revolution similar to the one triggered by the change from dialog operation to batch operation twenty years ago (Perez et al., p. 31).

The strategic importance of the internet to business management led SAP, at an early stage, to consider first-class solutions that provide a safe and high-performance approach to linking the SAP system with the internet. The internet transaction server (ITS) has been successful in enabling the use of SAP's high-performance system architecture on the internet (Figure 1.1.9-3). Since release 3.1, ITS has been delivered with the standard SAP system and it forms an essential component in the scope of technologies that open up the SAP system and make it accessible to intercompany and interplatform business management.

ITS is a link between both systems and should be visualized as a gateway bringing the different communication protocols and data formats of the SAP system and the internet into tune with each another. A user of the world wide web can trigger an internet transaction in the SAP system via a link on a certain HTML page. The web server passes the request directly on to the ITS which sets up a connection with the previously specified SAP system to start the transaction.

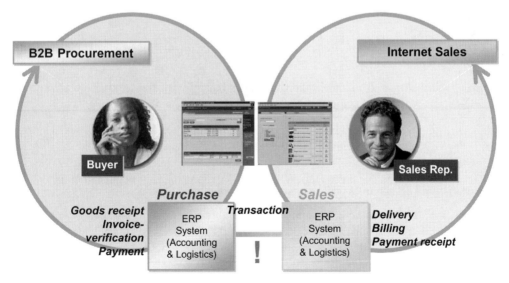

Figure 1.1.9-2:   One-step business
SAP AG

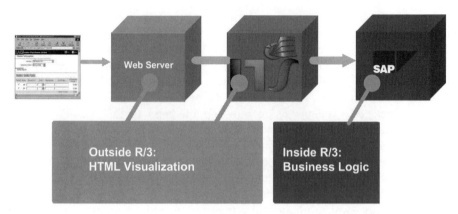

Figure 1.1.9-3:   Function of the internet transaction server
SAP AG

The ITS technique and the advantages of linking the SAP system with the internet become evident when used with suitable SAP-based internet applications. The SAP system is also delivered with internet application components. These are SAP internet applications that the customer can immediately use once the SAP system is installed. By using these applications, an enterprise can use the internet to process business transactions both internally and beyond the boundaries of the enterprise, making a variety of information available to a wide range of users. Release 4.0 includes as many as 35 separate configurable applications for B2B, consumer-to-business and intranet communication. These applications are not just for accessing information but are developed specially for the execution of business transactions.

For example, the following processes are available on the internet for the online store scenario.

- *Detailed view of a product:* portrayal of a product with descriptive text, picture, and sound in a product catalog.

- *Fill a virtual shopping basket:* if the customer is happy with the product and wants to order it, he places it in a shopping basket – this is a list of all products selected for the purchase order so far.

- *Create a customer:* if the internet user is a new customer, he has to register with the company before a quotation can be created. This basically means entering his address and any other relevant data. The online store then creates a customer master in the SAP system and assigns a customer number to the new customer.

- *Create a customer quotation:* as soon as the customer has been positively identified, a quotation is created under consideration of all details specified by the customer – the system also checks the current availability, and the delivery date is confirmed immediately online.

- *Enter a sales order:* if the customer is happy with the quotation he can convert it into an order – he receives confirmation of the order including information such as the product name, quantity, and availability, as well as the order number of the online order placed directly in the SAP system.

For the provider of this service, it means that order placement is no longer restricted to opening hours. Moreover, the company can react quickly to a sales order because it is entered directly in the SAP system. The online store is a direct link between the internet and SAP which provides the user with an optimal tool for the smooth and profitable processing of business transactions on the web.

1.2   What are knowledge maps?

Knowledge maps are based on the MindMapping method created by Tony Buzan; it was developed especially for representing knowledge using text and graphics. The left hemisphere of the brain is used for remembering words, while the right hemisphere can remember pictures. Both hemispheres are addressed and linked with the mind map. With MindMapping, you are able to portray your ideas and concepts in a growing graphical structure, using your maximum mental potential.

Knowledge maps apply the MindMapping method to business knowledge concerning a specific situation. All the relevant topics are visualized and structured in the form of a mind map. Knowledge maps can refer to general business situations but in this book they are specially adapted to R/3 functionality. Knowledge maps can be function-oriented, which means that a knowledge map is applied to a specific R/3 module, e.g. sales and distribution (SD), and all topics relevant to this module are represented and described in structured form. A knowledge map could also be used at a lower level, e.g. a certain sub-functionality of the module, such as SD-pricing. However, important processes and dependencies are not taken into consideration. For this reason, the use of knowledge maps to portray business cases only really makes sense within the framework of process-orientation. In his article on knowledge process re-engineering Dr. Thomas Allweyer states that collecting, presenting, transferring, and using knowledge is based on the activities of an enterprise, and that the essential requirement for targetted knowledge management can only be achieved with an understanding of the business processes (Allweyer, pp. 162–168). For this reason, knowledge maps are based on existing R/3 reference process modules and contain information about the R/3 process module they represent. The **main branches** (see Chapter 4.2.2) of a knowledge map represent important questions used in the process analysis, while the **side branches** (see Chapter 4.2.3) contain either further questions or possible solutions related to R/3. The presentation of a knowledge map is completed with texts and symbols indicating R/3 integration. For example, the process analyst can use the SAP symbols on the sales planning knowledge map (Figure 1.2-1) to see where there is integration with production planning.

The knowledge content of a knowledge map undergoes constant change with regards to R/3 and must be adjusted and updated accordingly. A knowledge map is a dynamic document and customer requirements can be added for project implementation if required. Users of knowledge maps may include information from their own project

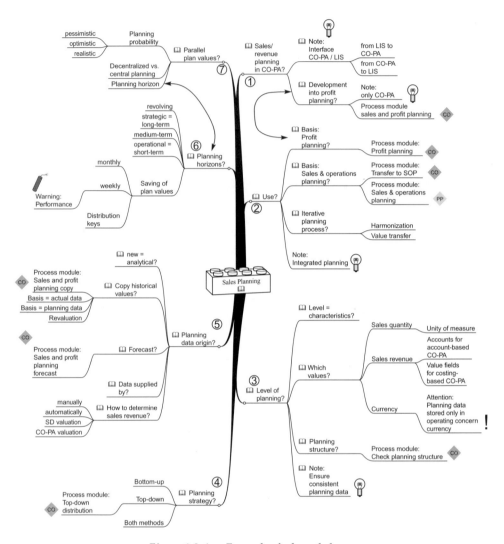

Figure 1.2-1:   Example of a knowledge map

experience as new knowledge components. The project manager can act as knowledge manager for an R/3 process analysis. Davenport calls this new role chief knowledge officer (Davenport, 1996). Combining knowledge maps with other information-processing media (e.g. overheads, videocams, etc.) enables knowledge to be presented in the form of a **master knowledge map** (see Chapter 6.2). For this, all the information required for a project is gathered together. The collection of knowledge is known as the **knowledge container** and is filed in a structured way for each process.

Further hyperlinks between different knowledge maps enable almost infinite linking of knowledge. However, knowledge maps must also be structured. Process chains for each process area enable an overview of all levels before looking at the individual knowledge map in detail and per process module. Knowledge maps are filed in a database which the consultant, customer or whoever is interested in R/3 as the basis of process analysis can access with the *MindManager* tool.

If we look at a knowledge map in detail, we can ascertain several syntheses regarding familiar R/3 topics, components or processes. A synthesis is created from existing questions from ASAP (Q&Adb), consultant project experience, R/3 documentation, R/3 reference model processes, and the transactions of the R/3 system. The most important syntheses are listed below.

- Synthesis 1: *Knowledge maps and R/3 organizational units*
  In the definition of organizational units (see Chapter 5.3.2) several aspects have to be considered which arise within an enterprise process area and also in the relationships between individual process areas. The MindMapping method can structure and add text to these dependencies and relationships. The project team is thus aided in the definition of organizational units and informed of possible interdependencies at an early stage.

- Synthesis 2: *Knowledge maps and R/3 reference model*
  A process mind map contains the process names from the R/3 reference model in its root and provides all information needed for a process analysis. This information may be in the form of questions, business explanations, notes, dependencies, or general definitions.

- Synthesis 3: *Knowledge maps and R/3 ASAP*
  Mind maps can be used for the definition of the enterprise scope as part of the creation of the business blueprint. In addition, the structured and hierarchical representation of questions and information and mind maps can be used to create the blueprint document (target concept).

- Synthesis 4: *Knowledge maps and R/3 documentation*
  Within the framework of a mind map, information is collected which helps to understand and explain certain business facts (process mind map, organizational mind map, etc.). Corresponding information and terms defined by SAP flow from the R/3 documentation in processed form into the individual mind maps.

- Synthesis 5: *Knowledge maps and R/3 transactions*
  By entering the transaction code in the mind map root of a process module, the project team can interact with the R/3 system. This forms a basis for transforming business concepts into concrete system flows.

- Synthesis 6: *Knowledge maps and R/3 business objects*
  Relevant business objects are identified within the framework of a process analysis. The structured representation of the mind map shows the master, organizational, and process objects per enterprise process area.

- Synthesis 7: *Knowledge maps and R/3 consultant project experience*
  Explanations, notes, questions, and instructions from various projects can be filed in the mind map and referred to for future projects.

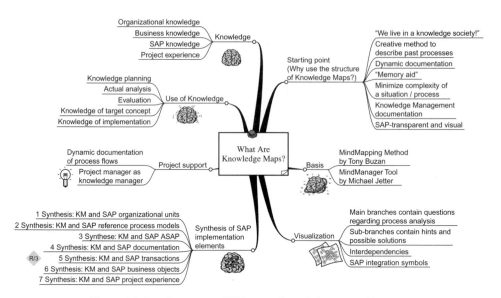

Figure 1.2-2:   Summary of 'What are knowledge maps?' in one map

The cumulation of all these syntheses turns the R/3 knowledge map into an integrated knowledge container (container = collection of different types of knowledge). Mind mapping forms a creative and structured **synthesis** between the existing questions from ASAP (Q&Adb), consultant project experience, R/3 documentation, R/3 reference model processes, and the transactions of the R/3 system.

1.3   Benefits of using knowledge maps

An enterprise can gain considerably from the consistent use of knowledge maps for process analysis or for business engineering as part of an R/3 implementation project, and also in supporting continuous engineering throughout the life cycle of the R/3 system. A distinction must be made between monetary and non-monetary values, which have equal importance for an enterprise. Figure 1.3-1 presents an overview of the potential benefits; these are then described in detail.

1. *Support of reference-based BPR with knowledge maps*
   The general principle of business (re)engineering was explained in Chapters 1.1.1 and 1.1.2. How the process analysis of business engineering is carried out, its aims and foundation are described in Chapter 5. The procedure presented here is based on reference-based business engineering and supported by the consistent use of knowledge maps within the framework of the LEGO principle of process visualization and design. Process analysis is not performed out of context, but is based on the reference processes provided by the R/3 system, reflecting **best business practices**. These processes, in turn, are made up of individual process modules which the reference model combines in a logical context in the form of the total/integrated

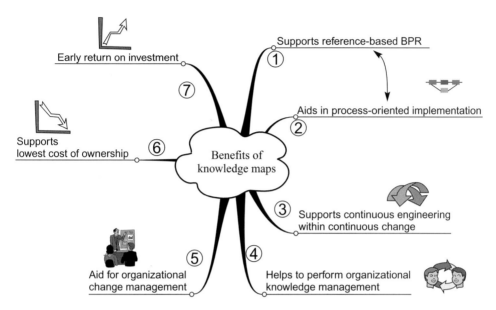

Figure 1.3-1:   Benefits of knowledge maps

process (scenario process), taking into account the best business practices of the corresponding industry. The process modules are generally individual transactions which can be put together according to the customer's personal requirements. The customer can select the relevant process modules (like LEGO bricks from a box) and put them together to form a logical process chain (LEGO chain) tailored individually to the enterprise. Each process module has its own knowledge map, which asks, or answers, the most important questions regarding the use of the process module, thus providing the basis for the mapping of customer-specific processes to the R/3 system and the adaptation of the R/3 system to meet customer requirements. The advantage of this is that you can tell exactly which processes and what optimizing potential can be expected prior to R/3 implementation. You can also see clearly which processes are carried out, and how, in the R/3 system and, if necessary, how these process flows can be adjusted to suit the individual enterprise.

For business engineering, knowledge maps are a synthesis of typical consultant questions about R/3 implementation, the ASAP method (Q&Adb), R/3 documentation, R/3 system transactions, R/3 process models, and, particularly, tips and tricks from consultants' experience (see Chapter 1.2). This enables the customer to carry out a process analysis quite independently with relatively little support from external consultants. This speeds up the whole implementation process and can help the continuous business engineering phase too. If consultants are involved from the very outset of the process analysis, knowledge maps are useful in leading both the consultants and the project team in a structured way through the business engineering phase. Regardless of whether or not external consultants are involved in processing knowledge maps, even at this stage the maps provide valuable tips and tricks which cannot be found in any documentation, but which are important for the adaptation and subsequent system implementation. The fact that knowledge maps contain structured questions **and** explanations ensures that R/3 knowledge is transferred to the enterprise employees. This, in turn, ensures quality and guarantees that goals are realized within a shorter time span. In addition to the potential benefits already described, the use of knowledge maps has a monetary value, for the benefits listed above can save considerable time and money.

2. *Knowledge maps to support a process-oriented R/3 implementation*
   Knowledge maps can, of course, also be used if the pure (re)engineering aspect is not necessarily the focal point of R/3 implementation, but the implementation should nonetheless be **process-oriented** (see Chapter 1.1.3). Naturally the same is true if business (re)engineering is to be supported by the process-oriented implementation which, in this case, is actually the prerequisite. In both cases, but particularly in the former, implementation is generally based on the best business practices represented in the R/3 system, in the form of the reference process. As far as the use of knowledge maps is concerned, and their use in the process-oriented procedure, the same applies as for the first point above.

3. *Continuous business engineering with knowledge maps*
   To meet the challenges of the 21st century, enterprises must be prepared for continuously changing conditions (see Chapters 1.1.4 and 1.1.5). Otherwise they risk losing customers, become disadvantaged over competitors, and fall behind on the ever-necessary innovation. The ability to constantly adapt to new framework conditions is often referred to in today's literature as **organizational leadership** (Moore, p. 219). The following are causes of constant change (see also Chapter 1.1.5):

   - shorter life cycles
   - more demanding customers (individual customizing of products)
   - increasing and tougher competition
   - increasing number of niche providers
   - economic changes
   - globalization.

These factors put considerable demands on the processes of an enterprise. Once defined, it does not mean that they will stay that way for the next few years. On the contrary, as soon as they have been defined it may be necessary to change certain processes, even if only slightly. This could mean a concrete change to, or extension of, existing processes. Knowledge maps are designed to support continuous change in several application areas.

   By documenting processes at different levels, made possible by the structure of knowledge maps in main and side branches, knowledge is made available in all phases of the R/3 system's life cycle and, as a result, also during **continuous business engineering**, and can be accessed by anyone who is interested. The main advantage, however, is that if additions become necessary to the implemented – or not yet implemented – processes or functionality during this phase, knowledge maps can also be applied. This option supports the CSE method favored by Thome and Hufgard (see Chapter 1.1.4): " ... the software library enables the enterprise to change [and extend] the functionality at any time" (Thome and Hufgard, p. 84). Such additions can take many forms:

- *New process modules, not in use up to now*
  If a concrete process module (e.g. customer inquiry processing) was not introduced during initial implementation, but becomes necessary or is required for continuous engineering, it can be analyzed and implemented quickly using knowledge maps because these contain all the information relevant to its implementation due to their system-inherent properties.

- *Process modules already used, but only with partial functionality*
  When processes are initially implemented, it is often the case that certain customizing options or functions of a process module are not yet relevant to productive use. If such an unused functionality should become relevant during the life cycle of continuous engineering, the knowledge map can be referred to. Here is an example, using the process module called customer inquiry processing. During the initial implementation, the decision was made not to include a credit limit check which is a subfunctionality of the customer inquiry processing process module. However, the customer wants to use it now. As it is structured in main and side branches, the knowledge map of the process module can be used here, because this functionality is included on the main branch (see Chapter 7.6).

As these examples show, accelerated analysis and implementation is possible in both cases. Why? Firstly because knowledge maps are created per process module, and secondly because the structured documentation and tips and tricks at each level enable their application in every phase of the R/3 system life cycle. This means that the continuous engineering phase also profits from knowledge maps. This is evident in the accelerated procedure in carrying out necessary tasks, in the higher quality of work, in the extensive documentation, and, of course, in the reduction of costs. This potential can be fully exploited if the knowledge map is extended to form a master knowledge map and used for active knowledge management as described in Chapter 6.

4. *Knowledge maps in knowledge management*
   The initials of knowledge map also form the abbreviation for knowledge management. As described in Chapter 1.1.6, this term has emerged over the past couple of years and cannot be ignored in today's increasingly knowledge-based society. The knowledge management described here, as explained in Chapter 6, refers only to process knowledge (which includes both the organizational and the process structures) as part of the organizational knowledge management of an enterprise. As the term suggests, knowledge maps support both general knowledge management (as described in Chapter 1.1) and R/3-specific knowledge management (as described in Chapter 6) in a number of ways.

   Knowledge management, if carried out emphatically, not only benefits the individual employee but the enterprise as a whole, because it is able to manage, support, and pass on this strategically important resource. In this way, current employees can be retrained and new employees trained quickly and thoroughly. Effectively planned and efficiently implemented knowledge management stems the loss of knowledge through, for example, an employee leaving the company. Instead, information remains within the enterprise and is accessible to newcomers. This naturally means both qualitative and quantitative (i.e. monetary) benefits. Chapter 6.2 explains in detail how knowledge maps can be implemented within the framework of knowledge management.

5. *Organizational change management with knowledge maps*
   Knowledge maps can also support change management as described in Chapter 1.1.5. The emphasis here is laid on the education and training of employees whose tasks are subject to constant change. The graphic representation and the written descriptions of each process module, which together make up the integrated process in the enterprise, knowledge maps particularly facilitate the process-oriented training of employees. This is achieved by using an intuitive and clear representation of business and R/3 relevant situations with the help of the MindMapping method. In addition, the LEGO principle enables representation of the overall dependencies and connections of processes in all areas of the enterprise by creating process chains (LEGO chains). The employee profits from this in a variety of ways. Process chains provide a simple and clear overview of all processes within the company, and employees can see and understand the part they play as individuals for the creation of value within the enterprise. They can see the input which a process module, and thus the employee responsible, receives from upstream process modules, or just what they provide for the processes which follow. Knowledge maps also explain the content of a process module, with regards to its functions and integration, to the employee responsible for that module.

   With knowledge maps, the important business task of change management can also be realized, not only faster but also in a process-oriented manner, thus achieving a better quality of knowledge transfer.

6. *Support of lowest cost of ownership with knowledge maps*
   In addition to the range of qualitative benefits which knowledge maps offer, the points listed above include quantitative advantages, such as the reduction of time and costs. Looking at the overall cost as part of a TCO approach (see Chapter 1.1.7), it is evident that alongside the many other initiatives to reduce the overall cost of the ERP system (on the part of SAP or the customer), knowledge maps can make an important contribution.

7. *Earlier and higher return on investment with knowledge maps*
   Particularly in the areas of business engineering, process-oriented R/3 implementation, and CSE, the use of knowledge maps accelerates procedures and reduces costs because it puts the customer in a position to react more independently. As shown in Chapter 1.1.8, lower costs result in a higher ROI. By minimizing the time factor, the customer can also profit from the earlier realization of an ROI, which in turn is reflected in a higher overall ROI.

2 mySAP.com

2.1 EnjoySAP

As of release 4.0, the functionality offered by SAP enterprise resource planning software covers virtually all areas, processes, and tasks required by today's enterprises for logistics, financial accounting, and human resources. Up to now, SAP users have been almost exclusively "expert users," i.e. users working with SAP functionality for the major part of their working day. This, however, is not the purpose of ERP software. Rather, all employees should be able to work with such a system, even those who need to use it only occasionally, e.g. to call a specific report. This aim puts additional demands on the visual design, flow logic, and customizability of software which was originally developed by engineers and has, so far, been based on the "gray" screens of the Windows era. Moreover, end users in general, quite independently of SAP products, now tend to have higher expectations of a business software, expecting it to be easy to use and customizable. This attitude has been nurtured by several trends which have become popular with many employees over the past few years. Many employees now have experience of the world wide web, new mobile devices (handhelds, palmtops, etc.), and self-service applications which are increasingly used by many enterprises as part of their intranets, e.g. for requesting leave. All these applications focus essentially on user-friendly features and intuitive use of software. These characteristics had to be transferred to the powerful functionality of the SAP system. This was all the more important in view of the evolving internet strategy with *mySAP.com*, because all of SAP's functionality will be contained in *mySAP.com* components and thus available on the internet.

Against this background, SAP started an extensive customer survey in the summer of 1998. A large number of developers visited customer sites to find out what they required of SAP software concerning user-friendliness. The ultimate aim was to make the software as easy to use, as intuitive, and as personalized as possible for end users, irrespective of whether those concerned used SAP software occasionally or on a regular basis. Basically, the aim was to ensure that all users have fun using the software and **enjoy** their work (hence EnjoySAP). Working with SAP software – e.g. viewing the master data or sales reports of a specific customer – should not be regarded as a chore. The end user becomes a V.I.P within EnjoySAP; this acronym not only implies that the end user will be treated as a very important person, it also describes the three main elements that make up EnjoySAP:

- *New visual design*
  The SAP user interface has been completely redesigned. From the very first moment, the user should find working with the system as easy as possible; the look and feel

effect is intended to give users a positive feeling. This is why all the elements of the user interface, including the background color of the frames, icons, buttons, scrollbars, controls, etc., have been redesigned in eye-pleasing colors. As a result, the end user sees and understands at first glance what a certain element or button does, and knows when to use it. Furthermore, the most important elements of a screen are now accentuated to make them stand out – new tasks/work items in the inbox (e.g. within an automatic workflow), required entry fields, or system messages can be seen clearly.

- *New interaction design*
  Simply revamping the screen, however, is not enough to make the system more user-friendly. If you look at some SAP functions, such as creating a sales order in SD or a purchase order in materials management (MM) (Figure 2.1-1), you will find that you frequently have to work your way through several screens to get to a certain part or piece of information within the transaction. It was this interaction, i.e. the way the user interacts with the system and navigates through screens in performing operations, that needed simplification. In addition, it must be possible to adapt this interaction to the specific needs and roles of different users. To find solutions to these problem areas, not only with regard to software-specific issues but also with respect to the business side of things, SAP interviewed a large number of end users in partner companies (including order takers, purchasing agents, auditors, etc.). The results of these interviews were

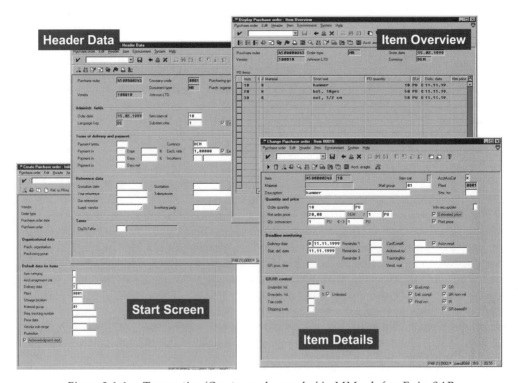

Figure 2.1-1:   Transaction 'Create purchase order' in MM – before EnjoySAP

considered for the EnjoySAP release. Moreover, the most up-to-date interaction technologies have been applied to rationalize SAP applications by using various screen elements such as tree structures, table controls, tabstrips, and drag and drop functions (Figure 2.1-2). This has significantly reduced the number of screens that the user meets in performing the task(s) assigned to his specific role within a certain process (business scenario).

● *Personalized (i.e. customized) user interface*
Very often, users do not need the whole range of functions within a transaction to perform the tasks assigned to them in their specific role. Yet these functions are required to perform the overall process within the context of the enterprise as a whole – although by different users who are assigned other roles within the same process. Therefore, it must be possible for the user-specific working environment to be easily adapted to different roles/employees so that it contains only the (personalized) functionality required by one specific user. Such a personalized, role-based user interface can easily be created in EnjoySAP. Instead of generic menus and screen layouts, EnjoySAP defines personal user scenarios tailored to a particular user's specific role and tasks within the enterprise, e.g. sales employee, purchasing agent, production planner. This fulfills the requirement of "what you see is what you need," as users

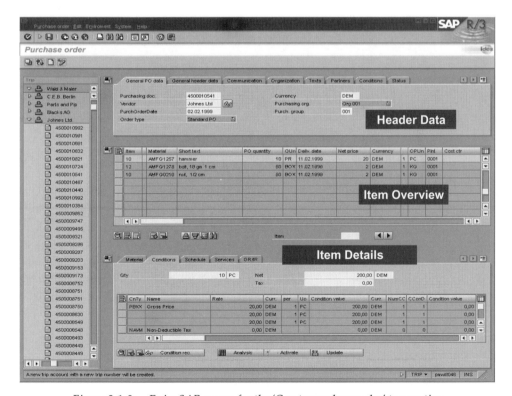

Figure 2.1-2:   EnjoySAP screen for the 'Create purchase order' transaction

are able to add the transactions they access most frequently to a favorites list (Figure 2.1-3).

To conclude, we would like to point out once more that EnjoySAP was a prerequisite for implementing the SAP internet strategy and the *mySAP.com* product (details in Chapters 2.2 to 2.4). All existing SAP functions will be contained in *mySAP.com* components and available on the internet (Figure 2.1-4). To enable universal use of the world wide web with all its options, the web browser and web pages should fulfill the same requirements envisaged by EnjoySAP:

- attractive visual design

- easy-to-use interaction

- personalized screens.

Imagine you are on the internet searching for information concerning shares, buying products, etc. If the web browser you are using or the web pages you visit are complicated to use or difficult to understand, you will choose another web browser or web page.

This transformation of the graphical user interface (GUI) installed on your client or front-end (desktop computer) is enabled by two new SAP software developments, SAPGUI

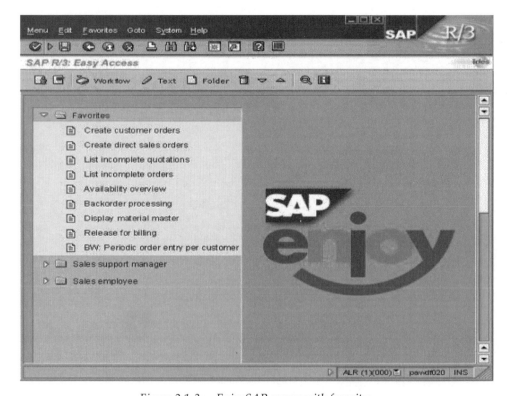

Figure 2.1-3:   EnjoySAP screen with favorites

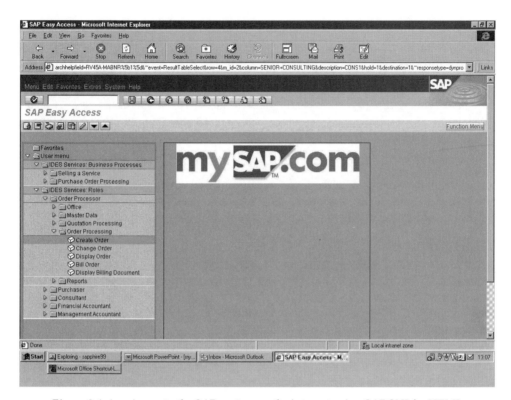

*Figure 2.1-4:   Access to the SAP system on the internet using SAPGUI for HTML
(EnjoySAP design)*

for HTML and SAPGUI for Java. Furthermore, users will no longer have to install a GUI on their local front-end unless they use the SAPGUI for Windows. A simple internet browser (currently Microsoft Internet Explorer) is all that is required to access SAP components from anywhere via a network without client installation of the GUI.

2.2   What is mySAP.com and one-step business?

mySAP.com is SAP's new internet strategy that presents the enterprise as a provider not only of a mere product but of extensive software solutions for inter-enterprise cooperation in the virtual marketplace. *mySAP.com* is SAP's extensive and open e-business solution made up of industry solutions, portals, business scenario-oriented and role-based internet applications, special internet services, as well as XML-based technology. These elements interact to enable all enterprises to participate in internet business and achieve the maximum benefit. *mySAP.com*'s aim is to enable enterprises to:

- involve employees more actively and directly in business processes, e.g. by giving them greater responsibility by means of employee self-services;

- supply complete, easy-to-use, customizable business solutions on the internet;

- integrate all business partners, such as customers and suppliers, directly in their processes across organizational boundaries;

- generate new values – this not only involves making processes more effective and efficient (which can be expressed in figures such as cost savings) but also means developing, for example, new customer groups or supplier sources, thereby creating a higher value added;

- implement one-step business transactions within a cooperative business environment.

This means that by using *mySAP.com* an enterprise should achieve the lowest TCO and a high ROI. However, the focus is on creating additional value, e.g. tapping new customer groups. Yet, to really generate new values and propel the enterprise toward a new kind of interbusiness cooperation, reaching out to new customer groups is not enough. Rather, the enterprise must be enabled to do business with these new customers immediately and without too much extra effort. This can only be done efficiently by means of effective communication and data exchange between the business partners' application systems. This is often summed up by the catchword "one-step business." One example is procurement of C materials or services via the internet (MRO – maintenance, repair, operation – e-procurement), as shown in Figure 2.2-1.

Within the e-commerce environment, supply and demand interact, for example in a marketplace. For e-commerce to develop on a B2B basis, we need a supplier who offers

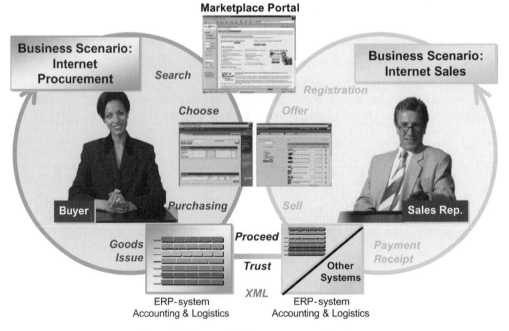

Figure 2.2-1   mySAP.com – one-step business

goods on the internet, for example in a marketplace or in his own online store on a web page. In addition, we need a customer who wants to buy a certain product over the internet, for example in a marketplace or directly by calling a familiar web page. In our example, the supplier offers his goods in his own online store.

In this case the online store is integrated with a back-end transaction system (ERP software) which can be either an SAP or an external system. Moreover, it is recorded in the business directory under www.mysap.com, and its software has been enabled for one-step business since, as described above, the internet software is linked to back-end transaction systems and uses the corresponding technical (e.g. XML, HTTP) and semantic (e.g. BAPI, e-SPEAK, Biz-Talk) internet standards. At the other end, we have a buyer whose B2B procurement software (e.g. *mySAP.com* B2B procurement) is able to display several different supplier catalogs, e.g. via an open-catalog interface. This internet procurement software is in turn linked to the back-end transaction system (ERP software) which once again can be either an SAP or an external system. The buyer's software must also be one-step business-enabled, which is ensured by the connection of the internet to back-end transaction systems and by using the technical and semantic internet standards described above. Let us assume, for example, that our lady in the purchasing department on the buyer side is looking for a new supplier of laser printers for her enterprise, as their current supplier has become too expensive. To find out which laser printer suppliers offer the most favorable conditions, she searches the SAP marketplace for suitable sources under www.mysap.com. She then contacts the chosen supplier and negotiates the exact conditions, either by telephone or by exchanging internet-enabled documents. After an agreement has been reached on prices, terms of delivery, and quantities, the supplier's catalog is integrated into the buyer's internal procurement system via the B2B open-catalog interface. From now on, whenever a department needs a printer, an authorized employee simply has to choose the relevant supplier catalog using the B2B procurement software, select the product, and place an order. In the "normal" procedure, i.e. without a link between the procurement or online store software and a back-end transaction system, and without using internet standards, several manual steps would then have to be carried out. The person placing the order would have to print out the order and submit it to the purchasing department, where the purchasing staff would have to enter it manually in the material management software and create a purchase order. At the other end, the supplier would have to enter and store the incoming purchase order in the internal order entry system. All following steps, such as exchange of delivery notes, invoices, etc., would be semi-integrated and involve the exchange of many documents and papers requiring manual steps.

The greatest benefit of *mySAP.com* is that, due to the one-step business environment, a purchase order is automatically created in the buyer's system the instant the order is placed. This is made possible by the integrated transfer of all the necessary parameters (e.g. supplier, article, quantity, price, etc.) from the procurement system to the back-end transaction system (ERP system). On the supplier's side, the corresponding data (e.g. customer, article, quantity, price, etc.) is transferred from the online store software to the back-end system (ERP system) at the same time. Similarly, the systems automatically exchange all additional data, such as the purchase or sales order number, as well as all relevant confirmations. There are two principal ways to ensure this communication between the two enterprises' back-end systems: either the two systems communicate and exchange electronic documents via the www.mySAP.com marketplace; or the internet applications involved (i.e. the B2B procurement software and the online store) are linked directly and exchange data directly (i.e. without taking the detour via the marketplace).

To illustrate the full potential of *mySAP.com* and to explain why, in this context, we talk of collaborative or cooperative business not just on a $1:1$ basis (i.e. between one recipient and one sender) but on an $n:n$ basis (i.e. between several recipients and several senders), we will take the example one step further. Up to now, when business systems were linked, we have used EDI as a communication medium. However, EDI is cumbersome and difficult to install (Hess, p. 195), and expensive during operation. What is more, EDI connections are usually $1:1$ links that generally need to be set up and defined separately for each business partner. The use of internet technology – SAP talks about the internet business framework – and currently evolving technical and semantic standards makes it easier and cheaper to integrate your own system with those of your business partners, provided that all systems are able to deal with one-step business scenarios, i.e. their back-end systems are also integrated with the internet applications and the required standards are used. You need to connect your own system to the internet only once. This link enables you to contact and communicate with any business partner and to integrate your business systems with no further steps, i.e. without explicitly setting up a new connection for each business partner. This explains why, at this stage, we no longer talk only of e-business but also of c-business, i.e. collaborative business. The aim is no longer to establish $1:1$ links between individual enterprises but to set up networks for whole communities, as described by Hagel and Armstrong (Hagel and Armstrong, p. 17). If we further consider Metcalfe's law (Zerdick et al., p. 116), which postulates that the value (V) of a network increases by the square number of participants (n), $V = n^2$, we soon realize that this is not just about inter-enterprise process optimization but about creating completely new opportunities and values, such as tapping a new, extensive range of customers.

2.3   mySAP.com – evolution phases

mySAP.com represents e-community collaboration, the paradigm of the coming years and decades for the integration, cooperation, and collaboration of business applications within a post-net e-business environment (Gartner Group, 1999). If we look at the evolution of this era of e-community collaboration, we can distinguish three main phases (Figure 2.3–1).

- *Phase 1: ERP systems*
  The emphasis at this stage is on integrating business processes within one enterprise to achieve maximum efficiency. Thus, these integrated systems make it possible, for example, for goods receipt entries in materials management to be automatically updated to financial accounts at the same time, even if the material received is immediately used for a production order. The SAP system represents this level of integration and the first phase of evolution. The enabling technology behind it is the three-level client/server architecture.

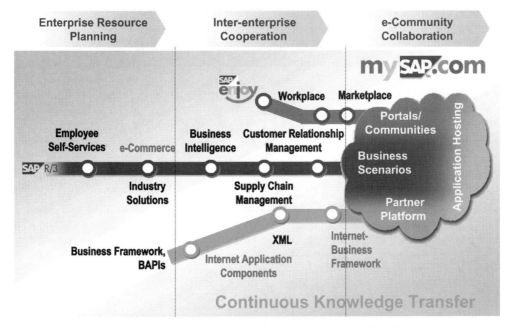

Figure 2.3-1:   Evolution of SAP business solutions and products

- *Phase 2: inter-enterprise cooperation*
  In contrast to Phase 1, the focus of this phase is on system integration across organizational boundaries, i.e. cooperation between several business partners. This means that the concept of integrated processes with the aim of increasing efficiency is extended to business partner systems. As well as the best-in-class SAP ERP system, this requires additional software to provide this kind of cooperation and integration. In this area, SAP offers products such as B2B procurement (buying on the internet), B2B sales (selling on the internet), supply chain management (advanced planner and optimizer), customer relationship management, etc. This type of software enables you to offer products on the internet to a wide range of customers and to integrate purchase orders directly in the ERP system. Another example of cooperation is joint production planning. Manufacturers of a certain product (e.g. automobiles) make their production plans immediately available to suppliers (e.g. suppliers to the automobile industry) to enable them to optimize their own planning and production. Apart from the additional programs mentioned, individual ERP system modules and objects are directly linked in this phase (e.g. via EDI) to exchange necessary data. In addition, the SAP system uses Intermediate Documents (IDOCs) and Business Application Programming Interfaces (BAPIs), which are linked via a direct connection or network. Again, a three-level client/server architecture is used, extended by the business framework (BAPIs).

Phase 3: e-community collaboration
At this level, the concept of integration achieved in Phase 2 is stepped up. This phase not only aims to increase efficiency and effectiveness but to create new values for

businesses. Integration across organizational boundaries is no longer limited to a small number of suppliers and customers, but can be extended to the whole of the "global village internet." This means that by using the required standards you will be able to cooperate, and thus link transaction systems (back-end ERP systems) via the internet, with any chosen partner with no extra effort. These business relations do not necessarily have to be long-term partnerships. While these are desirable, once-only cooperation is also possible. The technology offered by SAP is the *mySAP.com* product with its internal workplace and public www.mySAP.com marketplace, portals, web-enabled business processes (software components), and the XML and BAPI-enabled internet business framework.

2.4   mySAP.com – components

As we pointed out earlier, *mySAP.com* is much more than a simple product or software solution and we have already discussed the aims behind the new concept. We can

Figure 2.4-1:   mySAP.com components

conclude by saying that *mySAP.com* is based on four main "pillars" (Figure 2.4-1). These four components are now described in more detail.

2.4.1 mySAP.com: business scenarios

An important milestone on the way to the internet is enabling the complete SAP product range for internet use. The first step in that direction was the EnjoySAP initiative (see Chapter 2.1), in so far as in the internet era a piece of software needs to be easy to learn, adapt, and handle, so that every employee is able to use it. In the beginning, EnjoySAP represented a simplified way of working with SAP software. Since then it has been enhanced by SAPGUI for HTML and SAPGUI for Java and, in conjunction with a standard internet browser such as Microsoft Internet Explorer 5.0, it is now accessible on the internet from anywhere in the world. The internet also has significant implications for inter-enterprise process integration. This is where so-called business scenarios will be used in the future. *mySAP.com* business scenarios are role-based, industry-specific, end-to-end, integrated business processes that connect people within one enterprise (employees) and across organizational boundaries (customers, suppliers, and other business partners) via the internet. These business scenarios are implemented together with the components of SAP e-business solutions (Figure 2.4.1-1).

The business scenario displayed in Figure 2.4.1-1, "procurement of C materials via the internet (MRO e-procurement)" should be interpreted as follows:

- Karen is employed in the exemplar enterprise. In accordance with her tasks within the processes in which she is involved, she is assigned the principal roles "employee" and "service staff member." In her role as a service staff member she requires service-specific

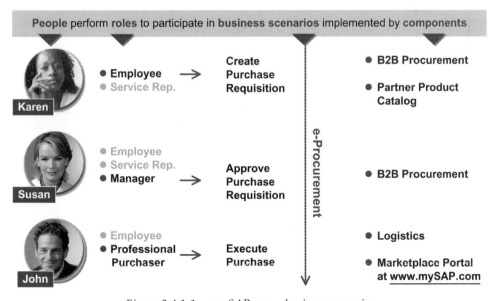

Figure 2.4.1-1:   mySAP.com – business scenarios

information, e.g. about certain customers and the products they use (particularly the service frequency, etc.). In her role as employee she needs certain information and services which are available to all employees regardless of their department, e.g. enterprise internal news, requests for leave, or purchase orders for certain C materials. In the example in Figure 2.4.1-1 she orders a product in her role as employee (e.g. a palmtop) which she does not need to perform her service-specific tasks but does in her capacity as "normal" employee, for example for time management. To place the order, she creates a purchase requisition via an intranet-based employee self-service function. This activity is part of the business scenario "procurement of C materials via the internet (MRO e-procurement)" and uses the *mySAP.com* B2B procurement component.

- Susan is also employed in the exemplar enterprise. She is Karen's boss and is therefore assigned the additional role "manager" in relation to Karen. As Karen's boss, she has to approve Karen's purchase order. Her approval is also part of the business scenario "procurement of C materials via the internet (e-procurement)", and the *mySAP.com* B2B procurement component is also used to carry out this activity. This scenario is supported by an enterprise internal business workflow, which notifies Susan (e.g. by a message in her mail inbox) that she is required to perform a certain activity ("approve purchase requisition").

- John is also employed in the same enterprise. Unlike Karen and Susan, he works in the purchasing department where he performs the tasks assigned to his roles as "employee" and "purchasing agent." In his role as purchasing agent, he deals with the purchase requisition created by Karen and approved by Susan, and transforms it into a purchase order that he places with a suitable supplier. This activity is also part of the business scenario "procurement of C materials via the internet (MRO e-procurement)." It uses the *mySAP.com* logistics component (materials management). The whole purchase order process is performed by the back-end transaction system after the relevant data has been integrated and transferred from the B2B procurement software. If our exemplar company's software was not linked directly to the partner company (supplier) but indirectly by document exchange via the www.mysap.com marketplace, the order would be integrated and transferred online to the supplier's transaction system via the marketplace (e.g. via BAPI in XML format).

Here are some further examples of possible scenarios.

- Cooperative (collaborative) and integrated planning and forecasts, e.g. vendor-managed inventory, customer-managed production planning.

- Sales and procurement, e.g. B2B procurement, MRO procurement.

- Cooperative (collaborative) applications, e.g. vendor cooperation, cooperative project management, procurement aggregation.

- Invoicing and payment, e.g. web-based invoicing, web-based repayment/compensation/reimbursement.

- Employee self-services, e.g. knowledge management, training.

- Strategic enterprise management, e.g. overview, strategic planning.

- Integrated sales and services on the internet (customer relationship management).

Chapter 2.6 gives a detailed description of how existing (e.g. the current SAP system) and future (e.g. business-to-consumer internet selling) software components are related to *mySAP.com* and its scenarios. This is essential in order to organize the process modules described in this series of books.

2.4.2 mySAP.com: workplace

The *mySAP.com* workplace is an intra-enterprise portal that provides users with web-based, quick, convenient, and easy access to all external and internal applications as well as their services and content (Figure 2.4.2-1). The entire workplace is based on the EnjoySAP design, which makes it easy to understand, adapt, and use. Being role-based and personalized, its user interface offers all the information that a particular employee needs to perform the tasks assigned to him within his role. The main characteristics of the workplace are listed and explained below.

- *Single point of access via web browser*
  The *mySAP.com* workplace is the central starting point from which the user has access to all the systems he needs to perform his daily tasks. This applies to both SAP and

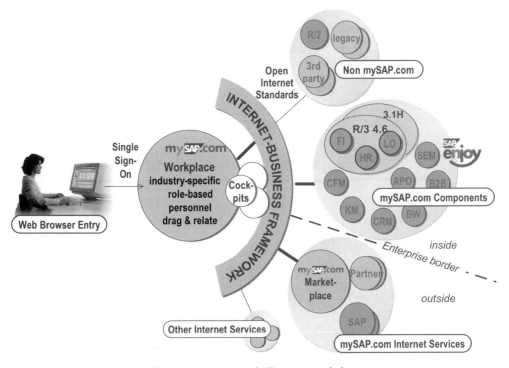

Figure 2.4.2-1: mySAP.com – workplace

non-SAP applications. The principal characteristics are that all applications can be started from one central point and that the required application or information will be displayed in a central window, the web browser. This means that the user no longer has to start several programs, for example from Windows, and work with a number of different user interfaces. In addition, as the workplace design is based on common **business management** roles, the user no longer needs to know which SAP or non-SAP systems to start in order to perform a particular task. To create a sales order, for example, the user now simply selects the link "Create sales order," or to display a specific report he selects "Report customers by region." When creating the sales order, the user will see the SAP SD functionality "Create sales order" (VA01) on the workplace user interface using SAPGUI for HTML. The "Customers by regions" report could be based on a report from the business information warehouse.

- *Personalized and role-based user interface*
  In an enterprise there are a number of users who require different information according to their roles (e.g. controller, employee, order processor, purchasing agent, manager). Therefore, the workplace comes preconfigured by SAP and can then be configured and adapted at all levels to meet the specific needs of an industry, enterprise, role, or individual user (Figure 2.4.2-2). This role-oriented feature of the workplace is particularly important, because in performing their individual roles, users are often part

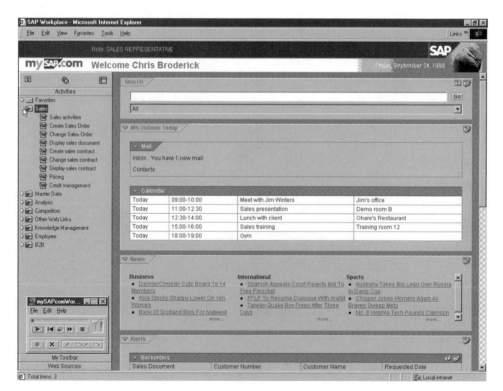

Figure 2.4.2-2:   mySAP.com – workplace configuration to meet individual needs

of the same business scenario but require different activities or information. For example, a user wants to order a certain product in his role as employee and creates a purchase requisition. By doing so, he participates in the business scenario "Order C materials via the internet (MRO e-procurement)." Another user in the role of purchasing agent is able to place the order but needs different functions and information compared to the person who creates the purchase order. A role-based workplace ensures that all employees involved are provided with the relevant information, functionality, and services they need to perform their tasks. Since the workplace is a centrally controlled application, end users can customize the central workplace to meet their personal requirements, e.g. add certain links they use frequently.

- *Convenient integration*
  Intranet, extranet, internet, office applications, business application software – the flood of information and technical possibilities offered by all these applications often overwhelms the user, who can easily get lost in the proliferation of information. This problem is particularly difficult for people who use certain applications sporadically. Consequently, users spend a lot of time typing in passwords, searching through vast amounts of data, and switching between user interfaces. In addition, a lack of integration between web-based resources (e.g. online tracking of supplier data) and business application software (e.g. monitoring a purchase order) frequently prevents employees from working productively. This challenge is met by the workplace's integrated drag and drop functionality. For example, a member of the sales staff can see in his workplace that a particular order is overdue. To find out why this is or where the ordered goods are at the moment, the employee clicks on the delivery note number and drags and drops it onto the express dispatch icon on the same workplace screen. The workplace automatically calls the forwarding agent's web page and, if it supports this function, the employee can see details of the overdue shipment. This kind of integration cuts out tedious steps, such as clicking on the web browser, entering the forwarding agent's web address, logging on with a password, and manually entering the order number.

- *Openness and flexibility*
  The workplace is a central and centrally managed application server that combines all the resources to suit the personal needs and roles of its user. This enables you to set up security mechanisms and a convenient single sign-on. In addition, the internet business framework supports new business collaboration possibilities on the internet via the workplace by providing a flexible and open infrastructure for all *mySAP.com* solutions based on web standards and supported by XML-based web messaging and web flow. Another benefit is that users need only a web browser and no further client installations. Since it uses the open internet standard HTML as its front-end communication protocol, the workplace is sometimes referred to as thin client computing.

- *Universal access to the system*
  As the front-end computer only needs a web browser, and as the workplace is a server-based application, the user can access his role-based, personalized working environment from any workstation.

2.4.3   mySAP.com: marketplace

From the historical point of view, a marketplace is a central square where supply and demand for products, services, and information meet. Moreover, the marketplace used to be the center of public life, e.g. the agorá in Greek antiquity was where people met for philosophical discourse, everyday gossip or political discussions (Rißmann et al., p. 142). Over time, particularly in the wake of industrialization which brought diverse and complex products and services, there evolved increasingly focussed and specialized markets (e.g. fish markets, car markets, grocery stores) and their derivatives (e.g. trade fairs for automobiles, computers, mechanical engineering, agricultural machines). The development of IT, particularly the internet, is now taking these markets one step further – the physical market is being transformed into the virtual cyberspace market of the future. SAP is meeting the challenge of this evolution with the development of its own marketplace under www.mySAP.com. The *mySAP.com* marketplace is an internet community, a central hub that can be used by enterprises of all industries and sizes to perform all their business transactions (Figure 2.4.3-1).

Before we describe the special services and business cooperation possibilities offered in the *mySAP.com* marketplace, we would like to discuss the following customizing options regarding general network effects, standardization, and business process integration on

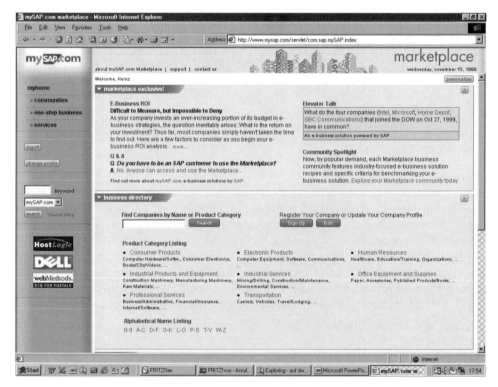

Figure 2.4.3-1:   The mySAP.com marketplace – initial screen

the internet. Internet-enabled software components are a necessary prerequisite for conducting business processes on the internet or any other network. They are the basis of any kind of business collaboration or cooperation. Unlike EDI, business collaboration does not represent a link between a few, usually long-standing, business partners (suppliers, customers, etc.) on a 1 : 1 basis. Rather, it is about actively leveraging the benefits offered by currently emerging networks and standards with regard to communication on the internet (e.g. XML). This means that in future we will also cooperate with business partners with whom no contacts previously existed. Partnerships may be formed just to carry out a certain business transaction and then dissolved. This practice can be compared to the founding of virtual enterprises (Wüthrich and Philip, p. 49). By developing and using only a limited number of semantic (e.g. BAPI, e-Speak, BIZTALK, W3C) and technical (e.g. XML, HTTP, COM, JAVA) standards we are able, without any extra effort, to integrate our business processes with any enterprise that uses the same standards. These two important developments enable business collaboration. But more than just implementing these business management and technical preconditions, we now – in this era of virtual networks – also need to find the right business partner offering suitable products, services, or information. SAP solutions and the SAP marketplace fulfill all these basic requirements.

The services and potential the *mySAP.com* marketplace offers for doing business on the internet are based on the "4 Cs" – community, commerce, collaboration, and content.

- *Commerce*
  Basically, the *mySAP.com* marketplace offers a business directory that works along the lines of the Yellow Pages. Here you find diverse information on buyers and suppliers,

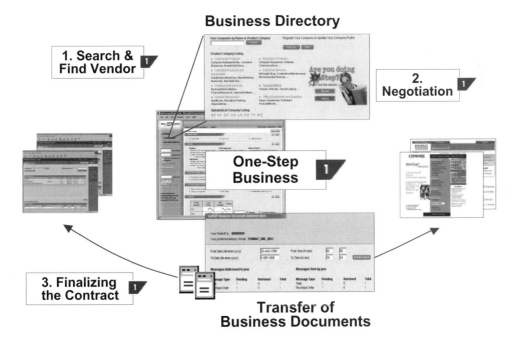

Figure 2.4.3-2:   E-commerce via the mySAP.com marketplace

such as general business data, product catalogs, contact addresses, target markets, etc. SAP uses the DUNS numbers of the business database supplier Dun & Bradstreet, which are linked to the SAP business directory. SAP thus actively supports e-commerce and focusses on the commerce part of the marketplace, i.e. buying and selling. Integration of business partners for specific processes beyond commerce (e.g. cooperative planning and forecasts) is described under "Collaboration". The SAP marketplace is far more than a simple business directory of the kind offered by many providers today in so far as you are not only able to find business partners but also perform business transactions directly via the www.mySAP.com marketplace and integrate the requisite data in a one-step business process. The only condition is that both business partners must have enabled their systems for one-step business by using the required internet standards and setting up links with the back-end transaction systems. If this has been done, the relevant business documents can be exchanged and a seamless exchange of information is ensured (see Chapter 2.2). We would like to emphasize the unique concept of the marketplace created by SAP. To speak of a mere "marketplace" would not be quite correct, as *mySAP.com* consists of several cross-industry marketplaces and, more importantly, of many vertical and regional marketplaces. Cross-industry or horizontal marketplaces offer goods and services that are required by virtually all businesses whatever their industry. The best example in this regard may be the marketplace for maintenance, repair, operation (MRO) materials which facilitates the procurement of C materials. Cross-industry marketplaces are further enhanced by applications such as auctions, matching requests for quotation issued to vendors, etc. In contrast, vertical marketplaces mainly pool the supply and demand of one particular industry, (e.g. the oil and gas industry) for specific goods, services, and information. The same applies to regional marketplaces, where regional supply meets regional demand. A marketplace for real estate, for example, only makes sense for a specific region, such as California. Such a marketplace should, of course, be connected to a real estate marketplace in the USA, and it should be possible to branch from one marketplace to the other.

- *Collaboration*
  Cooperative or collaborative business on the internet can assume many different forms, but it goes far beyond mere e-commerce, as described above under the heading "Commerce." The joint and ultimate goal of all *mySAP.com* components is to connect and integrate intra-enterprise processes with all business partners across organizational boundaries by using the internet. What is more, integration should be implemented not in the form of a $1:1$ relationship but on an $n:n$ basis. In other words, you can integrate your business processes with any business partner participating in one-step business without having to make additional implementations each time, which would be required with EDI. Some significant examples of business cooperation reaching beyond the classical form of e-commerce are described below.

  - *Distributor reseller management*
    The web-based business scenario distributor reseller management simplifies the individual steps of cooperation between manufacturers and distributors/resellers. Each process step is supported electronically and by XML – from drawing up an

initial contract and negotiating the business terms and contents, to concluding a corresponding agreement.

- *Request for proposal (RFP) and request for quotation (RFQ) matching*
  On the *mySAP.com* marketplace, RFQs issued to vendors can be entered, distributed, and matched. This reduces administrative costs for the purchasing and sales departments of the participating enterprises. Moreover, customers can enter their demands for preferred vendors directly in the relevant section of the marketplace. Suppliers can then give a quotation and negotiate terms. For those suppliers who are already participating, a classification system compares available capacities with the required quantity.

- *Cooperative sales and production planning and forecasts*
  Sales organizations or distributors define their sales plans and enter them in a special planning sheet on the internet. For example, they may use the advanced planner and optimizer which can be accessed via the *mySAP.com* marketplace. Manufacturers and vendors can then update and adapt their production plans accordingly (Figure 2.4.3-3). Several planning cycles may be run if required.

- *Content*
  Many internet pages have a single goal – to supply information. This is also often referred to as providing content. There are a large number of such content providers who offer either general information or specific content for certain target groups. *mySAP.com* also provides specialized information, which mainly consists of user group-specific content. This includes comprehensive business news as well as detailed industry news. In addition, general information such as sports news or politics, etc. is supplied.

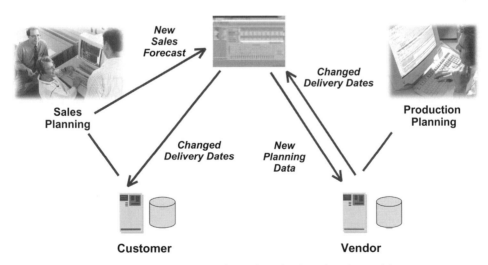

Figure 2.4.3-3:   Cooperative sales and production planning and forecasts

- *Community*

  Nowadays, IT is rapidly changing the way business is done, and how products and services are exchanged between enterprises. In today's competitive business environment buyers need to have access to information at all times and from anywhere in the world, e.g. prices and market alternatives for the products and services they need. Vendors, on the other hand, need to respond with quick, unlimited, and, above all, personalized and global access to information and best prices for their products and services. To help both business partners meet these challenges, SAP offers **business communities**. These are virtual locations where business partners from the same industry (e.g. consumer products) can meet and communicate, call specific content in the form of messages, find out about interesting events, and do business together. SAP supports nineteen such vertical business communities – one such is the consumer product community.

  To conclude, we can describe the *mySAP.com* marketplace as a combination of infrastructure, technology, web applications, and web services. For the protection of data exchanged via the marketplace, secure socket layer protocols are used to ensure data confidentiality, integration, and authenticity. In addition to Verisign, other certificates are supported. Data transfer in the form of transactions is secured via a message store service. In this case, SAP acts as a confidential, independent third party offering to log and store all B2B transactions (such as purchase orders or confirmations). Documents exchanged by business partners via the marketplace are processed by a messaging engine which receives, stores, and sends business documents in XML format with synchronous as well as asynchronous protocols.

2.4.4   mySAP.com: application hosting

Application hosting is the fourth "pillar" of the *mySAP.com* internet strategy alongside the marketplace, the workplace, and the business scenarios. Before we describe this service in detail, we would like to give a general explanation of the term application hosting. This is a service provided by application service providers (ASPs). The ASP runs enterprise solutions (applications, such as the SAP system, B2B procurement, or even *mySAP.com* as a whole) as well as the corresponding technology (network, database, operating system, etc.) within its own computing and data center and makes them available to customers on a network (e.g. extranet, virtual private network, or the internet). All the customer needs to access his personal enterprise solution is a desktop or network client (network computing), a web browser and a connection to the network, e.g. via an ISDN internet port. Depending on the specific provider, this solution can either be predefined (off-the-shelf), meaning that no customer-specific modifications can be made, or tailor-made, i.e. tailored to the specific needs of the customer. As a rule, however, we only talk of application hosting in the first case, as the ASP–customer relation is a $1:n$ relationship. The second case will usually be a classical outsourcing project. Furthermore, ASPs offer various services as part of service level agreements, e.g. upgrade cycles, several backups. Analysts give the following definitions of application hosting and ASP:

- "ASPs implement, host, and manage a wide range of applications for multiple clients networked into a central processing facility." (META-Group)

- "Hosted applications typically allow packaged software products or solutions to be delivered on a one-to-many basis ... where the application is purchased as a service. Responsibility for ... management and development is ceded contractually to an external service provider." (International Data Corporation)

To provide a basic classification of the various services offered by ASPs within application hosting, SAP, in accordance with the most common definitions given by analysts, has divided application hosting into the following three levels:

- *Platform services or IT outsourcing*: the customer delegates all, or at least a large part of, the activities connected with the IT infrastructure operation (e.g. networks, servers, operating systems, databases, internet basis, SAP basis) to the ASP.

- *Application services or application management outsourcing*: the customer delegates all activities related to applications such as the SAP system, the business information warehouse, B2B procurement, internet applications, etc. to the ASP. Activities may include application design, customizing, technical change management (upgrades), documentation, application helpdesks, etc.

- *Business operation services or business process outsourcing*: the customer delegates all or at least a large part of a business process or corporate function to the ASP. This means that the ASP is responsible for performing all activities related to the business process. For example, when hosting the HR (human resources) payroll, the ASP operates the total application, updates HR master records, and calculates and sends paychecks.

Within the *mySAP.com* solution, SAP and its partners offer a complete end-to-end hosting service that is available in its entirety on the internet as well as via conventional methods (leased line, extranet, etc.) (Figure 2.4.4-1).

- *Test drive your solution online*
  As part of evaluation, prospective customers are given an opportunity to "test drive" *mySAP.com* solutions before buying them. Within this "try-before-you-buy" approach, they can get an SAP user account on the internet to gain access to the *mySAP.com* system. Using an internet demonstration and evaluation system, enterprises can try out their typical, industry-specific processes. The evaluation system is an industry-specific, preconfigured system containing components such as SAP, B2B procurement, workplace, etc. and enables users to simulate the relevant processes in an integrated environment.

- *Compose your solution online*
  In the interface between evaluation and implementation, the (prospective) customer can design a preconfigured system to suit his organization's needs and industry requirements by filling in a web-based questionnaire. If he decides to become an SAP customer, he can add further customized details to this system online in the next phase.

- *We implement your solution online*
  Once a customer has created his own personal SAP solution, he can implement it in one of two ways. In the conventional way, he installs hardware and software on the

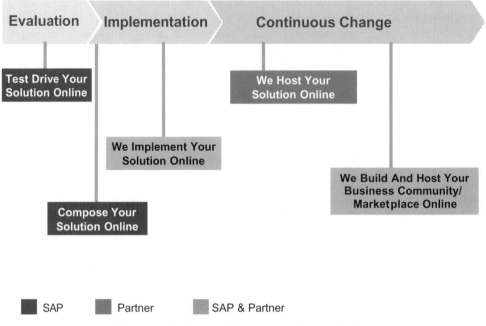

Figure 2.4.4.-1:   mySAP.com – application hosting

premises and also performs the detailed analysis (blueprinting) and configuration on site, supported by a project team. Alternatively, he can use online implementation, in which case he has the software installed on SAP/partner hardware in an SAP/partner computing center. The detailed analysis is also performed online on the internet. The customer may be supported by a project team on site, or can use a variety of additional SAP online services (e.g. e-learning, e-consulting).

- *We host your solution online*
  This means the operation of SAP solutions by ASPs, i.e. the classic case of application hosting. The customer basically has a choice of two ways of hosting for his solution. Either the customer contacts directly the SAP ASP partner who offers the exact solution for his specific needs without taking a detour via SAP services (e.g. *we implement your solution online*), or he entrusts his individual system – which he has previously configured to meet his specific requirements using SAP online implementation – to the SAP ASP partner for operation. This is necessary because SAP itself does not act in the market as an ASP operating SAP solutions.

- *We build and host your marketplace*
  Many enterprises participate in several marketplaces such as www.mySAP.com in order to optimize inter-enterprise processes, e.g. procurement processes. We distinguish between **closed** marketplaces, which are reserved for a few selected business partners, and **open** marketplaces, which anyone can access. In addition to participating in various open and closed marketplaces, many customers, particularly

large groups, are interested in building up and operating their own group-specific marketplace, e.g. to integrate their processes with selected suppliers and customers or other business partners. With this in mind, SAP offers additional services within *mySAP.com* to help these enterprises to establish and operate their own marketplaces.

2.5 mySAP.com software components – relationships

The current SAP product range essentially consists of the following independent products, all of which can be implemented individually. Nevertheless, the real benefit emerges in complete end-to-end (and easy-to-implement) integration with each other (e.g. SAP MM with B2B procurement). The product range includes:

- SAP as a back-end ERP system (financials, logistics, human resources)
- customer relationship management
- advanced planner and optimizer
- B2B procurement
- B2B selling
- business-to-consumer selling
- business information warehouse
- knowledge management
- corporate finance management
- strategic enterprise management
- employee self services.

These products can currently be bought and implemented individually and have different release cycles. *mySAP.com*, on the other hand, is a complete end-to-end solution. In concrete terms, this means that the individual software products listed above will become part of the complete *mySAP.com* package, and that in future we will talk of *mySAP.com* software components, such as *mySAP.com* customer relationship management or *mySAP.com* logistics. *mySAP.com* customers are offered a package of various software components which are installed on site and can be activated or deactivated according to their personal requirements on the business scenarios to be implemented in their enterprise. As *mySAP.com* is not a "pure" software solution but rather a complete end-to-end solution for cooperative business transactions, it contains service components in addition to software components. Figure 2.5-1 gives an overview of *mySAP.com*.

The most important resources of an enterprise are its human resources, and in particular their effective and efficient deployment. To enable these employees to perform their daily work, the necessary IT solutions supporting them must make all activities as

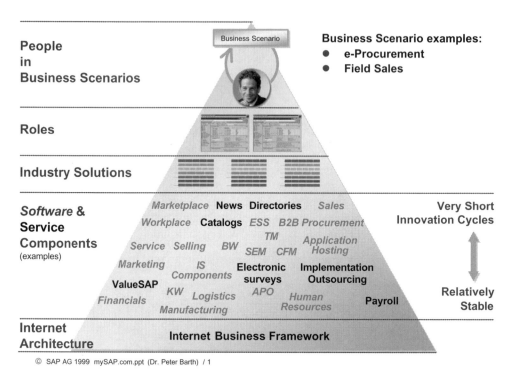

© SAP AG 1999 mySAP.com.ppt (Dr. Peter Barth) / 1

Figure 2.5-1:   mySAP.com – system and software components

easy to access and use as possible. How this is done largely depends on the kind of information required by each individual employee according to his role in the enterprise. This is why *mySAP.com* implementation is focussed on the end user as the center of all activities. As part of their jobs, all employees participate in different processes or business scenarios both within the enterprise (e.g. requesting leave using employee self-service, sales analysis, etc.) and beyond the confines of the enterprise (e.g. procurement on the internet, cooperative production planning, etc.). How an employee participates in such a business scenario and what kind of information or transactions he needs depends on his individual role. A purchasing manager requires different support to purchasing staff. Furthermore, the enterprise's branch of industry is another factor determining the specific type of information and customized settings required. Thus, a sales agent employed by an enterprise in the consumer goods industry needs different information and transactions than a sales agent in the aerospace sector. This is exactly why *mySAP.com* offers an industry-specific approach modeled on SAP industry solution maps. SAP industry solutions also form part of *mySAP.com*. These customized, role-based, industry-specific business scenarios are based on SAP software and service components which provide greater coverage than the software components listed above. An additional software application is the workplace. In the area of services, the marketplace, the business directory, business communities, general internet services, and application hosting are of primary interest.

As mentioned above, all *mySAP.com* components can be used both individually (i.e. as independent components) and collectively as part of a more extensive solution. In the latter case, the implementation sequence is of no importance. This means that the various scenarios needing more than just one software component can be implemented either by exclusively using *mySAP.com* components or by using third party software solutions as well. This is made possible by the internet business framework with its semantic standard BAPI and its technical standard XML.

Note: The SAP system and its functionality remain intact within the *mySAP.com* solution. When in future we speak of "*mySAP.com* logistics" or "*mySAP.com* financials," for example, we mean the functions derived directly from the SAP system. The SAP system is sometimes also referred to as a "back-end," "execution" or "backbone" system.

2.6   mySAP.com – process modules

In Chapter 2.5 we illustrated the individual components of *mySAP.com* and their relationships and showed how this solution differs from existing applications such as the SAP system and "new dimension products" (e.g. B2B procurement, business information warehouse). We also explained that the basic functionality of the SAP system as it stands today will be preserved, in so far as it will become part of the new complete *mySAP.com* solution. Finally, we described the strategy of business scenarios. If we look at the current situation with regard to software solutions, we find that SAP components can integrate an

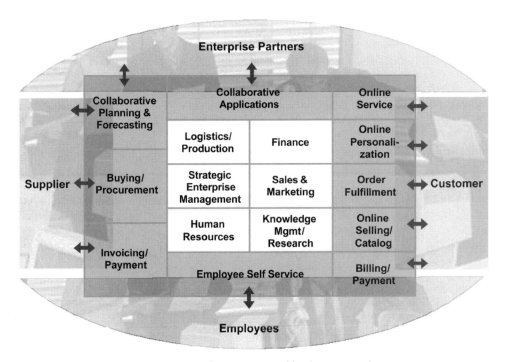

Figure 2.6-1:   Components and business scenarios

enterprise internally (intra-enterprise integration). To integrate processes across enterprises, we can use either SAP inherent internet application components (see Chapter 1.1.9) and BAPIs, or new products such as B2B procurement.

For comprehensive internet integration, cross-enterprise processes or business scenarios require different components, such as SAP as an execution system and B2B procurement as a product. This proves that the SAP system will continue to play an essential role in the future – quite contrary to the frequently voiced belief that ERP software will no longer be necessary. The SAP system and its complete functionality – though it may in the future be referred to in terms of *mySAP.com* components (see Chapter 2.5) – will:

- continue to be required to integrate processes within the enterprise;

- act as back-end/execution system to perform and control inter-enterprise business processes and scenarios taking place on the internet.

Figures 2.6.-1 and 2.6-2 show this very clearly. The dark fields in the center rectangle (logistics/production, finance, human resources) represent the *mySAP.com* components and functions currently provided within the SAP system. Each component shown here

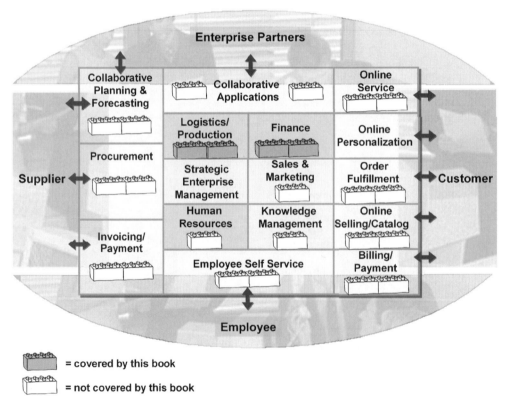

Figure 2.6-2:   Components and business scenarios

(see Chapter 2.5) contains a certain number of process modules (Figure 2.6-2) that can be put together.

The process chains created in this way may consist of processes that operate only within the enterprise. In the same way, such a process chain may represent an inter-enterprise business process (Figure 2.6-2). Consequently, the components listed in Chapter 2.5 comprise all the process modules existing in *mySAP.com*. *mySAP.com* business scenarios are made up of various process modules from one component lined up in a chain, or integrated process modules from various different components. Taken together, these modules enable a new approach to electronic commerce, cooperative business, and the supply of business information systems. Being components of internet-enabled applications, they help businesses to overcome functional and geographical barriers and maximize their individual and combined performance.

For internet sales to end users (business-to-consumer) for example, process modules of various *mySAP.com* components are integrated, i.e. the business system logic of the SAP sales module and the processes and functions of the SAP online store are combined in an interactive, multimedia online user interface. In this highly integrated approach, all relevant data (customer data, prices, and logistic information) is stored and maintained in the SAP system. In the online store, users have direct access to this data so it is no longer necessary to copy data. All data, such as production information, prices, and product availability, can be read directly in the system and is therefore always up to date. After changes to data, the online store need not be updated again. Sales orders and customer master data entered on the internet are automatically transferred to the central system for further processing. The SAP system acts as the business backbone of this process, i.e. it supports the complete order processing scenario. Consequently, all subsequent processes related to the order, such as shipping, billing, and processing payment forms, are mapped directly onto the SAP system. Processes in the online store, such as pictures of products, shopping basket management, customer entry, offer creation, or order status tracking, are directly integrated with SAP process modules.

In the following example we illustrate the interaction of process modules from different *mySAP.com* components using the online store and SAP system as above (Figure 2.6-3):

- *Selecting a product*
  When you select a product group in the online store, the various articles it contains are displayed. The list gives a brief description of each product (e.g. with a photograph and name) and its price. You can branch from the product list to a detailed view of each product which has more text, pictures, and possibly sound clips. The detailed product presentation in the online store uses the **document management system** or corresponding process module.

- *Filling the shopping basket*
  If the customer is satisfied with a product and wants to order it, he places it in a shopping basket. This basket is a list of all products selected for the purchase order so far. At this stage, no transaction is performed in the SAP back-end system.

- *Creating a customer*
  Internet users who are new customers of an enterprise have to go through a registration process before they receive a quotation. This process mainly consists of

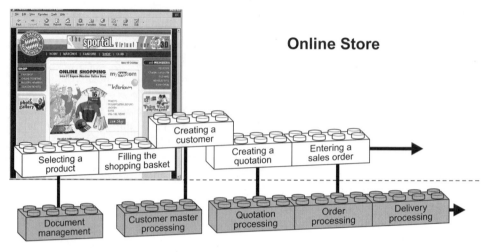

Figure 2.6-3:   Interaction between online store and SAP system

collecting customer address data. The online store then creates a customer master record in the SAP system and allocates a number to the customer. The interaction in the online store triggers the **customer master processing** process module in the SAP system.

- *Creating a quotation*
  Once a customer has been identified, a quotation is issued under consideration of all customer terms. In addition, current availability is checked and the resulting delivery date is confirmed directly online. Confirmation to the internet user is triggered by **sales order processing** in the SAP system. So far, however, it is only a simulated confirmation as the customer has not yet placed a definite order.

- *Entering a sales order*
  If the customer is satisfied with the quotation, he can convert it into an order. He will receive confirmation containing all the relevant information about the goods ordered (such as product name, quantity, and availability) as well as the number of the order which was entered directly into the SAP system online, i.e. the process module sales order processing is executed.

All further processing of the sales order, such as delivery processing and billing, takes place in the SAP system. Using the order number, the customer is able to see the current status of the order online in the internet application component **sales order status** (e.g. inquire how many or which of the articles in his order have been prepared for shipping or have already been shipped).

We would like to mention that in Books 2, 3, and 4 of this series, we explain and analyze the process modules of the *mySAP.com* components logistics and financial accounting (currently SAP LO and FI) using knowledge maps and EnjoySAP graphics for clarification. We have thus focussed on the **internal** integration of an enterprise, which still forms the basis of integrated (i.e. effective and efficient) processes and, therefore, an indispensable prerequisite for inter-enterprise process integration.

2.7   Example of a business scenario on the internet with mySAP.com marketplace, B2B procurement, and the SAP back-end system

The SAP B2B procurement solution provides ideal support for the entire procurement process of non-production-related products (primarily C materials) over the internet (Figure 2.7-1). As a result, today's business is considerably relieved of the need to place operational purchase orders for indirect goods and can thus strategically focus on goods and services that must be supplied directly by vendors. The advantages of using B2B purchasing are:

- it relieves purchasing managers of operational tasks;

- there are simple and straightforward processes between buyer and supplier (e.g. purchase order items, goods receipt, and invoices do not have to be entered but are processed directly via the internet and exchanged automatically);

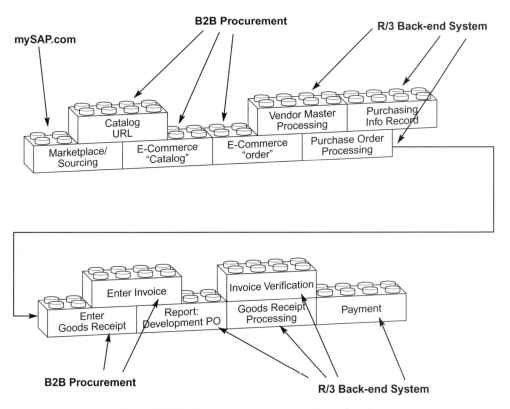

Figure 2.7-1:   E-commerce procurement – value chain

- many unnecessary and redundant process steps (double data maintenance) are eliminated;

- it gives increased transparency of pricing and improved ability to compare products;

- time-consuming approval procedures are electronically supported.

The integration of B2B components in the *mySAP.com* concept enables location of suppliers in the marketplace and inclusion of their catalogs in the B2B procurement system. Following the B2B procurement process on the internet, you are able to deal with processes such as goods receipt and invoice processing in the SAP business back-end system. The individual process steps of the scenario are now explained.

1. *Role (purchaser) looks for suitable suppliers in the marketplace using mySAP.com*
   Under the heading one-step business, the purchaser can find enterprises sorted according to different product categories. He can then compare several suppliers and include them at a later stage in the catalog selection as insuppliers. The online catalog (product catalog) for one-step business is only included if the purchaser is satisfied with the range of products offered, the prices, and delivery conditions. In our example (Figure 2.7-2), the purchaser is looking for a specific company: Grainger. He can view details about the company profile and tap into the Grainger catalog. In addition, SAP

Figure 2.7-2: EnjoySAP screen for mySAP.com marketplace

has, in this case, identified Grainger as a one-step business supplier. This means that the catalog can easily be transferred to the B2B catalog selection by entering the uniform resource locator (URL), login data, and the return URL. The data is entered for each catalog in SAP B2B procurement customizing (Figure 2.7-3). The supplier and purchaser can thus participate in open, cooperative, virtual marketplaces that enable one-step business processes.

The *mySAP.com* marketplace aims to enable "business community collaboration," i.e. it is an open marketplace where competitors can offer their materials, tools, and services. It provides the purchaser with a wider range of suppliers and better market transparency than ever before.

2. *Role (requester/purchaser) branches to the purchase environment of SAP B2B procurement*
   At the start of the ordering process, the requester sees an empty shopping basket which he can fill with goods or services. He can either enter the material number directly (Figure 2.7-4 – Material field) if he knows it and it is known to the back-end system (e.g. SAP), or he can branch to an online catalog. If he is not authorized to place an order then he can enter a description of his requirements (free entry) that can be further processed by the purchaser. In our example, the purchaser himself selects the **requisite** catalog and starts the purchase order process.

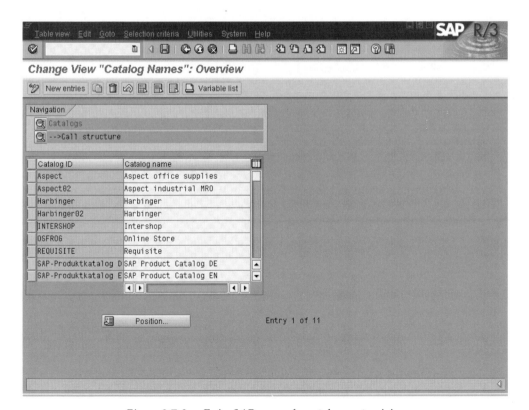

Figure 2.7-3:   EnjoySAP screen for catalog customizing

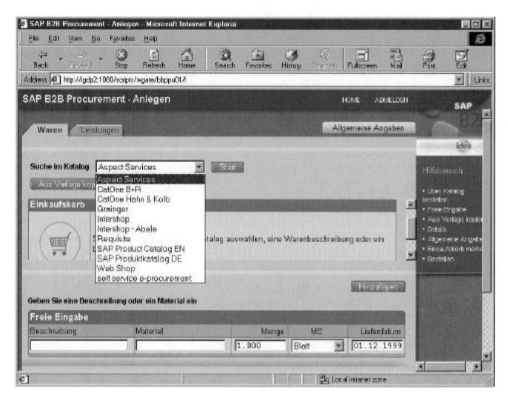

Figure 2.7-4:   EnjoySAP screen for SAP B2B procurement – shopping basket

3. *Role (purchaser) branches to the supplier catalog and selects goods for purchase requisition*
   The purchaser is generally able to enter the item description in the supplier catalog using
   a direct search (in this example a palm pilot), or he can select an item via the shopping
   list (Figure 2.7-5). In most cases, product pictures are not shown in the list as this would
   affect system performance. In the detail screen, however, the purchaser can see a picture
   of the product with further details, such as dimensions, tolerance levels, a more detailed
   description of the product, etc. (Figure 2.7-6). The advantages of web-based catalogs
   often lie in their simple structure and intuitive, well-received presentation. The following
   fields can be used to transfer items to the SAP shopping basket:

   - material number or description (short text)
   - quantity with unit of measure
   - price, price unit, and currency
   - delivery time
   - supplier
   - supplier material number (if required)
   - manufacturer with part number
   - material group.

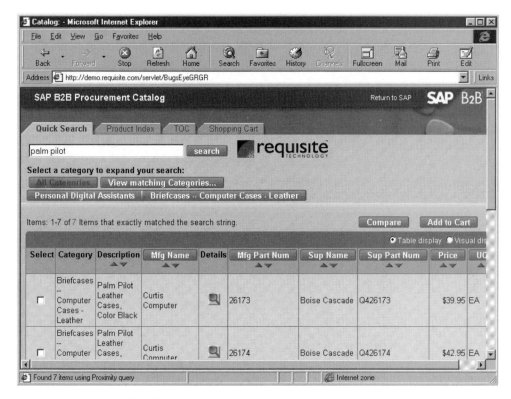

Figure 2.7-5:   EnjoySAP screen for goods selection from an online catalog

Data exchange, i.e. the integration of heterogeneous systems (such as different online catalog with the SAP B2B procurement system), requires standardization. Currently, there is a lack of uniform international standards that enable uncomplicated communication between different internet applications. In the form of the business connector (BC), SAP provides a basic method that enables defined data exchange between a number of partners with different systems (e.g. supplier product catalog) using XML (eXtended Markup Language) technology. XML is emerging as an increasingly accepted standard format within the World Wide Web Consortium. The SAP BC interface converts XML documents to a format that can be read by SAP system servers.

4. *Role (purchaser) transfers items to the shopping cart and places an order*
   The items (e.g. palm pilot) are copied to the SAP B2B procurement system using the **add to cart** menu option. Quantities can still be changed in the shopping cart, and the price is automatically recalculated if changes are made. In the shopping cart, you can check the ordered goods once more before finally transferring them to the shopping basket. The order can be completed from there. The SAP system creates the purchase order number and info record number in the background in the SAP back-end system.

Figure 2.7-6:   EnjoySAP screen for online catalog – item details view

Our example shows (Figure 2.7-7) the purchase order number 3000031323 for supplier 5400. At the same time, a workflow is started that checks whether approval is required. If it is, the people required to give approval receive a message (via e-mail). If approval is not necessary, purchase orders or reservations are generated in the back-end system as shown in the example. If the purchaser has stored the shopping basket (here basket 011299), he can use this as a personal template the next time he makes a purchase. He is also able to change the account assignment details at a later stage (cost center, line, project, sales order, network plan). In most cases he will use the account type C as in cost center and he can still change the cost center at short notice in the basic data of the SAP B2B procurement system.

5. *Role (purchaser) can view the generated info record, vendor master record, or purchase order in the SAP back-end system*
   The info record shows the purchaser the agreed data such as the price for a material, order conditions, terms of delivery, tolerance limits for over or under delivery, etc. Contrary to the price given in the material master, the info record can show the specific prices agreed with the supplier. If a net price has not been specified in the info record, the conditions of the last purchase order, or the last outline agreement, are copied to a

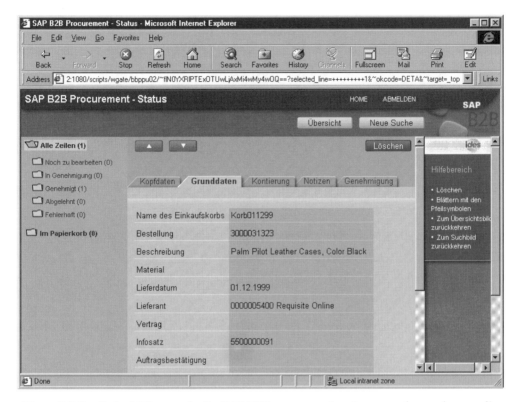

Figure 2.7-7: EnjoySAP screen for the SAP B2B procurement system – purchase order, supplier and info record number data

new purchase order. There is usually an info record and the conditions are transferred to the purchase order using a template. The catalog supplier from the SAP B2B procurement system is listed as a supplier (vendor) with name and address details in the SAP back-end system. Additionally, the purchaser can store the valid currency, conditions of payment, or the contact person in the master record. Following Step 4, a purchase order with the document type EC (electronic commerce) was automatically generated in the SAP back-end system. Figure 2.7-8 shows the items screen of the purchase order and its most important fields. The first field group shows the quantity and net price. If you differentiate between purchase order unit and purchase order price unit, a conversion is necessary. The next field group is used for scheduling – scaled deliveries are carried out in accordance with a predefined time schedule (delivery schedule line). Other important indicators can be found in goods/invoice receipt control. In our example, the indicators for goods receipt and invoice receipt have been set, i.e. we expect to receive both goods (see Step 6) and an invoice (see Step 7) from our supplier "Requisite Online." If you expect a number of part deliveries of your order, it makes sense to run an invoice verification based on the goods receipt

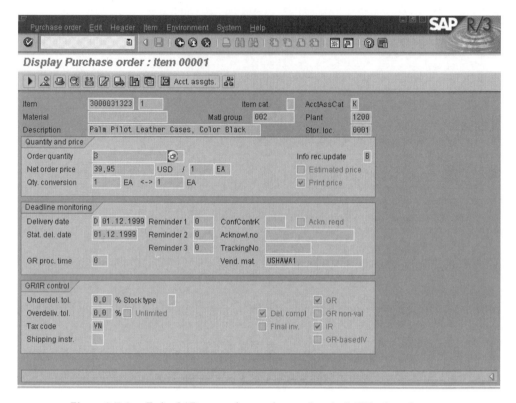

Figure 2.7-8:   EnjoySAP screen for purchase orders in SAP back-end system

(see corresponding indicator). In this case, the invoice is not based on the purchase order but on the individual deliveries (goods receipt document).

6. *Role (requester/purchaser) checks if the goods have been received and which cost center was debited*
   When the materials (here the palm pilot with goods receipt quantity of three pieces) have been received, the employee (requester/purchaser) has the following options. He can enter the goods receipt, or return the goods (e.g. if they are damaged), or he can cancel goods receipts that have already been entered. To determine whether or not the purchase order budget covers the amount sufficiently, a cost center analysis can be started in the back-end SAP system. Account assignment data is stored in the SAP B2B procurement system. In our example (Figure 2.7-9), cost center 1000 has been debited for the goods from shopping basket 011299. The purchaser can view the account assignment data and change it if necessary. Possible entries (cost center, line, project, sales document, order, and network plan) depend on the account assignment category.

7. *Role (vendor/catalog supplier) enters the invoice directly in the SAP B2B procurement system*
   The supplier either sends an invoice by post or enters the invoice for the purchase

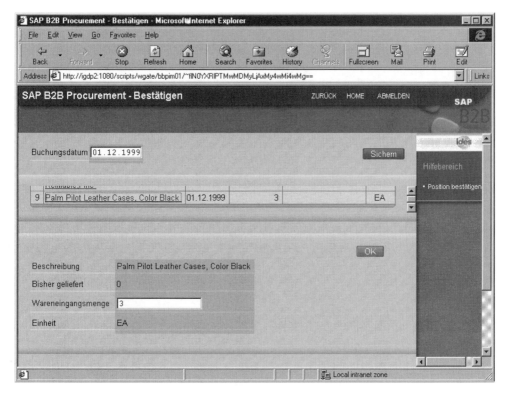

Figure 2.7-9:   EnjoySAP screen for SAP B2B – goods receipt

order directly on the internet using the SAP B2B procurement system. The invoice can then be subjected to an approval procedure. If the invoice is refused, the invoicing party is sent an e-mail. If the invoice is approved, it is released for payment. Figure 2.7-10 shows a selection of purchase orders for which you can enter invoices. You can limit the selection by entering a date. Only the purchase orders that correspond to the search criteria are displayed. The colors in the far right column, create invoice, show whether the purchase order has been released for invoice entry (green = released for invoicing, red = goods not yet received). You can then enter the invoice directly or view the details of the order, edit it if necessary, then enter the invoice.

8. *Role (purchaser) checks the development of the purchase order in the SAP back-end system*
The purchaser can use the **purchase order history** report in the purchasing system of the SAP back-end system to see whether goods and invoices have been received. The purchase order history documents all processes regarding an order item. In addition, delivery costs, down payments, etc. are listed for the goods receipts and invoices. Figure 2.7-11 shows delivery costs of DM16.83 for the goods entry. When displaying the purchase order history, you can switch between several views. The following

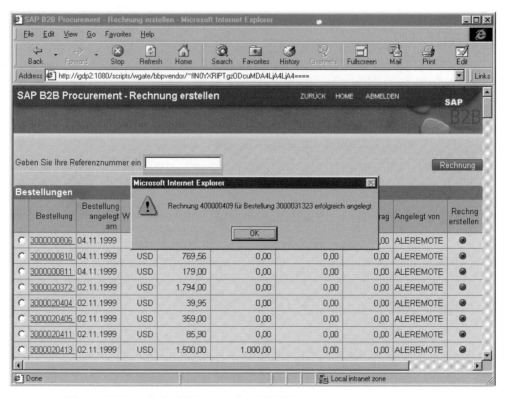

Figure 2.7-10:   EnjoySAP screen for SAP B2B procurement – invoice entry

are available:

- delivery costs
- invoice documents
- quantity of blocked stock
- the assignment of goods and invoice receipt documents for a goods receipt-based invoice verification.

9. *Role (accountant) checks the posted invoice for purchase order and goods received*
   The accountant can call up the material document, the accounting document, the profit center document, the special ledger, and the controlling document in the SAP back-end system. When the invoice is posted, the back-end system finds the accounts to be posted to. Account assignment is based on your entries for the invoice, and on stored information such as net and gross posting, the vendor account, and the general ledger (G/L) accounts. The material master contains further information necessary for posting, e.g. the evaluation class (to which account the material is posted), price controlling (standard price/moving average price). The accounts are also defined in a chart of accounts. The following accounts are particularly important for invoice verification.

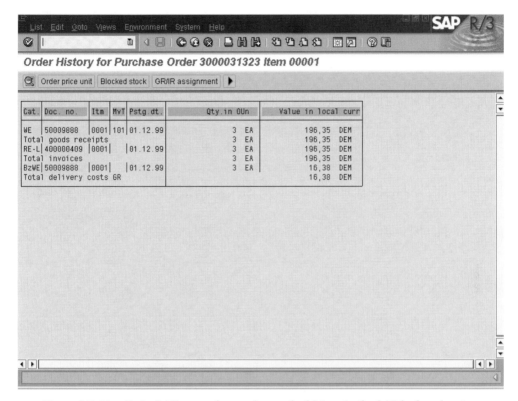

Figure 2.7-11:   EnjoySAP screen for purchase order history in the SAP back-end system

- *Vendor account (in the example, vendor Requisite Online with account 5400)*
  A separate account is created for each vendor in sub-ledger accounting to which all amounts relevant to this vendor are posted. A posting to the vendor account is not the same as a payment; this is carried out by financial accounting by a **vendor account to bank** posting.
- *Balance sheet account*
  A separate account is not set up for each material in the SAP back-end system. Different materials with similar characteristics are grouped in a joint account. The material master record defines the relevant account for a material.
- *GR/IR clearing account (in the example, GR/IR clearing account with $119.85)*
  The GR/IR clearing account is an interim account between the balance sheet account and the vendor account. When a goods receipt is posted, the system carries out the following account movements: the value of the delivery is credited to the balance sheet account (purchase order net price × goods receipt quantity), the GR/IR clearing account is debited this amount; when the invoice is posted, the GR/IR clearing account is cleared by debiting the vendor account (Figure 2.7-12). At the end of a settlement period, all purchases should have been posted to accounts in the back-end system. Combined with the posted invoice, the result is a settled clearing account.

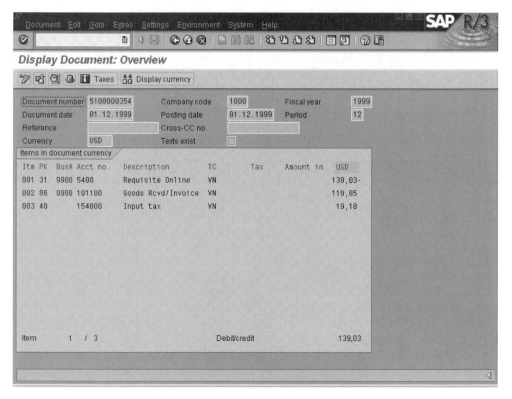

Figure 2.7-12:   EnjoySAP screen for accounting document in SAP back-end system

3 Basics

3.1 The MindMapping method

The MindMapping method is said to have been invented by the British scientist Tony Buzan. In the preface to his book, *The Mind Map Book* (Buzan and Buzan) he describes the difficulties he encountered during his studies. At the time, he felt overwhelmed by the flood of information rushing at him and he started looking for literature to enable him to cope better with the vast quantity of data. However, he could not find any information on how to use the capacity of the brain as efficiently as possible. He looked into the questions revolving around learning, thinking, creativity, and methods of thinking. From his exploration of these issues there evolved the concept of mind mapping in the seventies.

Based on the knowledge that thinking is a highly complex process in which new associations and structures are constantly being evolved, Buzan developed the MindMapping method, which tries to involve both hemispheres of the brain. The active use of both brain regions produces synergy effects which can be exploited to improve the performance of the brain dramatically.

The concept is such that information is no longer represented as linear lists or word wrap, but in a way which turns records and notes into a unique, memorable picture. Unnecessary fillers are deliberately excluded while the focus is on carefully selected keywords which serve to recall the message of the notes later on and stimulate a thorough analysis of the subject concerned. The methodical use of language, pictures, numbers, graphics, codes, etc., which exploit the ability to think in three dimensions as well as rhythm, is a very effective way of stimulating the potential of the human mind and utilizing the full range of its capacity and resources.

At first glance, mind maps may seem rather odd and confusing. Knowing how memory functions and understanding the workings of the human brain makes it easier to grasp the method and structure of mind mapping.

3.1.1 What we have in common with Mozart, Einstein, and Picasso

This is the somewhat provocative subtitle of a book by Robert W. Weisberg (*Kreativität und Begabung: Was wir mit Mozart, Einstein und Picasso gemeinsam haben*). The personalities discussed in this book are generally regarded as geniuses. The works and achievements of composers, inventors, scientists, and artists show a special creative gift. Their work is widely recognized, and they are generally admired for their creative talent. Yet creativity can also be found in children's dreams and games, in inventive solutions to problems at home or at work, in the constructive resolution of conflicts, in writing a letter, etc. Creativity is not something we find only in geniuses, we also see it in children, in all people in all kinds of everyday situations requiring unconventional, inspired ideas, new visions and concepts. Creativity, or being creative, is a challenge to all of us. What is creativity and how can we characterize it? Creativity is regarded as a complex phenomenon for which there is no clear definition. The word stems from the Latin *creare* which means "to generate, produce, breed" and indicates a dynamic process (origin and aim). In former times, creativity was also described as "creative power." From antiquity to the classical period, man with his creative power was regarded as an almost perfect being. Creativity was placed in the category of mysticism and religion, or it was "a sign of God's mercy" (Stocker, p. 11). As we will not find an unambiguous definition of creativity, let us turn to its characteristics. Scientists seem to have a clear idea of the requirements that must be met so that we can talk of a creative product. "The term 'product' comprises ideas and visions as well as their implementation, artistic designs and original acts of everyday life" (Preiser and Buchholz, p. 11). They continue by describing three requirements.

- The idea must be new or include new elements. It does not necessarily have to be unique. It must contain some novelty, something that is new for at least one person or in one specific situation.

- The second requirement is met when the idea contributes to the solution of a problem or triggers some kind of change, or if it makes people wonder or think. The idea must make sense.

- The tragedy of many artists, inventors, and discoverers may serve to illustrate the third requirement. Many revolutionary ideas were not recognized as such in their time. Their conceivers were honored only after their deaths. It may be that the conceiver of an idea is fully convinced of its value and his own creativity. Still, it will not necessarily gain him recognition. As long as an idea is not understood or accepted by the public, its conceiver may be called many things but probably not "creative." The novel and meaningful idea must be accepted by the social environment that surrounds it. Only through this acceptance can an idea have any effect. This process cannot be measured or recorded. Rather, this is about finding a consensus on the social acceptance of an idea. "The people who accept an idea as new and sensible form the social system which recognizes an idea as being creative" (Preiser and Buchholz, p. 12).

3.1.2   Basics of the MindMapping method

3.1.2.1   Radial thinking

"Radial thinking (i.e. thinking radiating from a center) refers to associative thinking processes which evolve from a central point or are connected with a central point" (Buzan and Buzan, p. 57). The process of thinking is not linear but a highly complex procedure in the brain during which new associations and structures are constantly generated. These associations are triggered by keywords. Every subject or word is linked with different ideas and conceptions for different people. Every sensation, memory, or thought triggers a multitude of associations in the human brain. Each association is linked to an infinite number of other ideas and associations. We can switch between different trains of thought. In our minds we can add, vary, or drop details as we please. We can easily establish and call up links with other fields of our knowledge, so that a network of interwoven bits of information is formed in the brain. They see the brain as " … a vast, ramified association machine …, as a super biocomputer with lines of thoughts radiating from an infinite number of data nodes" (Buzan and Buzan, p. 56).

3.1.2.2   Brainstorming

In the process of conceiving ideas, many of our thoughts do not fully emerge. We check ourselves, hold back and subject our ideas to the censorship of our brain, often rejecting an idea as not feasible or even crazy. Such an idea will no longer be considered in the analysis of our own thoughts. Creative problem solutions and ideas require not only using well-known paths but treading new, unfamiliar tracks as well. A suitable method for doing this is **brainstorming**. This method is frequently used in group work but the principles of brainstorming can also be applied to situations where ideas are collected by one individual. Brainstorming is a technique for creatively generating ideas. By stimulating spontaneous thoughts and chains of thought, this method contributes to breaking up existing structures and developing unusual, creative alternatives. Brainstorming is characterized by free association, a process of freely connecting ideas without censorship. Barriers and inhibitions are to be eliminated as far as possible. During brainstorming, ideas must not be commented on or explained, and by no means criticized. Based on existing ideas which have already been developed and voiced, these new ideas should stimulate each other and evolve further. All thoughts are recorded in writing. The immediate result is a collection of ideas, approaches, problems, etc. which can subsequently be put into order, assessed, specified, and developed further.

3.1.2.3   Combined method

Mind mapping builds on the processes of radial thinking and brainstorming, along with the proposition that "a picture is worth a thousand words." Buzan and Buzan list scientific studies (Buzan and Buzan, p. 71) which support the theory that our capacity to recognize a picture is almost perfect. If we consider the fact that a picture is composed of lines, colors, forms, multidimensionality and structure, all of which stimulate our imagination, it becomes clear that pictures trigger more chains of association than words and thus boost creative thinking and the memory. This raises the question of why, so often, no pictures are used in notetaking and learning processes. Buzan and Buzan have two answers to that question. "The reason why pictures are often dismissed is partly because, in these modern times, the word is overrated as a means of conveying information. However, this dismissal may also be rooted in the mistaken belief, by some people, that they cannot draw" (Buzan and Buzan, p. 73). The plethora of thoughts and ideas generated in the mind mapping process need to be given a structure. Ideas can be structured by forming hierarchies and categories. At the top level of the hierarchy are basic ordering ideas (BOI). The concept of BOI is applied, for instance, in building the structure of a book with chapters and sub-chapters. First of all, keywords are recorded with spaces left between them for further terms and concepts. As a mind map has a radial structure and can be extended infinitely, new keywords can be added and new chains of association can be formed. BOIs are expressed in terms that represent the simplest and most obvious concepts of categorization and trigger most ideas. The main ideas can be discovered by asking questions such as:

- What knowledge is required?

- What are the basic questions?

- What are the most important categories?

Fixing the basic idea makes it easier to find and build subsequent levels. Main ideas and related subordinate thoughts are represented as lines branching from the central topic. Each line is assigned only one keyword or picture. Thoughts can be grouped by connection lines. Notes should be written horizontally on the paper, as our eyes are more used to this angle than to the vertical format. Mind maps should be clearly structured to secure the transparency of all thoughts and ideas. Mind maps are the work of individuals and should be characterized by the personal style of the author. By developing your artistic skills you can boost the performance of your memory and creativity, making work more relaxing, less stressful, and altogether more fun.

3.1.2.4   Benefits of mind mapping

Compared to linear notes and records, mind maps have the following advantages.

- The main topic/basic idea is placed at the center, which makes it quicker and easier to grasp. A quick glance at your mind map tells you what the whole thing is about.

- The branch structure enables you to represent and classify thoughts and ideas according to their relative importance.

- By using keywords you can focus on the essential while saving time (for taking and reading notes) and paper.

- Mind maps are ideally suited to revising a subject. The basic ideas have already been understood. All you need to recall them are keywords which trigger associations.

- Mind maps have the capacity to grow organically; they can be extended at any time simply by adding another branch.

- Each mind map looks different, which makes its structure and content easy to remember.

- Related ideas/approaches/basic thoughts can be grouped by circling or highlighting them in the same color.

3.1.2.5   Problems

Initially, there may be some problems with mind maps. For instance, limiting yourself to keywords may take some getting used to. Basic ideas or concepts may turn out to be subordinate thoughts in retrospect. The sheet of paper you have chosen may turn out to be too small. Ideas placed at one level may be separated from other related ideas so that the chain of association is broken. The seemingly unstructured layout of mind maps may put the onlooker off. As with many other new and unusual methods and techniques, general acceptance is not always easy to gain in the beginning.

3.1.3   "Fire, thunder, and lightning"

3.1.3.1   The way our memory works

For a long time, scientists have been researching into the location of memory within the brain. Information is stored in the nerve cells of the brain and the links between them. There are some 100 billion of these nerve cells, and each of them is connected to up to 10,000 other cells. Thus, the brain may be pictured as a gigantic cable network of some 100,000 kilometers. As in an electric power cable, electricity travels along the nerves. When a nerve cell receives a stimulus, its status changes immediately. Either it is stimulated (it "fires") or it is inhibited. Whenever a cell fires, the underlying nerve cells are also induced to fire by neurotransmitters. One interesting point is how the brain knows that different bits of information belong to the same object. Scientists assume that it is to do with the firing time kept by the nerve cells. This would ensure that details of information arriving a long time apart could still be linked to form one coherent picture.

3.1.3.2   From awareness to memory

There are different memory systems. The most commonly known classification is that of short-term and long-term memory. Not quite as widely known are the sensory memory systems which enable us to perceive our environment.

When we distinguish between short-term and long-term memory, the essential difference is how long the information is stored. Over the past few years, however, the question of **what** is stored has come to the fore. The factor by which scientists now distinguish between different memory systems is not time but content. Scientists carrying out studies on people who had partially lost their memory found out that information can be stored in different ways. Such amnesia is caused by accidents or psychological strain. After observing and analyzing such cases, they determined these subdivisions of memory.

- *Autobiographical or episodic memory*:
  where all the details of our personal life history are stored, i.e. all memories which we can connect to specific times and places.

- *Semantic memory*:
  where everything we have learned is stored.

- *Procedural memory*:
  where movements and activities, such as riding a bike or swimming, are stored. This
  memory information is largely subconscious and is hardly ever destroyed or damaged
  in accidents.

3.1.3.3   Structure and function of the memory

Use of the memory can be divided into three principal phases – coding, storage, and
recall. The short-term memory has a capacity of about seven objects. This number varies
from one person to the next by no more than plus or minus two objects. This means, for
instance, that our short-term memory can remember a random sequence of five digits. If
the information is fed in only once, the duration of storage in the short-term memory is
very short, i.e. only a few seconds. If we want to store information for longer, we need to
repeat it in our minds. This is easiest when the information has the form of language. For
other types of information it is a little more difficult. If we do not take any special
measures, the short-term memory works like a queue. The first object to exceed the
capacity of the short-term memory will push out the object which has been stored
longest. This can be counteracted by selectively repeating the information, in which case it
is treated as new each time so that you can choose which object to discard first. While the
contents of short-term memory are stored as neuron activation (i.e. brain activity), the
contents of long-term memory are stored in the form of connections between neurons (i.e.
brain structure). Reality is more complicated and has not been fully explored, but this is
the basic mechanism. This mechanism also explains the two main characteristics of long-
term memory – its unlimited storage duration and its almost infinite capacity. The
functioning of long-term memory comprises two parts: firstly, we are able to recognize
things, and secondly, we store a great number of relationships involving these things –
particularly semantic relationships, such as a number of variants of "part of" or "is a," as
well as relationships between time and place such as the sequence of events in a story or
the digits in a telephone number. Information is always stored in the most abstract form
possible. In this way, many details can be left out and the information occupies less space.

3.1.4   "Left, right – right, left?" – the human brain

3.1.4.1   Simplified representation

The following description of the brain is highly simplified and schematic. It is only meant
to provide a basic understanding of how the brain works – many of its functions remain
unexplained. The main task of the brain is to receive, process, and respond to stimuli.
Receptors, such as the sensory organs, receive certain stimuli (light, pressure, sound,
temperature) and electronically transmit them as coded signals to the central nervous
system whose main control center is the brain. Here, the incoming signals are processed
according to specific patterns and, if required, forwarded as response stimuli to the
effectors (muscles, glands). Information is essentially processed in the cerebral cortex, the
grey matter, 2–3 mm thick. The human cerebral cortex, which looks like a lobe with

many furrows and convolutions, covers an area of approximately 0.2 square meters. Related associative abilities (motor movement, touch, sight, location) are linked and stored together in one part of the cerebral cortex. The elementary processing units are called neurons, cells which exchange signals electrochemically and stimulate each other. The human body contains about 10^{10} neurons, each of which has some 10,000 links to neighboring cells. All neurons exist from birth but with virtually no links between them. The connections are established only through learning. The optimum response to a given situation is correspondingly stored as a connection pattern between neurons. These connections can be strengthened by training. The brain works by association, i.e. concepts are stored in the form of interlinked groups of neurons called assemblies. Related concepts, such as thunder and lightning, have overlapping assemblies which activate each other. Concrete information is stored in a network of connections in our memory.

3.1.4.2   Memories via neural pathways

Learning processes leave trodden paths in the brain, which serve as the basis of memory. According to this image, the brain stores memories by nerve cells linking their communication paths particularly closely together. Information passes through individual cells as electric impulses. If the information is to be transmitted to a second cell, the sender cell emits a chemical messenger which travels to the receiver cell through a minute fissure. In the receiver cell, the chemical signal is then converted back into an electric signal. If you are memorizing a poem, for instance, you read it several times in a row, and each time a flood of information runs over the same group of nerve cells. This constant repetition causes the cells involved to react more and more sensitively to the chemical signal sent to them. Figuratively speaking, a path is made which is easier to walk on than high grass. This trodden path through sensitized nerve cells represents our memory. Since the sensitization persists for some time, scientists talk of long-term potentiation.

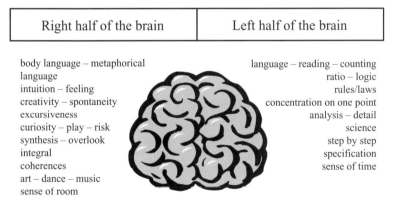

| Right half of the brain | Left half of the brain |

body language – metaphorical language
intuition – feeling
creativity – spontaneity
excursiveness
curiosity – play – risk
synthesis – overlook
integral
coherences
art – dance – music
sense of room

language – reading – counting
ratio – logic
rules/laws
concentration on one point
analysis – detail
science
step by step
specification
sense of time

Figure 3.1.4.3-1:   The functions of both cerebral hemispheres
www.ni.schule.de/~pohl/lernen/kurs/lern-02.htm

3.1.4.3   The cerebral hemispheres

The human brain consists of left and right hemispheres (Figure 3.1.4.3-1). Recent studies have shown that the two hemispheres perform different functions. In general, the left hemisphere is concerned with rational thinking, logic, language and speech, numbers, linearity, and analysis. The right hemisphere mainly controls the ability to visualize things in three dimensions, imagination, color, rhythm, form, recognition of patterns, and dimensionality. As the brain is highly complex, a strict allocation of each function to a specific area of the brain is impossible. However, the above representation is widely acknowledged.

3.1.5   Memorable pictures

This section illustrates the structure and effect of mind maps using two examples. Figure 3.1.5-1 was created manually and Figure 3.1.5-2 is a computer-generated mind map.

In Figure 3.1.5-1 the central topic is placed in the middle. A picture illustrates this topic and generates an association. From the center, radial lines branch off in all directions,

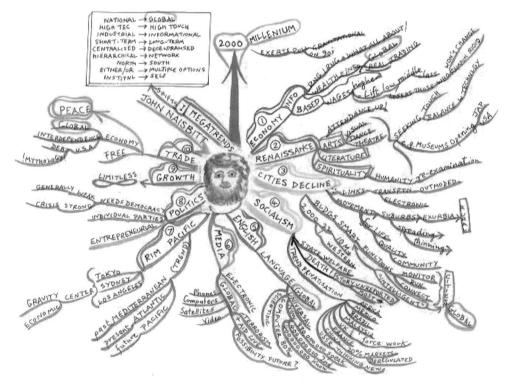

Figure 3.1.5.-1:   Mind map by Tony Buzan
(Buzan, p. 258)

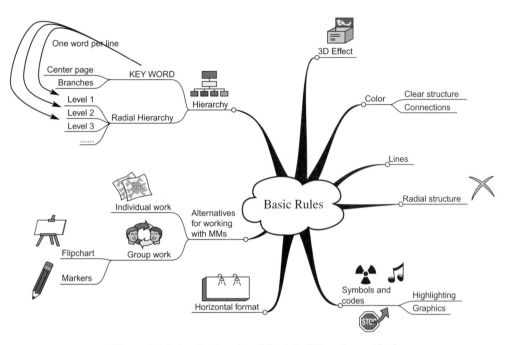

Figure 3.1.5-2:   Basic rules of the MindMapping method

thinning out toward the edges. The strongest branches represent the main concepts (BOI), i.e. the first hierarchical level. This first level is clearly organized by the different colors of the branches. Individual chapters are structured by thinner lines and further ramifications. Pictures, symbols, and frames underline the ideas and establish links between written words and pictures (right–left hemisphere). Arrows are used to connect ideas. The mind map can be extended by adding new thoughts and ideas at any time. The structure of the picture conveys the impression of three-dimensionality and depth.

With the aid of computer programs, pictures and symbols can be added to a mind map as required (Figure 3.1.5-2). This saves time and work. There are no mental blocks or inhibitions about drawing to hinder the creation of a picture. On the other hand, the creative process is clearly more limited. Hand-drawn pictures trigger more associations, boosting the performance of the memory. Computer mind maps can easily be inserted into other documents without having to use a scanner. While the variations in line thickness are easier to create by hand, this drawback is compensated by the opportunity to place elements freely and change them around as often as desired. (Figure 3.1.5-2 contains the most important basic rules as described in Chapter 3.1.6.)

3.1.6   Structure – basic rules

The MindMapping method is designed to involve the creativity and personality of an individual. Users of this method will develop a personal style and generate their own chains of association. The more individual the design of a mind map, the easier it is to remember the information it contains. However, there are certain basic rules which are helpful in building the structure.

- The sheet of paper should be worked on horizontally. In the center, you draw a memorable picture or a little sketch to represent the main topic. If a drawing does not seem useful, the keyword at least should be placed in the center of the sheet with a 3-D effect. You should always remember, however, that a picture is worth a thousand words.

- Emanating from the central picture, draw a bold line for each underlying thought or subordinate idea.

- Onto these lines, write the keywords summarizing these subordinate ideas. These words should be written in capitals to make the mind map more legible and easier to remember.

- Thinner lines may then be drawn, branching off from the main lines, to subdivide the individual main thoughts. These lines may then be branched further, and so forth.

- You should use different colors as this will enable a clearer overview. At the same time, it is useful to highlight related thoughts and ideas in the same color.

- Symbols such as arrows, geometrical figures, little pictures, exclamation or interrogation marks, and self-defined symbols should be used as often as possible. They make the information they contain easier to fathom and help to define or highlight certain areas more clearly.

- Hierarchies and classifications are helpful in designing and organizing mind maps.

- During the process of creative thinking, you should not spend too much time considering where to add certain information as this will stem the free flow of ideas. After all, we think faster than we can write. You can still rearrange and reorganize your ideas in a new sketch later. This also has the advantage that you reconsider the mapped topic once again, so that you will more easily remember and better understand the information it contains. Moreover, there is always a chance that a decisive idea might come to mind during this reorganization of thoughts.

3.1.7   Where to use mind maps

3.1.7.1   Individual work

The benefits we gain in terms of knowledge and insight from meetings, seminars, our environment, and other teaching/learning processes depend on our notetaking. Mind mapping is a highly suitable method to use for this task. Minutes and summaries can be drawn up faster. You can develop new ideas regarding complex issues for yourself and represent work schedules and problem solutions. Mind maps help to reconstruct memories and make future goals easier to plan.

3.1.7.2   Group work

In group work, mind maps are a suitable means of visualizing discussions, collected ideas, problem analyses, or work schedules. The results can be recorded on a large mind map. For such a group mind map, you need a sheet of paper or a flipchart and some thick markers. This mind map may serve as an overview and orientation for all participants. As all group members are involved in creating the map, they will be able to follow its development and information at all times. In building the mind map, only the main ideas and core concepts are recorded, so that participants are obliged to be brief and pointed in their comments and contributions. It often proves difficult to fit individual contributions into the logical consensus of the group discussion. By using mind maps you can solve this problem. Due to the graphic structure, group members can clearly see the current status of the discussion.

Linear notes require a lot more writing. Furthermore, mind maps offer the benefit that individual ideas can later be connected by lines. Discussion processes are visualized and thus made transparent, boosting the efficiency of group work. All relevant contributions are recorded, and by the end of the meeting the minutes are already completed.

3.2   Processes within the R/3 system

More and more companies are opting for the implementation of standard business management software. Often they decide in favor of the client/server-based SAP R/3 application system. SAP R/3 standard software has been developed from the experience of third party companies. The functionality provided by the R/3 system can be customized to suit different business scenarios. Before customizing, the respective business processes of each individual company should be checked against standard processes. Within SAP, a new term has recently been coined for this comparative analysis requirement which illustrates the process rather well. We refer to it as **mapping**. On initial contact, a company is shown a **solution map** for its particular industry, enabling a business process analysis to be performed as early as in the sales phase.

In his book *Working Knowledge: How Organizations Manage What They Know*, Thomas H. Davenport, professor at the Boston University School of Management, asks the following critical question: "Does your company suit the software?" He is referring to the requirement of carrying out a process analysis, including a description of a possible knowledge management method, before the actual implementation of the software. The results of such an analysis, given the required transparency, provide a sounder basis for a company's decision of how to represent all its essential business processes in the standard software.

Mapping people, processes, and products was the motto used by Henning Kargermann, spokesman of the SAP AG board, to illustrate the central role of this implementation requirement (Sapphire 99, Nice, France). A process analysis aimed at performing a mapping requires process orientation on one hand, and intelligent documentation in the form of knowledge maps on the other. Before we go into detail concerning knowledge maps in later chapters of this book, we would like to explain briefly the basics of SAP processes and some important business terminology used in business engineering.

3.2.1   What is a business process?

In his definition, Striening divides the term into two separate parts – business and process. First, he defines the term business as "the economically motivated exchange of goods or services." Then he gives the following definition of the term business process: "A sequence of actions and activities performed to create products or services, which are directly related to each other and which, together, determine the success of a company in the fields of business management, production, administration, and finance" (Striening, 1988, pp. 20–50). Davenport describes a business process as a customer-oriented procedure: "A business process is a series of events which can be structured and measured and which have been developed to generate a specific service for the customer or the market" (Davenport, 1993). Hammer and Champy also regard a business process as a customer-oriented activity: "A business process is defined as a bundle of activities which requires one or several inputs and whose result is of value for the customer" (Hammer and Champy, 1994). We can assume that between five and eight core processes contribute 80 percent of a company's turnover. A business process comprises several individual processes. A process is a business flow-oriented series of functions. It can also be described as a succession of individual elements. These elements can either be functions or processes in their own right. They are organized sequentially and logically, reflecting the order in which they are performed.

SAP AG started describing business management processes about five years ago, using the method of event-driven process chains (EPC). This method was developed at the Institut für Wirtschaftinformatik in Saarbrücken (Keller et al., 1992) and is characterized by the extension of events by symbols. Meanwhile, the SAP R/3 reference model comprises a total of 800 processes which are divided into scenario processes and EPC processes. SAP EPC processes are described in more detail in Chapters 3.2.4 and 3.2.5.

3.2.2   Enterprise process areas

For reasons of project organization, a general process analysis for the whole enterprise is not feasible. The ideal solution would be a process map, complete with all integration interfaces, describing and representing a model of the whole company. Desirable though such a model may be, it would be too complex. Therefore, a company is usually divided into manageable **enterprise process areas** (Figure 3.2.2-1).

Another reason is the organic structure of a company. Process areas often reflect the organizational structure of a company. For an enterprise process area **sales logistics**, for instance, there is a corresponding **sales department** or even an independent **sales organization** within the company. A representation of the organizational structures is based on a general description of the enterprise process areas (see Chapter 5.3.2, and particularly Figure 5.3.2-10). In the SAP reference model, possible enterprise process areas are provided as a structure. Scenarios (possible process variants within an enterprise area) are one level below the enterprise process areas and refer to individual process modules at a further process level (EPC process).

At the start of a project, the project scope can be defined by selecting the relevant enterprise process areas. It is important that the individual processes are not analyzed in

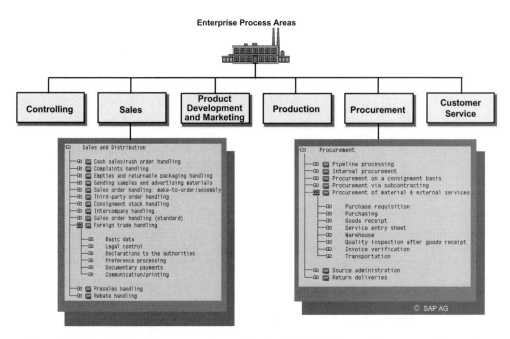

Figure 3.2.2-1:   Enterprise process areas with sales & distribution and procurement scenarios

detail at this point (Teufel, 1997). A medium-sized enterprise, for instance, will have process areas financial accounting, revenue and cost controlling, procurement, production, and sales & distribution, but no product development or marketing process areas.

3.2.3   Scenario processes

Each enterprise process area (as described in Chapter 3.2.2) comprises business flows which reflect different scenarios, depending on the structure and organization of the company. As a rule, each enterprise process area contains several scenarios, also referred to as scenario modules. For the enterprise area of production, for instance, you may want to select several different scenario modules, as you are producing different products in different ways (Figure 3.2.3-1). For the manufacture of product A, you may decide to use the scenario process **production by lot size**, while for the manufacture of product B, you choose **sales-order related production**. For product B you create a high surplus value, so that for cost reasons you cannot manufacture this product for the warehouse.

Selecting the right scenarios is an important step in the efficient implementation of business management standard software. You can make this selection in the ASAP Q&Adb, or use a modeling tool (such as *Intellicorp*) to choose your scenarios from the SAP R/3 reference model. You may select your scenarios based on the following questions:

- How high is the surplus value of a product?

- Can your product be manufactured continuously?

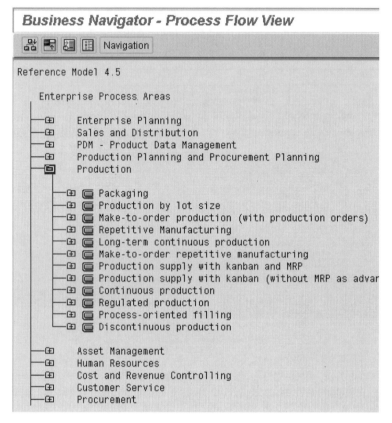

Figure 3.2.3-1:   Scenario modules within the production enterprise process area

- Do you provide service for your product?
- Etc.

If a preconfigured scenario for a particular enterprise process area of your company is not available, we recommend that you select a similar scenario. This saves modeling time, and you can still make any modifications needed during process analysis (see Chapter 5.3.3) such as including further scenario modules in the scenario process or building a new scenario process.

The SAP scenario processes are also described in the EPC terminology. They contain events, functions, process paths, and linking operators (for a more detailed description, see Chapter 3.2.5). It is important to realize that functions correspond to process modules. In the following chapters, we will refer to these functions in scenario processes as process modules and compare them to LEGO bricks for illustration purposes. To make matters easier, we have chosen a LEGO chain to illustrate the scenarios not contained in the SAP R/3 reference model. We therefore recommend extracting the functions from the scenarios, as described in Chapter 4.1, and adapting them to your company's situation in a simplified illustration.

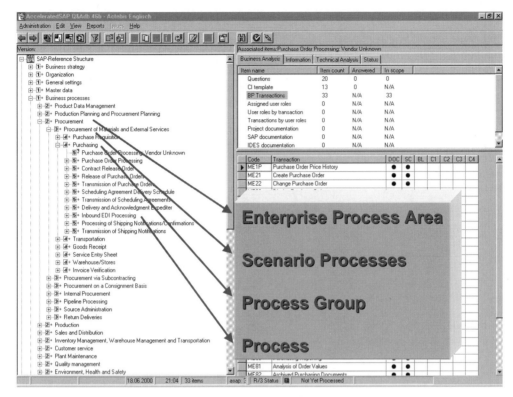

Figure 3.2.4-1:   Process group structure from the ASAP Q&Adb

3.2.4   Process group

A process group is a collection of process modules within a scenario. For example, processing of an RFQ issued to a vendor and vendor quotations processing have been grouped together in the process group RFQ/Quotation (Figure 3.2.4-1). Grouping several process modules together enables a condensed representation in the form of preconfigured value chains (Figure 5.3.2-11). The formation of groups is intended to be a navigation aid for the user. The individual areas have been named so that the user can tell which business aspect is referred to from the specialized field in question. Later on, these aspects will be analyzed in more detail with the aid of process modules.

3.2.5   Process

When we talk about a process, we need first to distinguish whether we mean the process module or the flow logic. The process module (used later on as a synonym for LEGO brick) is the actual name of the process, such as **purchase order processing**. Navigate to the EPC graphic within the SAP R/3 reference model to display the flow logic for a process (Figure 3.2.5-1). During consultation, a process illustration may be counterproductive, as

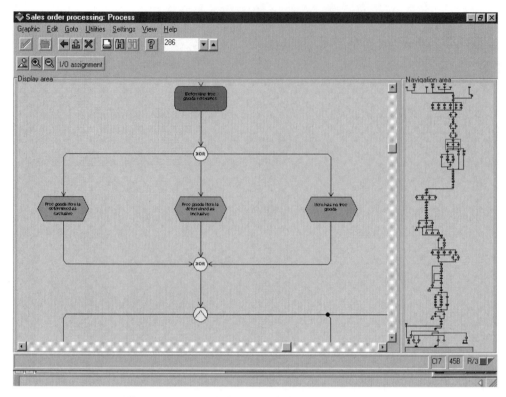

Figure 3.2.5-1:   EPC process 'sales order processing'

EPC graphics may appear too complex and need background knowledge to interpret them. We therefore recommend that you only use process modules (process names)! For a BPR project, EPC processes are useful only in some special cases.

The EPC method consists of the following elements: events, functions, process paths, and linking operators.

- *Event*
  The characteristic feature of an event is that its occurrence may trigger one or several functions. An event is a static condition which may or may not have occurred. The most important characteristics of an event are:
  - events can trigger functions
  - functions generate events
  - alternative results of functions are characterized by events
  - events represent an achieved status that is relevant to business management
  - events support consistency of process modeling.
  Events are not able to make a choice, i.e. they cannot start two or more functions alternatively. Figure 3.2.5-1 shows an example of the event **purchase order created** which triggers the function **release purchasing document**.

- *Function*
  A function is a business activity which entails the active performance of physical or mental processes. It is one step in a business process that describes the transformation of an initial status into a target status by reading, changing, deleting, or generating objects. A function is triggered by one or several events. Its result can also be one or several events. Thus, a function is able to choose with regard to subsequent functions (Keller et al., 1992).
    For the distinction between functions, the following rules apply.
  - *Semantic assignment rule*
    If functions have different semantic assignment rules, they cannot be the same (procedural rule). The reverse is not necessarily the case.

  - *Input/output rule*
    If one function receives different data to another function, we talk about a descriptive rule. If data output of one function is different from another function, the two functions are different. The reverse is not necessarily the case.

For a more detailed description of functions and events, additional information (such as the full name, processing time, and processing frequency) can be stored via **attributes** (e.g. attribute in the ARIS Toolset of IDS Prof. Scheer GmbH, Saarbrücken).

The EPC method contains link rules which define how events and functions can be linked with each other. If several events are linked to one function, we have an event link. Similarly, if several functions are linked to one event, we describe this as a function link (Keller et al., 1992).

Three logical linking operators are available for these two types of links.

- AND
  In a logical AND operation (conjunctive link) of events and functions, all events must have occurred or all functions must be active for the statement to be true (Schöning, 1989).

- OR
  A logical OR operation (disjunctive link) means that at least one of several alternative events must have occurred or functions must be active for the statement to be true. It is important to note that an event can never activate two functions alternatively (Schöning, 1989).

- EXCLUSIVE OR
  The exclusive OR operation (adjunctive link) means that exactly one of several alternative events must have occurred for the statement to be true. It is important to note that an event can never activate two functions alternatively (Schöning, 1989).

3.2.6   Method

In order to represent business processes in a simple form it is important to use a suitable method that can be abstracted from reality. Computer science in particular has evolved a variety of methods which are used mainly for the design and development of DP systems

(Balzert, pp. 30–65). The large number of methods, sometimes differing only slightly from one another, has led to a lack of transparency and hindered the evolution of a general concept for application development. Not every method is suitable for representing business processes. Some methods are data-oriented while others are more function- or organization-oriented. Then there are combined methods which, alongside their main focus, deal with other aspects to some extent. Due to the increasing use of DP-supported information systems, business processes themselves are now becoming the objects of analysis. There are different approaches for planning and implementing information systems. Scheer describes one such approach (ARIS – Architecture of integrated information systems) which contains several implementation steps or description levels. These description levels reflect a three-stage division, based on the proximity to IT. We distinguish between the following levels:

- process design level (level of semantic models)

- DP concept level

- implementation level.

By using **business solution maps**, and the future option of using *knowledge maps*, an SAP implementation project could be divided into the following levels:

1. Strategy, aims, and organization.

2. Finding one or several suitable SAP business solution map(s) for a company.

3. Selecting scenario processes/building a process LEGO chain.

4. Analysis of individual processes (LEGO bricks) with knowledge maps – building a target concept.

5. Examples using the R/3 system (application, prototyping).

6. Transport of a preconfigured client (80 percent solution–industry template).

7. Customizing and completion.

Between the levels there will be mappings, as follows:

- *Mapping between Levels 1 and 2:*
  Taking into account the targets and organizational structure of a company, a suitable business solution map, or several business solution maps, will be selected.

- *Mapping between Levels 2 and 3:*
  The preconfigured SAP scenario processes can be selected based on the modules of the business solution map. Depending on the business target, the individual scenario processes will be simplified by a LEGO chain illustration.

- *Mapping between Levels 3 and 4:*
  In connection with the process analysis, the process modules selected in Level 3 are discussed in more detail. The results of the discussion will be documented as the target concept.

- *Mapping between Levels 4 and 5:*
  The solutions predefined in the target concept are tested in the R/3 system. It may be possible to skip this mapping altogether and continue instead with a mapping between Levels 4 and 6.

- *Mapping between Levels 5 and 6:*
  After elaborating the target concept and performing the tests in the R/3 system, transport orders for a preconfigured system will be initiated (industry template). The customer starts his customizing activity with an 80 percent solution.

The levels described here may reflect the situation in an ideal world, admittedly. Still, with this representation of the different levels, we intend to show the problems connected with individual mapping activities and emphasize the fact that each mapping is an individual challenge, different from other mappings. Levels 1 to 4 reflect the business management side of a company, while Levels 5 and 6 reflect the IT world (R/3 system). Traditional business consulting is mainly concerned with projects from Levels 1 to 4, while software consultants are involved in Levels 4 and 5. If a project is to be successful, the focus should be on the mapping activities listed above to ensure compatibility of the worlds of business management (models) and IT realization (R/3 system).

3.3   AcceleratedSAP (ASAP)

The procedure of mapping and adapting your individual business *world* to the organizational units and business cases of the R/3 system described in Chapter 5.3.3 as well as the knowledge maps provided in Chapter 6 reflect the concept of the extended SAP standard strategy for an accelerated R/3 implementation, *Accelerated*SAP (ASAP). The same applies to knowledge management with master knowledge maps, as described in Chapter 6. The concepts described as well as the actual knowledge maps can be used as add-ons or extensions or as additional accelerators. It therefore seems appropriate to give a short overview of the procedure and basic concept of ASAP in this section.

3.3.1   Introduction

A company implementing R/3 wants to enjoy all the benefits and potential offered by a productive R/3 system as soon as possible. The relevant keywords in this respect are an early return on investment (ROI) and an early return on information. To meet these requirements, SAP has developed the implementation solution *Accelerated*SAP. ASAP is an extensive implementation strategy which is specially designed to provide a company implementing R/3 with all the benefits of a productive R/3 system relatively early on, while at the same time laying the foundation for a continuous optimization of all business processes. ASAP was introduced by SAP America in 1996. Due to its success, it soon became established as the SAP standard solution for an accelerated R/3 implementation.

This applies not only to projects carried out by consultants of the global SAP organization but also to projects led by SAP consulting partners. In the context of the SAP

*Team*SAP initiative, the ASAP process component provides a method of integrating and managing all activities performed by SAP, partners, and customer employees. As illustrated in Figure 3.3.1-1, *Team*SAP consists of three components – people (SAP employees, partner employees, and customer employees), processes (ASAP), and products (R/3 Business Framework, complementary partner software as well as partner hardware). The integration of these components is ensured throughout the life cycle of an R/3 installation. While ASAP was initially aimed at the R/3 implementation in companies with an annual turnover of between \$100 million and \$1 billion), it soon became clear that it was also a suitable solution for smaller companies with an annual turnover of less than 200 million. Large or medium-sized companies planning a worldwide rollout of the R/3 system can use *Global AcceleratedSAP*, which is an extension of the well-proven ASAP method for template and rollout projects.

ASAP is not a procedure designed by theorists in an ivory tower. On the contrary, behind *Accelerated*SAP and all its components stands an international team of experienced business process and technical consultants, project managers, and SAP global support managers. In years of experience with implementation projects, the team collected and assessed results and developed the ASAP concept from what they identified as the *best business practices* for R/3 implementation. In the process, redundant project activities have been eliminated and certain tasks and activities which were previously performed sequentially have now become parallel within the framework of an implementation project. The overall method is called a *Roadmap*, and is supported by various *accelerators* or *tools*.

What is important when looking at the overall concept of *Accelerated*SAP is that it is not always necessary to use all ASAP components in every project. Following the modular principle, individual components can be selected to support the aim of accelerated R/3 implementation. During an implementation project, the following tasks have to be performed:

- *Project management* (time, resource, and budget planning as well as planning and co-ordination of all activities such as training, tests, etc.).

People:
Solution-Competence (Quality)

- SAP
- Consulting Partner
- Complementary Software Partner
- Technology & Hardware Partner

Process:
AcceleratedSAP (Consistency)

- AcceleratedSAP or "Powered By" Method
- Quality Assurance
- Support, Consulting & Education Services

Products:
Business Framework (Performance ability)
- R/3-Product Family
- Solution Maps
- Products Technology Partners
- Complementary Software Products

Figure 3.3.1-1:   TeamSAP and ASAP

- *Adaptation and configuration of the business process and organizational structure* (business blueprint, setting relevant parameters in the R/3 system (customizing), authorizations, etc.).

- *Evaluation and set-up of the technical environment* (R/3 installation, networks, printers, interfaces, legacy data transfer, extensions, archiving, etc.).

To meet these requirements, SAP provides the following key elements:

- *Roadmap* – a step-by-step project plan containing detailed information on what tasks are to be performed when, by whom, why, and how.

- *Tools and accelerators* for *project management* (method/roadmap, spreadsheets, documentation forms, etc.), for the *business process consultant* (questionnaires, templates, checklists, tools for the R/3 configuration (customizing), etc.), and for the *set-up of the technical environment* (Interface Advisor, checklists for data transfer, archiving, infrastructure, etc.).

- *SAP services* in the fields of consulting, training, support, e.g. Hotline, Early Watch, Online Service System, InfoDB, training strategy for project teams and end users.

The *Implementation Assistant* provides all these elements directly (e.g. forms, checklists) or makes them accessible (e.g. Q&Adb).

The following points describe how *Accelerated*SAP differs from previous SAP implementation methods. *Accelerated*SAP:

- is the first implementation solution developed, supported, and marketed directly by SAP for its own use as well as for its implementation partners;

- provides an estimate of the project scope, time, cost, and resources required (internal and external), calculated on the basis of SAP standards and based on customer details;

- conveys a predefined, role-based method for coordinating project management, business process adaptation, and technology management for all R/3 projects;

- ensures global standardization of the R/3 implementation procedure;

- is an ideal basis for the challenges and activities of continuous change, e.g. upgrades or organizational change;

- recommends proactive quality assurance measures or provides its own.

ASAP is a desktop program and can thus be installed and used independently of an R/3 system. The general ASAP procedure follows the phases and contents illustrated in the roadmap in Figure 3.3.1-2, which will be explained in more detail in the following section. If a company has opted for R/3 implementation with the ASAP procedure, it has decided at the same time to use the existing R/3 *best business processes* to support its individual business processes. With this decision, a company sticks relatively close to the standard, although individual extensions or add-ons are possible at any time. At the end of each phase, quality checks are performed, supported by ASAP tools and accelerators. Should you require more checks or want an external opinion regarding the status of your project

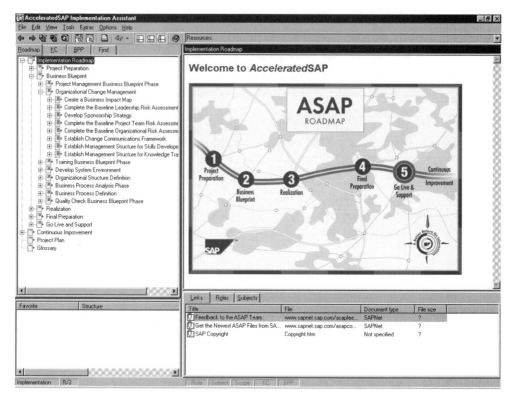

Figure 3.3.1-2:   AcceleratedSAP Implementation Assistant

by a person not involved in the daily project activities, you can benefit from the *SAP Review Program* service: an external consultant (experienced project manager) comes in to perform a quality audit at the end of each phase to check your project. The result of such checks could be the approval of the project so far or a recommendation to change certain procedures, basic conditions, etc. Furthermore, a quality auditor may recommend further checks should you desire them.

ASAP supports the following phases:

• Phase 1: Project preparation

Phase 1 is the project preparation phase which generally takes about two to four weeks. The aim of this phase is to make all preparations required for the overall project to run smoothly and to define all relevant basic conditions. This includes estimating the project scope, creating the project charter and project organization as well as a detailed project schedule including milestones regarding time, cost, resources, and deadlines. Furthermore, it includes planning the technical environment, defining project standards, such as communication plans, guidelines for the documentation of concept decisions or configurations, etc. This phase ends with the project kickoff, which at the same time signals the start of Phase 2.

- Phase 2: Business blueprint

The main goal of this phase is the creation of a business blueprint, i.e. the documentation of what you require from the R/3 system with regard to organizational, business process, and technical aspects. Depending on how complex your project is, this phase takes between four and eight weeks. It comprises not only an adaptation of your business processes to R/3 but also detailed "scoping" (detailed definition of the project scope). To determine how your demands on the organizational structure and business processes are to be represented in the R/3 system, detailed workshops are performed during this phase in close cooperation with the project consultants. Various questionnaires and graphical process chains may be used to support and accelerate the process. ASAP's *main tool*, the Question and Answer Database (Q&Adb), reflects most of these aids (Figure 3.3.1-3). Moreover, the Q&Adb contains the corresponding R/3 reference model for your release, e.g. reference model 4.0 or reference model 4.5. It is divided into general issues regarding business strategy, organizational structure, and organizational units on the one hand, and enterprise process areas on the other. Enterprise process areas are subdivided into scenario processes, process groups, and processes (see Chapter 3.2). Should an R/3 system be installed at this early stage, the consultant may run a demonstration of the facts discussed with the project team members using the *International Demo and Education*

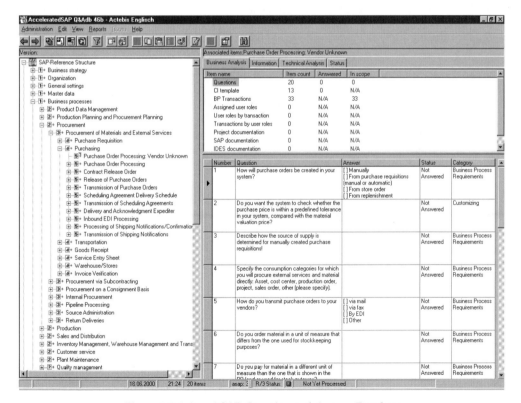

Figure 3.3.1-3:   ASAP Question and Answer Database

Systems (IDES), a fully functional and configured model enterprise provided by SAP. The result of this phase, the business blueprint document (target concept), is the blueprint for how your company is to be represented in R/3. It is the central document on which all following activities are based. Other important aspects of this phase are that project team members receive basic R/3 training (Levels 1 and 2) and that the system environment is determined in detail and ordered from the manufacturer or – if it has already been provided – installed.

- Phase 3: Realization

In this phase, a number of different activities run consecutively. The main task is the configuration of the R/3 system on the basis of the blueprint and according to the requirements you have laid down. For this process, you can use another important ASAP tool, the *Business Process Master List (BPML)*. The BPML is a predefined, process-oriented table which enables you to manage the whole configuration process including documentation, milestone monitoring, testing, etc. and the person responsible for each step. The actual configuration of system parameters is carried out with the process-oriented *Implementation Guide (IMG)* which can be accessed directly from the BPML. ASAP particularly supports a two-step realization procedure. First, a *baseline system* is configured, which includes 100 percent of your corporate structure and about 70–80 percent of your principal business processes. As a rule, you can calculate between four and six weeks for this phase. This gives you enough time to simulate all relevant business processes. The baseline system is not a *prototype* that will be discarded after the simulation. Rather, it serves as a basis for the productive system, which contains the remainder of your requirements and is configured in one to four cycles, as required. This part of Phase 3 usually takes between ten and fourteen weeks. In the meantime, project team members receive detailed training (Level 3), and the technical system environment is implemented and optimized.

If required, interface programs, and the company's own reports, extensions, and forms (e.g. invoices), will be created/programmed. Authorizations are set up with the aid of a role-based procedure, and the end user documentation is generated. The phase is completed with a comprehensive integration test.

- Phase 4: Final preparation

The last phase before the big moment, going live, has only one aim – to prepare your R/3 system for going live as smoothly as possible. In this phase, which usually takes about four to six weeks, the integration test performed in Phase 3 for the individual enterprise process areas is extended to the whole system. It tests, for instance, whether an invoice is smoothly processed by the system in all process areas – i.e. if it was generated in Sales and Distribution, was all data transferred correctly to Financial Accounting and Controlling? Furthermore, there will be mass and stress tests designed to simulate the expected data volume (workload) with the planned number of users under performance aspects and live conditions. All interface programs, reports, forms, etc. will also be tested. End user training is carried out based on a train-the-trainer approach, i.e. power users of the specialized areas or DPs train end users. A detailed plan for the transfer of all relevant data and settings (cutover) into the productive system is drawn up (transfer of system settings, master data, legacy data, data conversion, etc.).

- Phase 5: Go live and support

Once you have arrived at this phase, you will work with your *live*, customized R/3 system for the first time. During this phase, it is very important that end users are adequately supported by an internal support organization within your company (helpdesk) to help them with any questions or problems. Furthermore, the R/3 system should be continuously checked regarding its performance as well as its functionality and acceptance within each area. This phase merges with the tasks and activities of the continuous change phase, so it is therefore difficult to say exactly how long it lasts. You can assume, however, that the first four weeks of going live will require the most intensive support. At the conclusion of the project you should compare the expected benefits of your R/3 implementation recorded in the project charter in the form of the business case against the actual results, to evaluate to what degree the goals have been accomplished. After all, you implement the R/3 system to increase your business benefits with regard to *value generation*, which, in turn, will be reflected by a higher *shareholder value*.

It is important to note that after successfully going live, your company enters the phase of continuous change, i.e. continuous improvement process. Changes may be due to technical reasons (e.g. release upgrade), business reasons (e.g. extension of the R/3 functionality employed or acquisition and integration of a new company), or legal reasons (e.g. new bill passed by the Ministry of Finance, etc.). During this phase, you can also rely on the support of *Accelerated*SAP, e.g. Upgrade Roadmap, Continuous Change Roadmap, Implementation Guide, etc.

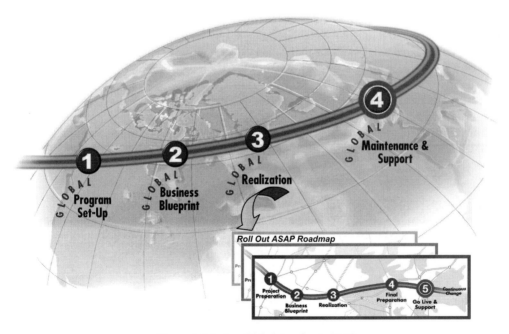

Figure 3.3.1-4:   Global AcceleratedSAP

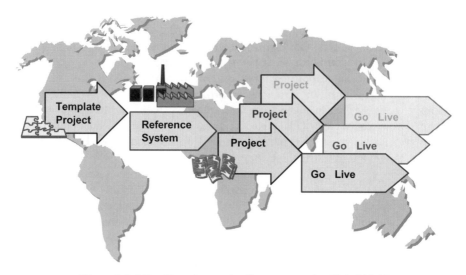

Figure 3.3.1-5:   Template and rollout support by GlobalASAP

In addition, *Global Accelerated*SAP has been available since May 1999 (Figures 3.3.1-4 and 3.3.1-5). It is a useful and relevant method for those customers for whom a baseline system is to be set up from a template or pilot project and then rolled out to further subsidiaries. This is called a multi-project environment.

This is supported by a *Global Roadmap*, which is used to make decisions on program management procedures within the global project, e.g. whether a template or pilot project is to be carried out, how extensive the standardization of organizational structures or business processes should be, how centralized the system's technical IT environment should be, etc. During generation of the Global blueprint, the business cases and organizational structures identified for standardization are designed. In Global ASAP the (global) blueprint also serves as the basis of (global) realization. Thus, the configuration of standardized processes and structures is based on the concept decisions recorded in the blueprint.

The results and decisions arrived at regarding standardization are transferred from here to local projects, several of which may run at the same time, where they are adapted to local conditions and extended in a local ASAP project.

3.3.2   The concept behind AcceleratedSAP

The ASAP solution is based on three principal concepts which will now be briefly described.

- *Process orientation*
  Compared with traditional implementation strategies, ASAP is strictly process-oriented and supports cross-enterprise area thinking and cooperation. This is shown by the fact that all tools, such as Q&Adb, BPML, IMG, are process-oriented in their design. Moreover, only a process-oriented procedure can exploit the optimization potential of the R/3 system.

- *Reference-based implementation*

  By opting for an ASAP project, a company decides in favor of a *reference-based implementation* of the R/3 system. In Chapter 5.2, you will find a detailed explanation of the concept of reference-based implementation (see branch 2 in Figure 5.2-1 and particularly Figures 5.2.2-1 and 5.2.3-1). The description makes it clear that our solution strategy and ASAP are both based on this concept. However, this does not mean that only standard functionalities will be implemented and that you cannot integrate individual processes or changes. Naturally, this concept also leaves enough room for individual business cases. However, ASAP does not support re-engineering out of context.

- *Big bang implementation strategy*

  As opposed to conventional procedures, ASAP favors the *big bang implementation strategy* (Figure 3.3.2-1). This is mainly due to the strict process orientation it adheres to. This method does not employ the traditional step-by-step implementation of components (modules), i.e. Project 1: FI, CO; Project 2: SD, MM; and Project 3: PP, PS, SM, etc. Instead, selected principal process areas are implemented globally, i.e. sales order processing for sales and distribution, production, procurement, financial accounting and controlling. With this process-oriented strategy, a number of components such as SD, MM, PP, CO, FI, etc. are implemented in one go (big bang). However, this solution means that some details or *nice-to-have* functions will not be

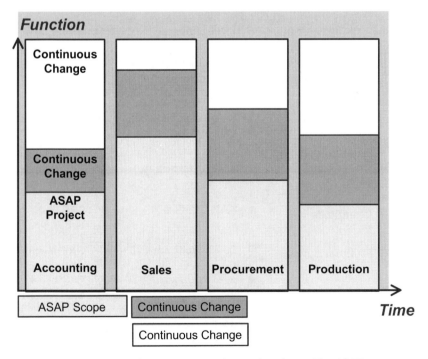

Figure 3.3.2-1:   Big bang strategy and procedure favored by ASAP

available immediately. In an initial project, only the essential components are implemented, to ensure that a process can be run throughout the enterprise. At a later stage, this process can be extended due to the inherent flexibility of the R/3 system.

3.4   Business solution maps

3.4.1   SAP industry-oriented solutions

To meet the various requirements of different industries, we need industry-specific integrated solutions which provide the necessary infrastructure for end-to-end support of all core business processes. SAP industry solutions have met these requirements since the early nineties and now have a basic structure. Industry business solutions comprise not only an R/3 system extended by industry-specific components but also additional elements along with the software, such as the integration of complementary software modules, ASAP, and a comprehensive support concept. Industry solutions are reflected within the SAP organizational structure in the form of industry business units (IBUs) that offer their solutions on the market. The industry solutions listed in Figure 3.4.1-1 are currently available for 18 industries, with additional solutions to be added over the next few years.

Frequently, IBUs can adopt large parts of the processes and functions from core development with virtually no modifications. The scope of specific extensions or adaptations varies from industry to industry.

In addition to this focus on selected industries, SAP generic business units cover cross-industry overlapping topics. By way of example, we would like to mention the SAP business information warehouse in the field of products, knowledge management for services, and the business framework architecture in the area of technologies.

Figure 3.4.1-1:   Industry business units

3.4.2   Business solution map structure

For each of its industry solutions, SAP has developed a solution map, a business and planning model with a detailed description of the functional requirements of these industries at different levels (Figure 3.4.2-1). This was presented at the SAPPHIRE conference in September 1998.

In these solution maps, SAP and partner products are directly matched with industry requirements. This affords customers and prospective customers an overview of how SAP and SAP partners view business processes and functions within an industry, and of the support SAP and its partners provide with their customized solutions both for today and in the future (Mezger, 1998). The business and planning models in the solution maps have each been developed for one particular industry in cooperation with SAP specialists, experts from the respective industries, partner companies, and users. Diagrams have been used to illustrate the IT scope of a company and help to provide an end-to-end structure instead of a patchwork solution.

Solution maps offer companies an overview of industry-specific business processes and show the functionality required to control these processes. This is done at two levels. At the first level, extensive process categories and their related basic processes and functions are defined for a particular industry. The second level provides a detailed view of these processes. In the case of the high tech & electronics IBU, level 1 of the solution map comprises nine process categories (see also Figure 3.4.2-1). These are enterprise

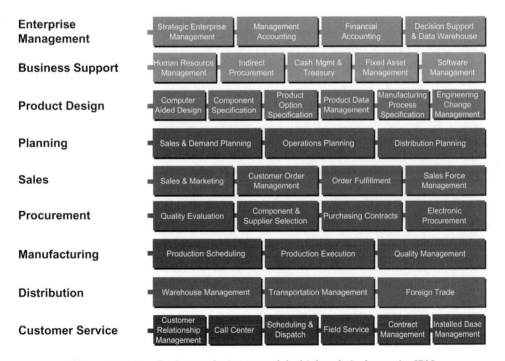

Figure 3.4.2-1:   Business solution map of the high tech & electronics IBU

Warehouse Management	Transportation Management	Foreign Trade
Planning and Monitoring	Transportation Scheduling	Import Processing
Receiving of Goods	Transportation Processing	Export Control
Storage Management	Transportation Monitoring	Preference Processing
Physical Inventory	Costing	Export Declarations
Shipping of Goods	Invoicing Customer	Communication/Print
Facility Management		Letter of Credit
Warehouse Technology		

Figure 3.4.2-2:   Business solution map of the high tech & electronics IBU, distribution process category

management, business support, product design, planning, sales, procurement, manufacturing, distribution, and customer service.

Each category is divided into basic processes. For the distribution process category, for instance, these are warehouse management, transportation management, and foreign trade. Level 2 contains the detailed functions of these processes (Figure 3.4.2-2).

Business solution maps use the open component architecture of the SAP business framework and the *Team*SAP concept to illustrate the combination of people, processes, and products in developing industry-specific end-to-end solutions. The end solutions consist of components partly made by SAP, partly provided by partner companies. The seamless integration of SAP and external solutions is ensured by the open structure of the SAP business framework with its standardized BAPIs and application link enabling functionality. With the *Team*SAP concept, SAP has accepted responsibility for integrating, coordinating, and certifying its partners and third-party suppliers.

SAP plans to update its industry solutions on an annual basis in order to adapt to the changing requirements and business needs of individual industries. For this purpose, SAP has developed an infrastructure that supports the development, implementation, and continuous expansion of its industry solutions. Cooperation with customers, partners, and industry experts ensures that SAP industry solutions and solution maps always meet the demands and business requirements of each individual industry.

4 Knowledge maps

In Chapters 1.2 and 1.3, we introduced knowledge maps and their benefits. In this chapter, we will describe the **structure** and **different types** of knowledge maps. This general description of knowledge maps will serve as a basis for Chapter 5, Process analysis with knowledge maps, and for the knowledge map database. Users will be introduced to the subject of **unfamiliar** pictures and learn how to read knowledge maps. Chapter 4.3 describes the different types of knowledge maps and their links with the SAP R/3 system. The relationship between knowledge maps and ASAP, SAP's official implementation procedure, is described in Chapter 4.4.

4.1 LEGO chain structure

LEGO chains reflect certain business scenarios, providing the reader, and in practice the enterprise, with an overview of the relationships and links between individual process knowledge maps ("keynote"). The idea of showing modules as LEGO bricks was chosen because virtually everyone has played with this toy as a child (J. Gaarder in the novel *Sophie's World*: "The most ingenious toy in the world"). In the same way as we used to put LEGO bricks together at random, standard modules can be combined freely for different business cases. Applied to SAP, this means that the LEGO bricks are standardized but can be adapted and selected individually to suit a company's needs.

In principle, an *entire* company could be represented by a single LEGO chain. However, to minimize complexity, LEGO chain graphics are limited to individual process areas (Figure 4.1-1). Our example shows parts of the process area of procurement, focussing on the warehouse materials procurement scenario. In practice, you can refer to the preconfigured scenario processes of the R/3 reference model. As described in the process analysis workshop (see Chapter 5.3.3 and Figure 5.3.3.2-2), you can omit the event symbols and condense the scenario process into the form of a LEGO chain (Figure 4.1-2).

In our LEGO chains in the knowledge map database, we will use three types of LEGO bricks. The white bricks represent the process modules (e.g. invoice processing) for the respective process area and contain the process knowledge maps in the background. A light grey brick indicates that no process knowledge maps exist as yet. Dark grey bricks represent modules with links to other process areas (e.g. accounts payable accounting). Should you require modules not provided by the R/3 standard, or which involve add-on solutions to R/3, you can complement the LEGO chain with shaded bricks (Figure 4.1-3).

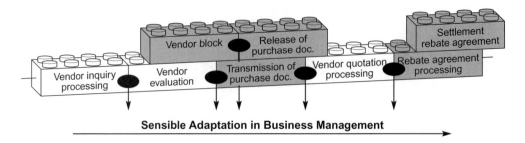

Figure 4.1-1:   (Chrono)logical sequence of LEGO bricks

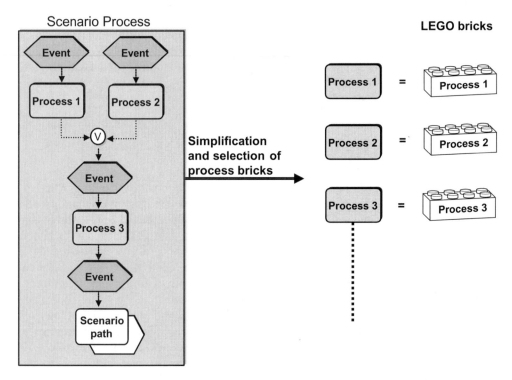

Figure 4.1-2:   Selection of LEGO bricks from preconfigured R/3 scenarios

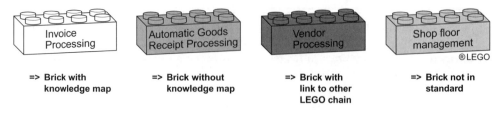

Figure 4.1-3:   Types of LEGO bricks

4.2   Knowledge map structure

A knowledge map can be designed and developed freely. The basic structure of knowledge maps is determined by only five general design guidelines, which are essentially based on the principles of the general MindMapping method devised by Tony Buzan (Chapter 3.1).

- *The root* represents the central topic of the knowledge map.

- *Main branches* form the fundamental chapters or basic ordering ideas of the main topic.

- *Side branches* subdivide basic ordering ideas.

- *Symbols* highlight individual branches/ideas.

- *Links* between the individual branches indicate important relations and inter-dependencies.

The combination of these design characteristics enables the viewer to quickly understand broad and complex topics such as those which arise within process analysis in the framework of an SAP R/3 implementation project. In particular, the graphic visualization of the structure provides the user with a quick overview of the topic. In just a small area, a knowledge map summarizes highly complex issues, questions, and facts regarding process analysis. Users work with keywords or associative terms which are carefully selected to embody another complex of complexities in the background. With the aid of these keywords (or anchor words), huge amounts of information are memorized easily. These design guidelines will be explained in principle to familiarize the reader with the structure of knowledge maps.

All the knowledge maps in this book have been developed with the *MindManager* software (Version 3.5) by MindJET LLC. Using *MindManager*, the authors have been able to produce high-quality graphic design, which ensures a high level of acceptance among users.

4.2.1 Root

The root contains the central topic of the knowledge map in a single keyword. In Figure 4.2.1-1, this keyword is billing, a process module from the sales and distribution business process. The 📖 symbol indicates that some text has been stored behind the root for additional information giving a brief summary of the knowledge map's central topic. This applies to all types of knowledge maps (see Chapter 4.3). During the process analysis, this summary may serve as a brief introduction to the topic.

The knowledge map in Figure 4.2.1-1 shows a sales and distribution process module. The topic represented by the root for this type of knowledge map (process knowledge map) corresponds to one brick in the LEGO chain (Figure 4.1-3), and therefore enables easy navigation from the root to the respective scenario process.

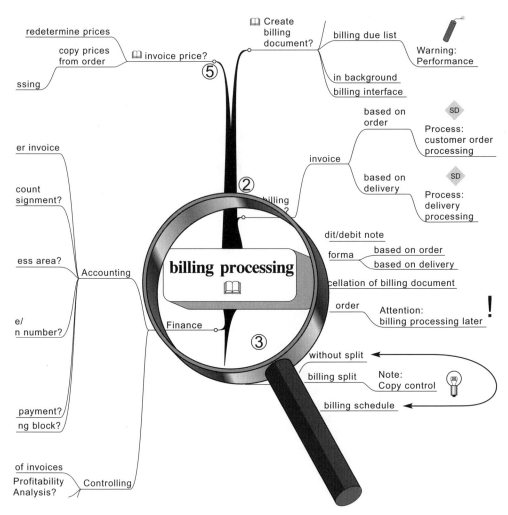

Figure 4.2.1-1:   Knowledge map root – billing process module

4.2.2   Main branches

The vast number of questions and topics which arise during process analysis or, more generally, when dealing with a complex subject need to be given some kind of structure. Questions may be organized in the form of hierarchies and categories, with the main branches representing the principal chapters or ordering ideas of the knowledge map's central topic.

Main branches consist of one or two keywords representing the most simple and obvious basic ordering ideas of the respective chapter. By reducing the topic to a few keywords you enhance its transparency and thus make it easier to memorize. The keywords selected for the main branches should **not** be abbreviated as this could lead to ambiguity and confuse the user. Due to the radial structure of the knowledge map, a variety of additional ordering ideas or keywords may be linked to the root. In Figure 4.2.2-1, five terms have been included representing the basic subdivision of the above process module for the purpose of a process analysis. These main branches facilitate finding and/or creating subsequent levels more quickly. The basic ordering ideas and their side branches cover all important aspects, questions, tips, and recommendations concerning billing (see Chapter 4.2.3).

A keyword followed by a "?" indicates that a question concerning process analysis has arisen at the level of the knowledge map main branch. In this book, questions arising in the individual knowledge maps have been highlighted by printing the keyword in **bold** letters. In the knowledge map graphics, the 📖 symbol indicates hidden text (i.e. a question) in the background of the main branch. With the *MindManager* tool, this text can be displayed simply by highlighting the branch. The questions concerning the ordering ideas do not stand alone but are explained in the text. Possible solutions or alternatives are depicted as applicable. If an answer to a question is negative, all further issues and questions may be excluded at this point. Due to the hierarchical structure, all dependent side branches then become irrelevant.

The number of main branches in a knowledge map depends on the degree of complexity involved. Branches are numbered in chronological order, starting from ① and illustrating a maximum of nine basic ordering ideas per map. The main branches are arranged starting, with ①, at the top right corner and moving clockwise. The texts indicate

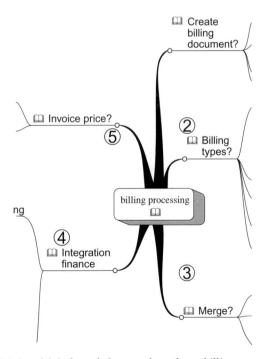

Figure 4.2.2-1:   Main knowledge map branches – billing process module

which question refers to which basic ordering idea by the numbers ① through ⑨. If the question is on a main branch, the number alone is used for reference. If, on the other hand, the question arises on a side branch, it will be referred to as "regarding ①." The maximum number of basic ordering ideas per knowledge map should not exceed nine. If more than nine basic chapters are needed to illustrate a complex subject, it should be split into several knowledge maps.

4.2.3   Side branches

The main branches, which represent the basic ideas, have ramified side branches, which subdivide these ideas. These side branches may also have smaller side branches and so on. This hierarchical structure develops into a whole tree of topics and questions with clearly marked connections between them. In the same way as on the main branches, keywords are also used for side branches for clear and concise organization of the topic or question. In Figure 4.2.3-1, the side branches of the integration accounting main branch are financial accounting and controlling. These side branches represent a clearly defined and complete substructure of the main branch and do not allow further side branches at the same hierarchical level. However, though this is not the case in Figure 4.2.3-1, questions concerning process analysis may be added at this level behind the keywords.

As a rule, questions regarding process analysis may be raised at all side branch levels, marked by a ? or the 📖 symbol. Of course, these questions will only be relevant if they lead to answers at a higher hierarchical level, and if these answers require further details to be added to the hierarchy in the form of side branches. The relative importance of each question is clearly expressed by the radial arrangement of the knowledge map. Important questions and issues can be found close to the center, less important ones towards the edges. The number of hierarchical levels/branches is not fixed. As shown in Figure 4.2.3-1, side branches may easily be arranged over five hierarchical levels for complex chapters without losing the structure of the topic. On the contrary, the precise relationship of each keyword to the main branch and topic is always maintained. At the same time, the consistent hierarchical organization ensures, at all levels, that with a negative answer all subsequent side branches automatically become irrelevant.

The side branches of a principal chapter can be classified into three different types.

- *Topics* which structure the chapter at the next hierarchical level and may entail further process analysis questions.

- *Notes, tips or warnings* regarding process analysis, marked by symbols (see Chapter 4.2.4).

- *Process modules* which show logical links between processes within an enterprise process area or across areas in the form of path symbols.

4.2.4   Symbols

Like the general MindMapping method, knowledge maps are based on the belief that "a

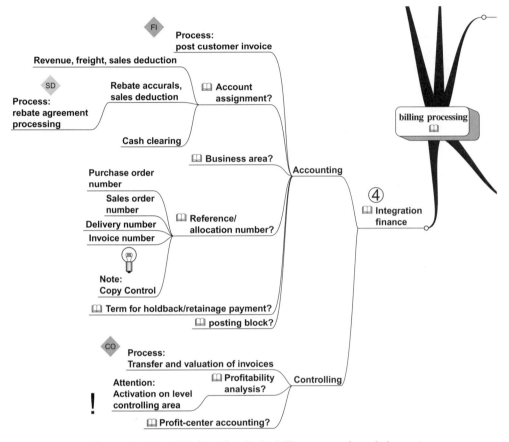

Figure 4.2.3-1:   Side branches in the billing process knowledge map

picture is worth a thousand words." Symbols help to convey the message and may be useful for separating or highlighting individual areas. On the whole, they make knowledge maps easier to grasp. For reasons of consistency and clarity, three symbols have been used in our knowledge maps:

Warning – when implementing this process or function attention should be paid to certain conditions and requirements to avoid problems such as long runtimes or undesired side effects. These recommendations are derived mainly from experience with other consulting projects and can therefore be taken into account even at an early stage of process analysis.

Attention – important information about the concept or system configuration. This information is based on inherent system restrictions, which must be allowed for during implementation. This enables you to set the right course for your implementation project at an early stage of process analysis.

Note – help and recommendations for the design of business processes and subsequent implementation during the realization phase, e.g. for concrete customizing in the implementation guide. Notes help project team members to build on the experience of existing solutions and thus speed up implementation.

When drawing up knowledge maps for process analysis, you frequently need to consider how they are integrated with other enterprise process areas. In process knowledge maps this is ensured by the side branches which are assigned the actual name of the integrated process module. In addition, special symbols from other enterprise process areas are used for process modules to highlight this cross-integration. These symbols have been chosen to resemble the SAP component symbols:

HR	Human resources	BC	Basic components
CA	Cross-application components	CO	Revenue and cost controlling
FI	Financial accounting	IM	Asset management
TR	Treasury	MM	Materials management
LO	Logistics (general)	PP	Production planning
PM	Plant maintenance	SD	Sales and distribution
QM	Quality management	PS	Project system
CS	Customer service		

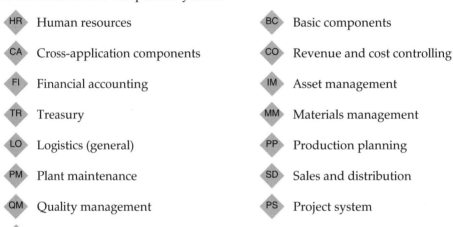

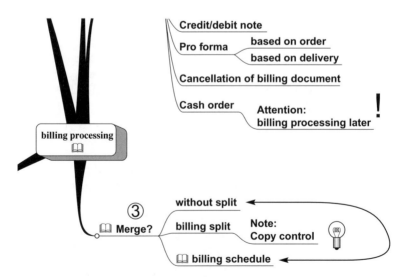

Figure 4.2.5-1:   Links knowledge map – billing process module

4.2.5 Links

Due to the integration of processes and functions in a knowledge map, there may be important interdependencies between main and side branches. These relations are clearly indicated by links. Figure 4.2.5-1 illustrates this principle for the subject of billing by the link between collective invoice and the question of invoice dates under the basic chapter summary. This serves to inform the reader or user about important integration points early on. The texts complementing the individual branches provide an additional detailed explanation of these links.

4.3   Knowledge map types

Different types of knowledge maps are used for process analysis. Depending on the timing of your analysis and the basic questions you would like to answer, you can choose from the following types:

- *Overview knowledge maps* for an introduction to an enterprise process area

- *Scenario knowledge maps* for selecting SAP business scenarios

- *Organizational knowledge maps* for enhancing a customer's personal organizational structure

- *Business object knowledge maps* for representing documents and master data per enterprise process area

- *Process knowledge maps* for a detailed process analysis.

4.3.1   Overview knowledge map

The overall business scope of SAP R/3 is subdivided into enterprise process areas (for a complete list see Figure 4.3.1-1). They have been delimited in such a way as to ensure that the individual areas are homogeneous units with a process-oriented structure. An enterprise process area contains defined task areas which, as a rule, do not overlap.

Tasks are listed under the enterprise process area in the form of business scenarios which all share the same basic pattern. Overview knowledge maps give the reader or user an initial, structured introduction to enterprise process areas and thus to process analysis (see Chapter 3.2.2).

The categorization and organization of overview knowledge maps into basic concepts helps readers and users to gain an overview of the business scope of an enterprise process area very quickly. The structure of enterprise process areas has been chosen to reflect the component view which already exists in SAP R/3. The basic ideas are condensed to one meaningful keyword, supplemented by the text of a general business management explanation. Very few overview knowledge maps have a branch hierarchy involving several levels. Such a complex hierarchy has been deliberately avoided as at this early

```
Enterprise Process Areas

    ┌─⊞    Enterprise Planning
    ├─⊞    Sales and Distribution
    ├─⊞    PDM - Product Data Management
    ├─⊞    Production Planning and Procurement Planning
    ├─⊞    Production
    ├─⊞    Asset Management
    ├─⊞    Human Resources
    ├─⊞    Cost and Revenue Controlling
    ├─⊞    Customer Service
    ├─⊞    Procurement
    ├─⊞    External Accounting
    ├─⊞    Finance Management
    ├─⊞    Retailing
    ├─⊞    Master Data
    ├─⊞    Inventory Management, Warehouse Management, and Transportation
    ├─⊞    Maintenance Management
    ├─⊞    Environment, Health & Safety
    ├─⊞    Project Management
    └─⊞    Quality Management
```

Figure 4.3.1-1:   Enterprise process areas

stage of process analysis it is sensible to provide an initial general introduction to the topic at the highest level. Further details about enterprise process areas will be provided by the knowledge map types (described in the next four sections).

4.3.2   Scenario knowledge map

At the next level down, enterprise process areas are subdivided into business scenarios which describe the business process flow along a business typology. A scenario such as that illustrated in Figure 4.3.2-1 is the model of a business process taking place within a certain enterprise process area. All the processes required for the completion of the tasks involved are linked in logical and chronological order. The business scenario provides the framework for all the elements or objects involved in the processes. Business scenarios can be graphically represented as LEGO chains or EPCs. The preconfigured scenario processes provided by SAP serve mainly to ensure rapid analysis so that frequently used business processes need not be remodeled every time.

Scenario knowledge maps illustrate all the scenarios of a particular enterprise process area in one graphic, and help users with the initial allocation of their company's business processes to the SAP R/3 system. Each scenario is represented by a branch and keyword and is explained in the corresponding text. Before a detailed analysis can be performed (see Chapter 4.3.5), process areas must be defined as a basis at an aggregate level. Even if you may never be able to select scenarios to cover all aspects of your business processes, you should be able to choose similar scenarios. For further details on using scenario knowledge maps, see Chapter 5.3.3.

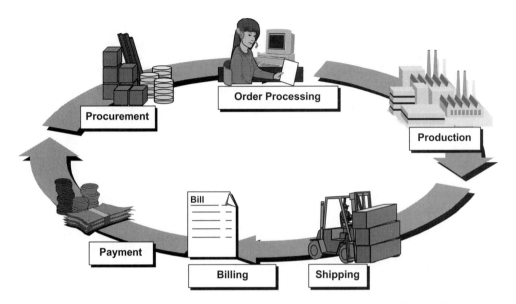

Figure 4.3.2-1:   Business scenarios – sales order processing, assembly-to-order

4.3.3   Organizational knowledge map

Flexible organizational units in SAP R/3 also make it possible to represent very complex corporate structures. A large number of organizational units serve to portray the legal and organizational structure of a company from different viewpoints, e.g. purchasing, sales, financial accounting, cost accounting (see Chapter 5.3.2). This means that specific organizational units may be defined for sales logistics, and others for procurement logistics and financial accounting. The different enterprise areas are integrated through links between the individual organizational units (Figure 4.3.3-1).

The definition of a **customer-specific organizational structure** as part of the organizational workshop is a prerequisite for user-specific system settings. The decision to use and customize certain organizational units is influenced by a number of factors. Organizational knowledge maps enable users to consider factors per organizational unit and adapt them specifically to their business needs. The individual knowledge map branches represent the decisive factors which influence the layout of a customer's organizational structure. The main branches classify basic questions, while the side branches subdivide these main points into topics and questions at several hierarchical levels, as required. Branches are always supplemented by texts which give examples to explain the topic and describe different customizing options in detail. Two variants of organizational knowledge maps have been developed for process analysis.

- *Process area-oriented organizational knowledge maps*
  Show all the relevant organizational elements required for processes within one process area. The process area (e.g. procurement) appears in the root, and the

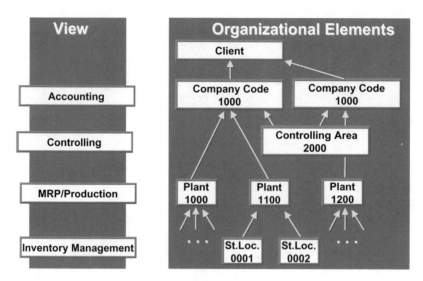

Figure 4.3.3-1:   Organizational structures

influencing factors, relationships, and interdependencies between the organizational elements required are displayed. This is particularly important with regard to links between organizational elements. Within the sales process area, for instance, the organizational element sales office is used for the external sales force. It is important to show the interdependency with the sales organization, i.e. the concrete organizational element of sales area.

- *Organizational element-oriented knowledge maps*
  Show all the relevant influencing factors for the layout of a customer's organization which have to be considered across process areas. The concrete organizational element is the central topic that appears in the root. Some organizational elements, such as the plant, have essentially different meanings in different process areas. It is important to include all the different viewpoints with all influencing factors to arrive at a well-balanced result across all process areas in the process analysis.

4.3.4   Business object knowledge map

R/3 business objects describe complete business processes. In a business application system like R/3, real objects, such as an employee, a purchase order, or a sales order, are represented as business objects. SAP business objects may be described as "black boxes" that contain R/3 data and business processes and thus incorporate structural and implementation details of the underlying data. This helps to reduce complexity, as the business object's internal subdivision into further stacked objects remains hidden.

Although this is not obligatory, it may often be useful in gaining an overview of the documents and master data within a process area as part of the process analysis. Business object knowledge maps show all the business objects of a particular subcomponent in one representation and can be used during the process analysis workshop, as required. This view of process areas is becoming increasingly important, particularly due to the business framework architecture of the SAP R/3 system. The business framework, an open, component-based architecture which enables interaction and integration of SAP and third party software components, is increasingly gaining importance. Business objects, the core elements of the business framework, provide an object-oriented view of the R/3 business functionality. SAP business objects can be accessed via stable, standardized methods called BAPIs.

4.3.5   Process knowledge map

Processes and process modules describe the smallest self-contained business tasks within the SAP R/3 system (see Chapter 3.2). Processes show in detail how individual functions of the R/3 system are sequentially and logically linked in performing a business task. Each process is carried out in transactions in the SAP R/3 system.

The actual detailed process analysis is based on process modules, for which process knowledge maps offer useful help (see Chapter 5.3.3). The root of the knowledge map provides a quick introduction to the central topic of the process module, while main branches reflect the principal chapters summarized as keywords and ramified as side branches over several levels. The keywords on the branches have been chosen to encompass a group of complex subtopics. Due to the radial structure of the knowledge map, the important subjects and questions appear close to the center (root), less important ones towards the edges, i.e. on smaller side branches. The questions recorded on the knowledge map branches can be used in the process analysis workshop to discuss the essential elements of a process. In the actual knowledge map, an explanation is attached to each question so as to provide the necessary background information for dealing with it during the analysis.

The relationship between process modules (i.e. their sequential and logical order) is highlighted by means of path symbols on the side branches. Thus, integration of a topic

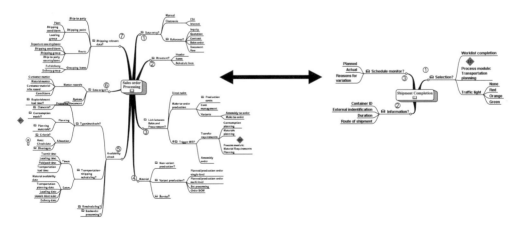

Figure 4.3.5-1:   Process knowledge map scope

with process modules of either the same or a different enterprise process area is immediately clear and can be considered during process analysis. Experience from other implementation projects has also been included in the form of additional information (warnings, attentions, notes) on side branches of the process module's main chapters and questions.

The scope of processes within SAP R/3 can vary widely. Figure 4.3.5-1 compares two process knowledge maps within sales – shipment completion (left) and sales order processing (right). At a glance you can see how diverse process modules can be. The number of basic chapters and hierarchical levels provides a gradation without impairing structure or transparency.

4.4   Knowledge maps and AcceleratedSAP

Process analysis with knowledge maps can be used for a wide range of tasks. As part of the R/3 implementation, we need to distinguish first of all which projects will be implemented using the SAP standard method, ASAP, and which will use another method. As a general rule, the process analysis method and related business engineering that we propose can be used for any R/3 implementation project. As process analysis with knowledge maps is an independent concept of its own, it may be integrated into any project management method currently available for R/3 implementation. Particularly in view of the SAP standard method illustrated in Chapter 3.3, ASAP, we regard the knowledge map database as an additional accelerator of an ASAP project. This chapter has therefore been dedicated to the use of knowledge maps within an ASAP project along the roadmap. Please refer to Chapter 3.3 for a general description of this implementation method, Chapter 5.2 for the concept behind process analysis, Chapter 1.3 to find out about the benefits of knowledge maps, and Chapter 6 to review the potential of knowledge maps. With particular regard to knowledge management, the importance of organizational and process knowledge maps by far exceeds that of an accelerator.

They could even be seen as an extension of the ASAP procedure, since they may be developed into a master knowledge map and used for organizational knowledge management, as described in Chapter 6. In an ASAP project for the implementation of an R/3 system, knowledge maps may be used in the following phases (Figure 4.4-1):

- presales or feasibility study
- business blueprint
- realization.

4.4.1   Feasibility study

The organizational and process knowledge maps described in the process library may also be used for an initial feasibility study, provided that such a feasibility study is process-oriented and based on the R/3 standard processes of the reference model.

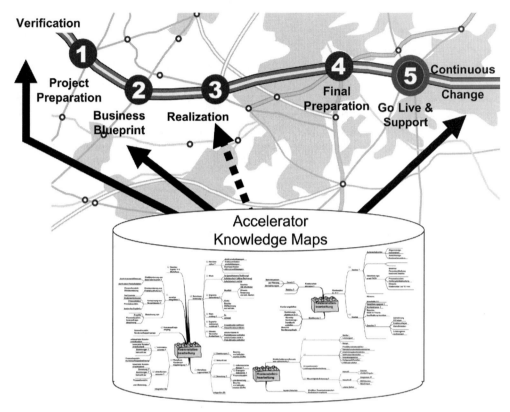

Figure 4.4-1:   Arrangement and use of organizational and process knowledge maps within an ASAP project

During this phase, the benefits of knowledge maps become very evident. In the past, checklists were used during the feasibility study for each application. The questions in these lists were not always as detailed as required by the subsequent target concept. With clearly defined representations of these questions and their interdependencies within a tree structure, knowledge maps can be used as early as in the feasibility study phase. During this phase, you can either only deal with relevant branches, or consider all branches only to a certain degree of detail, e.g. down to the second level. The results of this study will form the basis of all the following activities. The knowledge map status after the feasibility study will be the starting point for all further considerations.

4.4.2   Business blueprint

During the business blueprint phase, knowledge maps can be used without restriction. A major benefit of using knowledge maps is that users can prepare the process analysis or business (re)engineering workshops themselves, saving a lot of time and money for the actual workshops. We also recommend using organizational and process knowledge maps during the organizational and process analysis workshops to ensure a well structured organization. Moreover, you may add data to extend the knowledge maps provided if you require more information. In this case, the structure and principle of knowledge maps also offer many benefits, as information can either be supplemented at each level of the tree structure, or added as a completely new branch. Please bear in mind that during the organizational and process analysis workshops a lot of the knowledge involved and discussed is not explicit (i.e. documented) but implicit. To transform such information into explicit knowledge, you can also use knowledge maps. This is a first and very important step in the direction of organizational knowledge management. For more information, please refer to the description given in Chapter 6.

4.4.3   Realization

Now, following process analysis, how can you benefit from using knowledge maps during the realization phase? In Chapter 1.2, we mentioned that knowledge maps are a kind of synthesis between the experience of R/3 consultants, R/3 standard documentation, ASAP, R/3 transactions, R/3 business objects, R/3 organizational units, and the R/3 reference model. So, while they mainly serve the representation of your company in the framework of business engineering, knowledge maps are useful aids because of their clear structure and also because of the tips and tricks they provide concerning the configuration of the R/3 system. Due to their documentary character, they can help to gather important additional information during the configuration of organizational structures or business processes.

4.4.4   Continuous change

Due to the characteristics described above, knowledge maps also support system optimization during the continuous change phase with regard to several aspects. Once again, the benefits of knowledge maps are evident.

In the structure of a knowledge map, organizational units and processes are recorded at different levels on main and side branches, which means that this information is available throughout the life cycle of the R/3 system, in all phases including continuous change. Should extensions to the implemented (or not yet implemented) processes and functionality become necessary during this phase, knowledge maps may be used in the same way as in the initial project. Extensions may be new process modules which have not been used so far, or process modules of which only some functions have been in use. In the first case, a concrete process module, such as RFQ processing, was not implemented during the initial implementation. However, it turned out to be required during continuous engineering. In this case, the complete knowledge map for this process module can be used in the same way as in the initial implementation. In the second case, a concrete process module was included during the initial implementation but certain customizing features or functions running within this process module have not been used productively yet. Should these unused functions become relevant during the continuous change phase, the knowledge map may serve as a point of reference. In this case, you will refer only to the branches and side branches that have not yet been used or taken into consideration. Let us look at the process module *condition processing*. During the initial implementation, it was decided to not implement *scales*, which is a subfunction of *condition processing*, but now it is to be implemented retroactively. Again, the process module knowledge map can be used here, as this particular functionality is represented on a main branch as a question (see Figure 7.6.1 – Example: condition processing).

4.4.5   Knowledge management

In addition to supporting individual phases of an ASAP project, knowledge maps extend the ASAP procedure by enabling organizational and process knowledge management throughout the company. This knowledge is then available not only to consultants but also to all users and employees within the company. The use of knowledge maps in itself is a knowledge-based approach to the adaptation of enterprise-specific processes to the R/3 system and can be regarded as a first step towards extensive knowledge management. If the knowledge maps we have provided are extended and evolved into master knowledge maps (see Chapter 6.2), comprehensive knowledge management throughout your company becomes possible. This is achieved by allocating all materials, results, etc. which emerge or are developed during business engineering to the corresponding process or organizational knowledge map. Such information includes training materials, standard documentation, test data, process chains, technical data, etc. (see Chapter 6.2).

5 Process analysis with knowledge maps

5.1 Process analysis results

A SAP implementation, and its attendant business engineering or process analysis, entails certain concrete goals which should be defined, together with the corporate strategy and corporate targets (see Chapter 5.1.1 and Chapter 5.3.1). In order to achieve these central goals and targets using process analysis during the SAP implementation, the output (i.e. the results) must be known before business engineering. Figure 5.1-1 shows these results which will be explained in detail in the following.

5.1.1 Detailed process selection (scoping)

The SAP system is a standard ERP software that provides a wide range of processes and functions across all enterprise process areas. This functionality is designed to cater for as many customer requirements as possible. There are, of course, many other factors which also play a role, such as the manufacturing processes, the business planning philosophy, the industry, the corporate environment or market situation, etc. Naturally, not all of these aspects are relevant for all customers but only those which are part of the customer's business environment have been defined as relevant to implementation (e.g. human resources will not be relevant if a customer does not intend to use the SAP system for this particular process area), or those which have been identified as relevant during business (re)engineering (Davenport, 1993, p. 27). The processes of the enterprise in question must be compared with the SAP functionality and the processes that have been realized, or can be realized, within the SAP system (Kirchmer, p. 113). Based on this comparison, components are then selected from the available software solutions to best suit the individual requirements of the company (Thome and Hufgard, p. 93). For this selection, you can refer to SAP reference models or processes (see Chapter 3.2). As a rule, the overall functionality required by the enterprise is defined during the sales cycle or feasibility study before the project kickoff, so that the processes to be implemented can be selected at a very early stage. A detailed analysis defining which of these processes and functions will ultimately be used should be performed during the process analysis phase. For example, in company X, the feasibility study results established, before project kickoff, that the process areas production, sales and distribution, revenue and cost controlling, procurement, and financial accounting are relevant to the implementation of the core

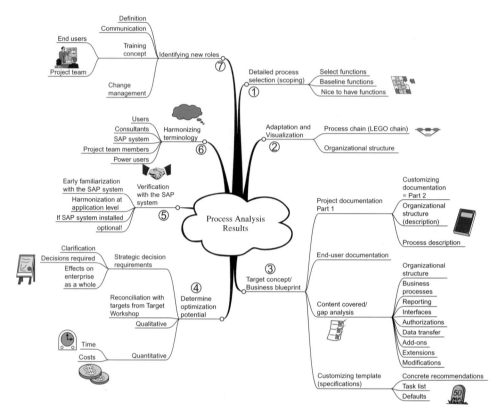

Figure 5.1-1:   Process analysis results

process sales order processing. Other areas are not included in the scope. In addition, according to the type and industry of your company, you may decide that different scenario processes are to be used for different areas, e.g. direct sales to industrial customers for the sales process area, sales order processing for the production area, etc. (see Chapter 3.4).

Scenario processes consist of process groups and individual processes (= process modules). These process modules or LEGO bricks (see Chapter 5.3.3) are arranged in a logical sequence. The detailed analysis serves to find out which of these components are of relevance to the enterprise. Scoping is therefore limited to the following structural elements (scoping in the ASAP Q&Adb):

- process areas (enterprise process areas)

- scenario processes

- process groups

- processes

- functions (to some extent).

After selecting the process modules, you should verify whether they are really necessary or just nice to have and which may therefore be implemented as part of a later project during continuous change (Bürkle, p. 13) or continuous system engineering (Thome and Hufgard, p. 61).

5.1.2   Adaptation and visualization of process chains and organizational structures

The aforementioned scoping alongside SAP reference processes goes hand-in-hand with the mapping and adaptation of customer requirements and processes to the SAP process world. The procedure during this adaptation is an essential part of process analysis and is described in Chapter 5.3.3. It can be seen as a conceptual process description supported by visualization and documented in the blueprint. Mapping will always raise the question of what is adapted to what – the SAP system to the company or vice versa. One thing is certain, however: the analysis will entail changes to existing business processes, e.g. by automatically triggering follow-up activities, eliminating redundant business processes, creating integrated teams, or setting up a process-oriented work organization. For complete process documentation it is not sufficient, however, to describe all processes in text form only. Rather, they should be visualized in the form of process chain graphics to make them more transparent and easier to understand. Processes should be illustrated or modeled at one specific level only (for instance, at scenario level), and the graphical representation should be kept as simple as possible. As we have found in many different projects, EPCs are not always suitable for this visualization, and we recommend using a simple process chain such as the LEGO chain (see Chapter 4.1 and Chapter 5.3.3). To facilitate process analysis, SAP reference models have been applied at scenario level and, to simplify representation, events have not been included.

An essential prerequisite and part of every process analysis is the adaptation of the enterprise structure to SAP organizational units, considering all the consequences entailed and bearing in mind that process flows are directly linked to the underlying organizational structure (Thome and Hufgard, p. 56). This is best accomplished by describing and defining the organizational structure of an enterprise using the organizational units available in SAP. As is the case with process flows, this is also done in the blueprint. The organizational structure should also be visualized, and the choice of representation form is left up to you.

5.1.3   Target concept/business blueprint

The terms (business) blueprint and target concept are used synonymously in this discussion. The blueprint generally defines what is required of the organizational structure and processes to be implemented (Grupp, p. 16), and provides the concrete design concept for implementing these requirements in SAP (Scheer, 1998a, p. 152). In other words, the blueprint represents and documents the organizational structure and the process description (process structure) adapted to SAP. This representation can be either textual or visual. Thus, the blueprint is the first part of the project documentation (i.e. the description of the corporate concept) which will be defined in more detail by means of customizing settings in the course of the project. The blueprint can be based either on the results of an as-is-analysis (Scheer, 1998a, p. 150; Bancroft et al., p. 168) or on re-engineering carried out previously (Hammer, 1994, p. 50; Davenport, 1993, p. 27). In business practice, as well as in publications by renowned authors, the as-is-analysis is discussed controversially before the target concept is drawn up (see Chapter 5.2; Thome and Hufgard, p. 18). Just as controversial is the discussion about re-engineering in the run up to an SAP implementation (Figure 5.1.3-1).

In connection with software implementation, we often hear people talking about the process design or technical design. How does this relate to the blueprint/target concept? When individual developments used to rule the business world, the DP implementation of business requirements was carried out as illustrated in Figure 5.1.3-1.

In this procedure, the process design described what was required of the information system from the user's (i.e. the technical) perspective using the technical business language of that area. This description was then used by the programmer/system analyst as a basis for a technical design, split into programmable units, or flowcharts, and translated into program code as part of the technical implementation. Today, this procedure has been replaced, at least in part, due to the increasing availability of standard business application software. Ultimately, the SAP standard software is nothing more than a realized technical design to be adapted to individual customer requirements in customizing, i.e. by system parameterization. The blueprint's aim is to describe the customer's business requirements with a view to adapting them to, and implementing them in, the SAP system. The creation of the blueprint includes mapping the preconfigured technical design of the SAP system to the customer's process design. In the framework of SAP implementation, the blueprint can therefore be seen as a combination of technical and process designs in one. The blueprint should include the following details.

- *Organizational structure*
  Detailed documentation and explanation of the organizational structure to be represented in the SAP system using SAP organizational units for logistics (e.g. sales organization, plant) and accounting (e.g. company code, controlling area).

- *Business processes*
  Detailed documentation and explanation of the process flows to be represented in the SAP system, using all the function variants provided in SAP and displayed as processes in the reference models.

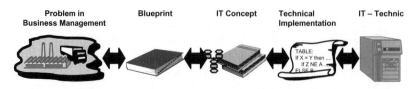

| Problem in Business Management | Blueprint | IT Concept | Technical Implementation | IT – Technic |

Figure 5.1.3-1:   How to define an information system
(Scheer 1990, p. 15)

- *Reporting*
Detailed documentation of the reports and analysis options required by the enterprise and their representation in the SAP system. In this early phase, you should verify whether the standard reporting options provided by SAP are sufficient or whether you will require additional reports.

- *Interfaces*
Detailed description of the interfaces required. For lowest cost of ownership (see Chapter 1.1-7; Kidler, p. 20) we recommend that you do not create too many interfaces. In most cases, however, it will not be possible to do without interfaces altogether. This is mainly due to the fact that additional information systems are usually running parallel to SAP.

- *Authorizations*
Detailed description and specification of authorizations for employees who will work with the SAP system in different enterprise areas. Roles, such as asset accountant, production planner, purchasing agent, auditor, warehouse manager, overhead cost controller, profitability and sales accountant, should be defined accordingly.

- *Data transfer programs*
Detailed documentation and specification of data transfer programming. This may include master data (e.g. cost elements, cost centers, accounts receivable, accounts payable, materials) and transaction data if required (open items in financial accounting, sales orders in sales and distribution, production orders in production, etc.). Possible data conversions also have to be taken into account (e.g. format and length of cost center keys, material numbers, or customer numbers). Most of the business objects described in the examples are mass data available in the legacy systems and required for the new SAP system. Corresponding programs have to be written for them.

- *Add-ons*
Detailed documentation of add-ons. The open architecture of the SAP system based on the business framework (Möhrlen and Kokot, p. 46) enables cross-company business processes (e.g. internet scenarios), links with complementary software systems (e.g. archiving programs), or decentralized implementation via application link enabling. These add-on functions also need to be described in detail.

- *Extensions*
Sometimes the SAP functionality does not completely cover all the requirements of an individual enterprise. For such cases, the SAP system provides clearly defined points called user exits (Buck-Emden and Galimow, p. 142) which enable users to program any additional functions themselves (e.g. enterprise-specific, sophisticated pricing mechanisms). As user exits are predefined points in the standard system, their upstream compatibility is ensured. Apart from preconfigured user exits, extensions also include programs which are added to the standard SAP system but do not affect the flow logic as modifications do.

- *Modifications*

  If the SAP system does not cover all enterprise-specific functions and process flows, and if none of the above mentioned options (extensions, user exits, etc.) meets these requirements, you may need modifications which have a tangible effect on the flow logic of the SAP system. As such modifications are not compatible with upstream functionality, they should be avoided if at all possible. Should they become indispensable, however, they need to be documented and specified.

Finally, the blueprint is a template for customizing. The processes identified during process analysis must be mapped onto the SAP system later including all the customizing settings described. The blueprint provides the customizing definitions for the system and concrete recommendations for implementing certain settings. In many cases it contains a task or project administration list which is used to set parameters for (customize) processes. This list specifies, for each process module, any open questions which need to be clarified during realization. It also includes information regarding the process owner and the consultant in charge; when parameterizing is to begin and end; who is to perform tests; and when and where there is a need for harmonization. In the ASAP method, all these points are covered by the creation and use of a business master list.

5.1.4   Determining optimization potential

The objectives of the SAP implementation are determined in the framework of the strategy and target definition (see Chapter 5.3.1). Most of the time, this is not just about replacing the old DP system but about defining concrete, central corporate strategies and optimization requirements (Bancroft et al., p. 161; Österle, p. 36; Heinrich and Burgholzer, pp. 179–184). These can be either qualitative or quantitative. For example,

- *qualitative*: improved customer service by optimizing service processes; accelerated product delivery by means of more efficient processes, which in turn results in a higher level of customer satisfaction;

- *quantitative (time factor)*: shorter production order throughput times; faster creation of financial/income statements;

- *quantitative (cost factor)*: 10 percent reduction of stock levels due to early warning systems and sophisticated inventory management concepts; quicker response to market changes or cost fluctuations by means of an up-to-date and detailed profitability analysis.

During the process analysis phase, target processes are defined in line with the goals and optimization potential which were defined beforehand. In addition, further optimization potential is usually identified during process analysis while handling the process chains. As opposed to the general strategic aims defined during the corporate strategy or corporate target workshops (see Chapter 5.3.1), this potential is described in a more concrete and detailed form. Even without an explicit as-is-analysis before business engineering, it is vital to give some thought to the actual situation during process analysis. As you are trying to achieve the greatest possible improvement in designing your target processes, you need only compare the actual situation with the defined target situation to identify the potential benefits of using the SAP system. The target business processes derived from such a comparison entail changes in many areas regarding the actual organizational structure and affecting the enterprise as a whole. For this reason, it is essential to communicate with the corporate management at an early stage in order to harmonize these processes. Depending on the scope of the project you must define which organizational change decisions are to be taken by the project team and which should be deferred to middle or top management. In the latter case, changes need to be presented to the management because they are responsible for making strategic decisions about adopting them, e.g. in the framework of a steering committee meeting.

5.1.5   Verification using the SAP system at application level (optional)

If an SAP system is in place at the time of process analysis, certain questions arising during the discussion on business process or function variants may be dealt with at the same time as the SAP analysis. Another benefit of this early availability is that project team members and power users can familiarize themselves with the SAP system at an early stage. However, we regard this as an optional step (also see Chapter 5.3.3).

5.1.6   Harmonizing the terminology of the department and SAP system

The SAP system uses a specific language, users within the company speak another language, system analysts/DP staff speak yet another language, consultants speak their own (SAP-influenced) language, etc. In addition, different companies often use different

Term	Meaning in SAP	Meaning for the customer
Business area	Detailed view of income and financial statements in financial accounting	Subcomponent of sales market, i.e. business area = division
Sales area	Combination of the organizational units of division, distribution channel, and sales organization	Marketing or distribution channels
Material number	Material number = key of a material	Purchase order number; customer means material number
Plant	Can also be a logical unit subdividing the physical plant into several logical plants	Physical unit/location

Figure 5.1.6-1:   Examples of different use of terminology

terminology to describe the same business situation. In process analysis workshops, several people sit round a table and discuss the same business aspects using different words and this necessarily leads to terminological "collisions." If the team is aware of this fact, a frequent side effect of process analysis is that after the workshop everybody involved tends to speak the same language in future. This is an essential prerequisite for efficient communication between consultants and project team members. Consultants should pay particular attention to harmonizing terminology, as they have the additional role of trainers who pass on IT/SAP knowledge (Thome and Hufgard, p. 90). Figure 5.1.6-1 illustrates some examples from practical consulting experience.

5.1.7   Identification of "new" roles (change management)

As a rule, every time business (re)engineering of a company's processes is carried out in combination with the implementation of integrated standard ERP software, it is accompanied by new organizational structures. This usually entails changes in the working environment of some employees (Davenport, 1993, p. 171), i.e. a new understanding and concept of roles. During process analysis (see Chapter 5.3.3) a decision is made regarding who will be responsible for a process and who will actually perform the process in the system later on. It is thus possible to develop a role concept even at this very early stage and to assign these new roles to the employees. However, change management not only involves defining new roles but also requires informing the staff concerned as early as possible (Bancroft et al., p. 220). The results can also be used during the process analysis phase to identify and create detailed documentation of the training requirements for project team members, power users, users, managers, etc. as all these people must be able to fulfill the tasks assigned to them during the role definition early on in the project. To this end, relevant training materials should be allocated to the corresponding process modules. These will enable target-based, process, and end user-oriented training preparation and activities. Easily comprehensible conveyance of the necessary skills, knowledge transfer, and communication of future work fields are the main requirements to be met during change management (Bancroft et al., p. 221).

5.2   The concept behind process analysis

Before we describe the procedure we recommend for process analysis with knowledge maps, we will explain the basic concepts behind it. These concepts form the basis not only of our procedure but also of many other widely known methods.

Whenever we talk of mapping or adaptation in the following, this refers to assigning the customer's processes to the SAP system and, conversely, the adaptation of the SAP system to customer requirements. In our particular case, this does not so much concern the software architecture and functionality but primarily refers to the level of processes. "The SAP project team will need to understand ... [SAP] ... well enough to judge where and how the system will be able to accommodate the required changes" (Bancroft et al., p. 171).

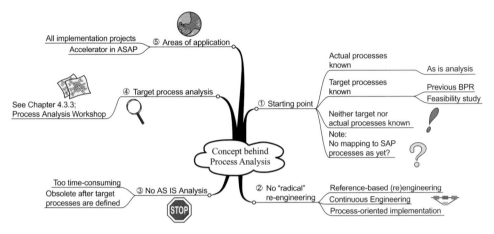

Figure 5.2-1:   The concept behind process analysis with knowledge maps

5.2.1   Starting point

The status of existing processes and of integrational thinking differs in each enterprise implementing the SAP system. Most enterprises have a purely functional organizational structure, since process organization as described by Gaitanides (Gaitanides, p. 10), for instance, has not gained wide recognition. Irrespective of whether an enterprise organization is process-oriented or function-based, the fact that the SAP software requires interdisciplinary and process-oriented thinking should be taken into account during the implementation of the integrated SAP system. In general, process-oriented thinking must first be introduced, as most enterprises have been function-oriented up to now. This requires various skills on the part of the employees. It is therefore not surprising that, more often than not, there is no, or only a very vague, knowledge of the processes which exist in an enterprise. Yet, whether or not an enterprise thinks in terms of processes largely depends on its level of evolution, on its corporate philosophy, and on the management. Ultimately, the implementation of new, integrated DP causes a small internal revolution in the company (Meinhardt and Teufel, p. 71). All this shows that it cannot always be taken for granted that an enterprise thinks in terms of processes or acts in line with the processes which exist at the start of the implementation project. There are three possible scenarios for an SAP implementation.

- *Actual processes are known*
  The actual processes which exist within the enterprise can be well known. This is usually shown by the fact that employees, when asked about the current system flows and processes, can give precise answers, feel responsible for specific processes, and differ only slightly in their statements. This is typically the case when an as-is-process analysis has been performed and documented in the company. Documented process flows can also be found in enterprises which have analyzed and described processes as part of a DIN ISO 9000 certification. Many companies have already turned to process orientation, and employ people in central or decentralized departments who are

responsible for continual process analysis and documentation, either full-time or in addition to their usual work. Actual processes must then be mapped (allocated) to the SAP system during a process analysis workshop. Processes may either be adopted without modification (if possible) or optimized using the full optimization potential of the SAP system, which usually results in optimized processes and business flows.

- *Target processes are known*
  If this is the case, then actual processes are usually also known. The implementing company has a definite idea as to how processes should be realized in the SAP system. This initial situation can often be found if an enterprise has performed BPR before the SAP implementation project. It is also important in this respect to know whether BPR was performed, at least partly, in consideration of the processes available in SAP, or independently without any link with the SAP system at all. In the latter case, it might turn out that the concept developed cannot be realized, or only with additional programming or modifications. Knowledge of the target processes may also have been gained through a feasibility study carried out using SAP reference models in the run up to an SAP implementation project. Once the target processes have been defined, they are mapped to the SAP system in the framework of a process analysis. If the target processes were defined in consideration of the process flows to be represented in the SAP system, mapping will be relatively easy. If this is not the case, you should determine which process flows are more efficient – the target processes defined independently of the SAP system, or the SAP standard processes.

- *Neither target nor actual processes are known*
  Very often, neither target nor actual processes are known. This does not mean that there is no knowledge at all about processes and process flows within the company. Rather, process knowledge is very vague or limited to a specific area and not related to the whole company, and has usually not been documented. In this case, SAP reference processes can be taken as a basis for mapping during process analysis. If an as-is-process analysis is not desired, business engineering can be initiated immediately on the basis of best business practices provided by the reference processes. Even without an explicit as-is-analysis, current process flows will come up during the discussion, so that a somewhat leaner but generally adequate as-is-analysis is still performed.

5.2.2   No re-engineering

BPR comprises various approaches to (re)designing business processes. In this context Hammer and Champy, in particular, talk of a radical redefinition of business processes (Hammer and Champy, p. 31) starting from scratch. Davenport favors the same radical change, which he calls business process innovation (Davenport, 1993, p. 132). According to this approach, IT is regarded as a mere enabler (Hammer and Champy, p. 83; Davenport, 1993, p. 37). Harrington, on the other hand, describes a business process improvement which is not as radical as the aforementioned approaches but aims at rationalizing existing processes followed by continuous engineering (Harrington, p. 23), as also described by Thome and Hufgard (Thome and Hufgard, p. 78). In real life, you do not often find the perfect conditions described by Hammer and Champy or Davenport, because business (re)engineering is usually considered for the first time when SAP is being implemented. Besides, the Hammer and Champy or Davenport approaches have not been successful in practice for pragmatic reasons (Müller, p. 180), or the optimization aimed at cannot be achieved (Thome and Hufgard, p. 61). Many companies do not really want to radically rethink their existing structures but to optimize, rationalize, and streamline existing business processes and organizational structures. Thus, a company's actual goal in performing business (re)engineering hovers somewhere between incremental rationalization and complete reinvention (Bancroft et al., p. 116).

The SAP system with its reference processes (also called best business practices) is particularly suited to meet this goal, as it provides optimized, industry-specific process flows which the implementing company can use as a reference for its organization instead of having to reinvent it from scratch. For this reason, and those mentioned in Chapter 1.1.1, the SAP system is to be regarded as an enabler and, at the same time, as a driver of substantial change during business (re)engineering and subsequent continuous engineering. This is shown by the process illustrated in Figure 5.2.2-1, before and after SAP implementation at Nokia. Bancroft et al. emphasize this fact: "With this force in hand [SAP], even companies which simply want to replace their ... will do some level of re-engineering because of the structure of SAP itself, and probably more than they imagined was needed" (Bancroft et al., p. 122). In principle, there are three different SAP implementation procedures serving to achieve the overall aim of process optimization.

Firstly, there is the purely process-oriented procedure in which business processes need to be defined before SAP implementation and SAP software is implemented later. The aim is to achieve an independent and individual business process design entailing very efficient and effective processes. However, this can only be achieved at the cost of longer project times and complex projects. The approach is labeled "1" in Figure 5.2.3-1.

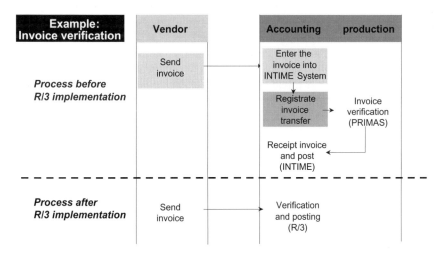

Figure 5.2.2-1:   Process invoice verification before and after SAP implementation at Nokia
IWI-HSG Faculty of Information Management of St. Gallen University: AcceleratedSAP – 4 Case Studies,
Research

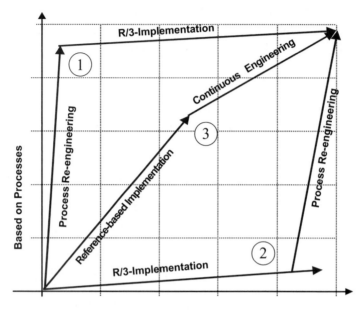

Figure 5.2.3-1:   Different approaches for an SAP implementation
Source: IWI-HSG Faculty of Information Management of St. Gallen University:
AcceleratedSAP – 4 Case Studies

Then there is the purely DP-oriented approach in which the enterprise aims at quick IT implementation on the basis of its actual processes without using SAP reference processes, at the expense of major improvements. The focus here is on short project times, and these are achieved at the cost of less than optimal processes. In order to realize the goal of a high level of process optimization, the implementation phase is followed by re-engineering within the continuous change phase. This approach is indicated by "2" in Figure 5.2.3-1.

Both of the extreme strategies described above have their advantages and disadvantages. The third procedure is an attempt to combine the advantages of both strategies while compensating their disadvantages. This method is called reference-based implementation. It uses the SAP reference processes, i.e. best business practices. The apparent drawback of this approach is that a company implementing SAP, basing its organization on the standard processes of the SAP system, loses the uniqueness and individuality that make it stand out from competitors. This argument does not hold water however, as the wide range of customizing options provided, in addition to the open architecture of the SAP system (business framework), is designed to preserve the individuality of an enterprise. As part of this procedure, business (re)engineering based on reference processes is performed at an early stage of SAP implementation. This enables the enterprise to utilize the optimization potential of the SAP system quickly and to shorten project duration. Further improvements can be realized during the continuous change phase. This third procedure is indicated by "3" in Figure 5.2.3-1.

Our process analysis description thus refers to a reference-based analysis performed with the aid of knowledge maps as part of a feasibility study of the actual implementation and optimization project, and during the subsequent continuous engineering phase. The ASAP procedure described in Chapter 3.3 is based on the same premise.

5.2.3   No as-is-analysis

The proposed process analysis does not explicitly include an ex ante as-is-analysis. An as-is-analysis usually takes too long and may adversely affect the subsequent definition of the target concept, as it may focus too much on the actual situation. Besides, such an analysis becomes obsolete after the definition of target processes (Thome and Hufgard, p. 20). Hammer also believes that a detailed as-is-analysis would be too long and complex, and that an assessment of the actual situation should mainly be about understanding actual processes without, however, analyzing them down to the smallest detail (Hammer and Champy, p. 41). Such a general as-is-analysis is automatically carried out during process analysis as a rule, i.e. when the improvement potential is determined, as described in Chapter 5.3.1. Understanding the actual processes is sufficient, there is no need to document or analyze them in detail.

5.2.4   Target process analysis

The above discussion shows that a target process analysis is performed as part of the recommended procedure for a process analysis with knowledge maps. In a nutshell, this means that the following steps are performed during a process analysis.

- Mapping and adaptation of the "customer's world" to the "SAP process world."
- Reference-based mapping, using the best business practices from the SAP reference model.
- Adaptation of SAP processes to customer requirements (i.e. blueprinting as a basis for parameterization).
- Business (re)engineering to identify optimization potential.
- Use of a specific questioning technique.
- Use of knowledge maps.
- Visualization of processes according to the LEGO principle.
- Consistent prioritization of and adherence to integration aspects from the start.

The actual procedure is described in detail in Chapter 5.3.3.

5.2.5   Areas of application

Process analysis with knowledge maps can be applied in a wide range of areas. First of all, SAP implementation projects need to be separated into those using the SAP standard method (ASAP) and those using another method. We have already stressed the fact that we regard knowledge maps as powerful accelerators in an ASAP project by giving a detailed description of their use along the roadmap in Chapter 4.3. What is more, process analysis using knowledge maps can be carried out in any project, whether it is ASAP or non-ASAP. Furthermore, knowledge maps can lend support not only during an implementation project but over the whole life cycle of an SAP system; more precisely, whenever a process analysis is required and mapping customer business processes to the SAP system becomes necessary. The following concrete phases usually require this business (re)engineering support, even if the names of the phases differ from one procedure model to the next:

- presales or feasibility study

- blueprinting, i.e. target concept definition

- realization – only partial support, e.g. concrete recommendations regarding do's and don'ts, which are stored in the knowledge maps

- continuous change – mainly if functional enhancements of the SAP system become necessary during continuous engineering because of new processes or functionality that need to be analyzed.

5.3   Workshops

A process analysis performed as part of process-oriented SAP implementation must be based on clearly defined corporate goals, well-known enterprise process areas, and a specified organizational structure. Current SAP system implementation projects are more than mere representations of the current business situation of an enterprise. They seize the opportunity to improve processes within an adapted organizational structure in line with the corporate goals. In the following chapters, dealing with enterprise analysis, we will describe several workshops that may help you develop a target concept within the framework of an SAP implementation.

5.3.1   The definition of strategies/goals

At corporate strategy level, management defines the business areas (market/product combinations), organizational structure, and related processes of an enterprise. The illustrations of processes and organizational fields drawn up during strategy planning are usually not very detailed, as the focus is placed on the absolutely essential. Strategies are the guidelines for an enterprise and are mainly concerned with economic aspects. Modern management, however, will not only try to consider rational, economic aspects, but will also take sociological and social aspects into account. In business management theory, this has become known as the turning point in the trend of strategic management, which was formerly a purely economically-oriented discipline (Wöhe, pp. 97–122). In the following, we will describe the two workshops (strategy workshop and target workshop)

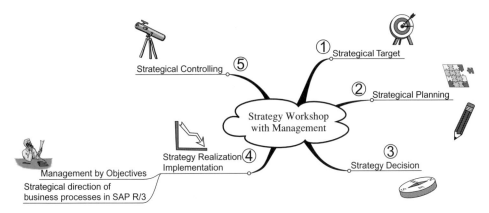

Figure 5.3.1-1:   Topics of the strategy workshop

that a company may perform to prepare for the subsequent organizational design (Chapter 5.3.2) and as a basis for process analysis (Chapter 5.3.3).

1. *Strategic objectives*

   Corporate management's principal task is to determine the strategic goals of the company and to adapt these strategies to changing market conditions if required. This enables employees to familiarize themselves with these strategies, which in turn helps them to recognize the value of their own work and to identify with their company. Existing problems within a company, such as high stock levels, may lead to the definition of corresponding solution strategies in the framework of a strategy workshop. These strategies involve targets and activities designed to deal with the problem. Whereas only a few years ago companies pursued global strategies, today more and more enterprises focus on core competencies in order to keep on top of problems and thus achieve maximum profits. While a sole enterprise will need to make an enormous effort to achieve the strategic corporate goals of, for example, growth or market leadership, merging is an efficient way to achieve this goal. Current examples include the mergers of Daimler and Chrysler, EXXON and Mobil, or AOL and Netscape. Daimler/Chrysler's strategy focussed on a higher level of market penetration in the US and the completion of its passenger car range, EXXON/Mobil is using the merger to further the implementation of its strategy to fight the oil price decline, while AOL merged with Netscape with a view to becoming the market leader on the internet.

2. *Planning a strategy*

   Once the management has defined its strategic goals, these are arranged in a time schedule. Strategies are either implemented in the form of goals or used to represent the corporate philosophy, which means that they are permanently rooted in the enterprise. Strategic planning allocates defined strategies to business areas of products, services, and customer groups (Scheer, 1998a, pp. 150–153). Each business area is described by critical success factors, as well as a target hierarchy (qualitative and quantitative goals) based on the strategies, and presented to the top management who then select a strategy. An enterprise may have defined several strategies – it makes sense, however, to implement only two or three of them. We will discuss the decision to implement a small number of strategies in the next step of the strategy workshop.

3. *Selecting a strategy*
   To select a strategy, middle management first defines the goals (decision portfolio) in a parallel workshop. In this target workshop, the strategies are supported by qualitative and quantitative goals, and ways of implementing these goals are shown. This puts top management in a better position to decide which strategies can be realized fairly easily, and which will be more difficult to implement. The implementation of SAP software opens up new possibilities for strategies which have only become possible with this new functionality. For example, if cost reduction has been defined as a strategy, it can then be implemented with SAP marginal costing.

4. *Implementing a strategy*
   Once the strategies have been selected and determined by the management, they will be translated into concrete goals (Chapter 5.3.2). In this regard, management by objectives and KPI are well-known terms in business management, which provide for a target agreement/measurement with employees. While many enterprises focus on the principle of management by objectives, most of them quantify these objectives. In order to be able to measure success based on objectives, we must determine the key figures of the individual enterprise areas. In the sales department, employees can easily be assessed in terms of their sales targets, whereas in other enterprise areas key figures are difficult to determine (Brenner and Hamm, pp. 24–27). An enterprise can only realize its strategies together with its employees if they do their daily work in accordance with business process definitions. If the business processes in SAP are oriented toward the defined goals, we can talk of a strategy implementation. The individual process analysis workshops (see Chapter 5.3.3) will be based on and defined by the results of the strategy workshop.

5. *Strategic control*
   Ultimately, the important thing is that the defined strategies and their objectives have been realized. To find out whether or not this is the case, business flows and tasks need to be monitored by the people performing these tasks. In addition, an external auditor (e.g. a business consultant) can give an objective assessment of the strategies, which is interesting for those who would like a neutral point of view. For monitoring quantitative goals, it is important to have the support of SAP financial accounting aids (accounting, financial statement, cost accounting, statistics, and other reports), the business information warehouse (key figures), and logistics information systems (stock situation, open item management, etc.).

In addition to the strategy workshop, there will be another workshop involving the management (plant manager, head of department, etc.), which is aimed at specifying the strategies and their goals and subgoals (Figure 5.3.1-2).

1. *Presentation of different kinds of goals*
   An introduction to the target workshop is not essential but may be useful for introducing the various objectives. It provides an overview of monetary and non-

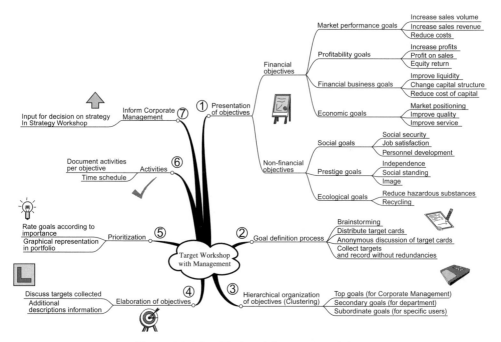

Figure 5.3.1-2:   Topics of the target workshop

monetary goals (Wöhe, p. 111). The enterprise focusses primarily on monetary objectives to secure its existence. Non-monetary objectives are mostly those seen through the eyes of employees or trade unions. It makes sense, therefore, to ensure during the subsequent steps of the workshops that monetary goals further non-monetary objectives. For instance, the objective of profitability (profit increase) could be linked to the non-financial objective of social security. Individual objectives may depend on each other but they may also compete. A reduction in costs, for instance, may well be to the detriment of quality assurance. The introduction of the various objectives serves to motivate the participants in the workshop and shows the importance of a target workshop.

2. *Goal definition process*
   In the target workshop, participants will be encouraged to discuss the enterprise's problems using the brainstorming method. Problems identified at this stage will serve as a basis from which to evolve the improvement objectives later on. An important part of the goal definition process is that the workshop participants suggest objectives anonymously. This is done with cards: participants in the workshop are given three cards each, on which they should note improvements (goals) that they personally consider important for the enterprise. The participants must not necessarily fill in all the cards. Completed cards are collected and pinned on a board. Redundant goals are immediately removed or grouped together. Figure 5.3.1-3 shows how goals can be grouped and organized.

```
┌─────────────────────────────────────────────────────────────────────────┐
│ Title of the Target Workshop: _____  │
│                                                                           │
│ ┌──────────────────────┐ ┌──────────────────────┐ ┌────────────────────┐ │
│ │ Organization         │ │ Who?                 │ │ SAP relevant?      │ │
│ │                      │ │                      │ │                    │ │
│ │ ☐ Depart. A  ☐ Sales │ │ ☐ Audience           │ │ ☐ Organizational   │ │
│ │ ☐ Depart. B  ☐ Plant A│ │ ☐ Affected by       │ │ ☐ Can be solved with SAP │
│ │ ☐ Depart. C  ☐ ......│ │ ☐ Interested in      │ │                    │ │
│ └──────────────────────┘ └──────────────────────┘ └────────────────────┘ │
│                                                                           │
│ Description:                                                              │
│ .......................................................................   │
│ .......................................................................   │
│ .......................................................................   │
│ .......................................................................   │
│ .......................................................................   │
│                                                                           │
│ ┌──────────────────────┐ ┌──────────────────────────────────────────┐   │
│ │ Numbers:             │ │ Related Documents or Master Data:        │   │
│ │                      │ │                                          │   │
│ │ Costs: ............. │ │ 0 Working List      0 Vendor Master      │   │
│ │                      │ │ 0 BOM               0 ................   │   │
│ │ Revenue: ........... │ │ 0 Material          0 ................   │   │
│ └──────────────────────┘ └──────────────────────────────────────────┘   │
└─────────────────────────────────────────────────────────────────────────┘
```

Figure 5.3.1-3:   Form for the definition and organization of objectives (target card)

3. *Hierarchical organization of objectives*

   The objectives identified are then grouped in clusters according to the strategies identified in the strategy workshop. Objectives can be grouped hierarchically into top, secondary, and subordinate goals – strategies should be classed as top goals, and the goals on the pinboard divided into secondary and subordinate goals. Figure 5.3.1-4 shows an example of a hierarchy of objectives.

4. *Elaboration of goals*

   The target cards can be recorded in a table (database) to be described in more detail. Objectives are expanded in a discussion between the participants. During the discussion, some of the objectives may suddenly appear to be irrelevant and be dropped. With a view to helping the subsequent SAP implementation, it makes sense to try to map (allocate) objectives to SAP components. The following table should give you an idea of how this mapping might be performed (Figure 5.3.1-5). This very general allocation of SAP components is also the starting point for the organizational analysis described in Chapter 5.3.2 and the process analysis discussed in Chapter 5.3.3.

5. *Prioritization*

   Top goals can be prioritized using the aspects relevance and urgency in a portfolio. The rating of goals is agreed among the workshop participants. Figure 5.3.1-6 is an example of a portfolio comprising eight top goals which have been reduced to four after

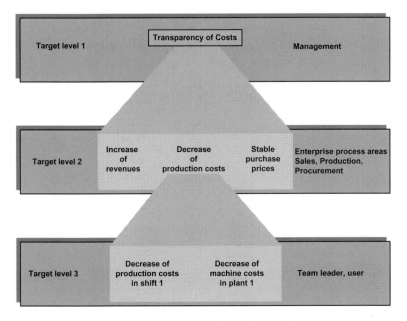

Figure 5.3.1-4:   Example – hierarchy of objectives

Activity	Description	Time horizon	SAP Relevant?	Expense	Expected Benefit	Unit / Time	Areas Concerned	Contact	Current Project
Disclose key figures	-Access to value flows is to be based on role (process) -Supply business key figures -Control & reduce overhead through cost transparency -Cost responsibility through decision basis -Who has access to what key figures? -Teach correct interpretation of business figures -Supply business key figures -Control and reduce product costs -Cost transparency & basis of decisions (costing. CMA. revenue controlling) -Determine key figures required and to be released -Show CM to sales staff, so that turnover is not the only basis of assessment -Release key figures (or use by areas concerned based on roles and teach correct interpretation of key figures/data -Introduce confidentially agreement & non-disclosure obligation for disclosed data	Medium-term, to be implemented with SAP Project Short-term – release available data today! Release available figures for use by Project Team	Yes – top priority!	Funds Required data/key figures are defined by SAP Teams and submitted to steering committee for decision			All areas you need (decision makers?) Cost transparency in the areas: SD. Administration Production – all areas. Not just CGM in Production	Management	SAP Project
Increase cost transparency	Within the Process Workshop, the data required for processes should be determined and processed. The SAP system should be set up accordingly	SAP Project	yes	Within Process Workshop	-Cost transparency -Cost responsibility can be delegated Target: Cost reduction	SAP Project	all	Management approves cost transparency approach - SAP Project Manager monitors implementation	SAP Project
Budgeting	-Define scope of costs within budgeting -Cost responsibility -Project-related budgeting (role-based planning)	For SAP Project	yes	High, as budget needs to be defined	-Cost transparency -Cost responsibility -Cost reduction				SAP Project

Figure 5.3.1-5:   Describing goals and mapping them to SAP

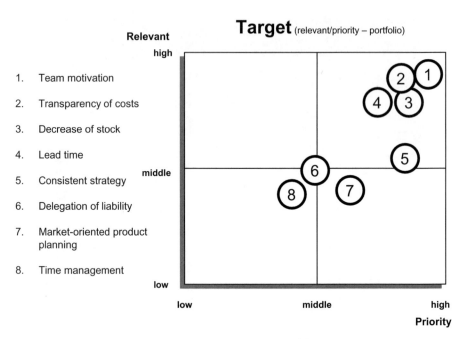

Relevant

high

1. Team motivation
2. Transparency of costs
3. Decrease of stock
4. Lead time
5. Consistent strategy
6. Delegation of liability
7. Market-oriented product planning
8. Time management

low

Figure 5.3.1-6:   Target portfolio

Decision Form

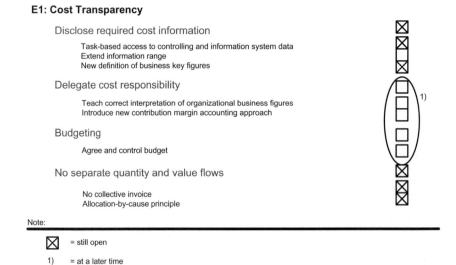

E1: Cost Transparency

Disclose required cost information

    Task-based access to controlling and information system data
    Extend information range
    New definition of business key figures

Delegate cost responsibility

    Teach correct interpretation of organizational business figures
    Introduce new contribution margin accounting approach

Budgeting

    Agree and control budget

No separate quantity and value flows

    No collective invoice
    Allocation-by-cause principle

Note:

    ⊠   = still open

    1)   = at a later time

Figure 5.3.1-7:   Decision on cost transparency

Decision Form

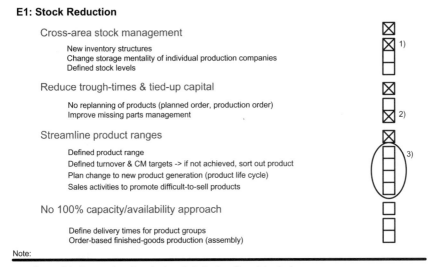

E1: Stock Reduction

Cross-area stock management

    New inventory structures
    Change storage mentality of individual production companies
    Defined stock levels

Reduce trough-times & tied-up capital

    No replanning of products (planned order, production order)
    Improve missing parts management

Streamline product ranges

    Defined product range
    Defined turnover & CM targets -> if not achieved, sort out product
    Plan change to new product generation (product life cycle)
    Sales activities to promote difficult-to-sell products

No 100% capacity/availability approach

    Define delivery times for product groups
    Order-based finished-goods production (assembly)

Note:

1)   = Introduce new inventory structures including benefits and drawbacks
2)   = Missing parts management is implemented together with the SAP system
3)   = Need for discussion

Figure 5.3.1-8:   Decision on the reduction of stock levels

prioritization in line with the strategic planning defined in the strategy workshop. The bubbles in a portfolio can be allocated different sizes according to their importance – however, this has not been done in Figure 5.3.1-6.

6. *Activities*

Based on the prioritized top goals, secondary and subordinate goals are now described by activities which are allocated an estimated time input. This estimate is made and agreed by the workshop participants. Describing activities is very time-consuming and should only be done after the four top priority goals have been determined. Two columns are added to the table from the elaboration of goals step: activities and input.

7. *Informing the corporate management*

With regard to the strategy selection step of the strategy workshop, the management needs to know the results of the target workshop. These prioritized goals, along with the descriptions and activities, are presented to the management in the form of a checklist. Figures 5.3.1-7 and 5.3.1-8 show a summary card for top management taken from consultancy experience for the prioritized goals of cost transparency and reduction of stock levels.

5.3.2   Workshop on the definition of an organization

"In the case of standard software, the organizational model or structure is often not as clearly defined as data, functions, or processes. It may be hidden behind names such as sales group, company code, or plant, for which specific fixed responsibilities are laid down in the respective programs. For the practical implementation of a standard software, however, the harmonization of organizational structures is particularly important" (Scheer, 1998b, pp. 52–66). This is why an organizational workshop is a necessary prerequisite of a successful SAP implementation. The knowledge map below (Figure 5.3.2-1) shows the procedure followed to define the organizational structure.

5.3.2.1   Determining enterprise views

An enterprise that has decided to use SAP software has its own existing organizational structures, which are also called enterprise views. These enterprise views are the starting point for an organizational workshop aimed at defining an organization with the SAP organizational units. Branch 1 in the organizational workshop knowledge map describes the various enterprise views required by the customer. Note that the terminology used by the customer to describe his organization is different from that of SAP organizational entities (e.g. a customer uses the term operational facility, whereas SAP calls this an operational facility plant). In the following, the individual enterprise views will be described briefly. If the enterprise failed to document these views at the beginning of the organizational workshop, they should evolve during this workshop.

- Legal enterprise view

Enterprises are subject to different disclosure obligations in different countries, and these are illustrated in a legal enterprise view. The MM Group, for instance, has companies in Berlin, Munich and Frankfurt (e.g. with the legal form GmbH), which are subject to different legal regulations from companies located in Spain (Madrid, Barcelona).

During the organizational workshop the customer must first of all inform the consultant about the organizational structure and explain the characteristics of each

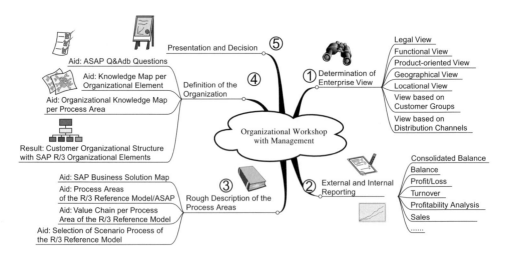

Figure 5.3.2-1:   Topics of the organizational workshop

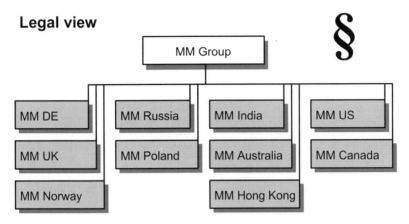

Figure 5.3.2-2:   Legal enterprise view

company (e.g. production company, selling company, selling and production company, or R&D company). If the enterprise comprises a large number of legally independent companies, it may be useful to select just a few as examples (Figure 5.3.2-2).

- Functional enterprise view

The functional enterprise view with its function-oriented organizational units provides an overview of areas such as research and development (R&D), procurement, sales, etc. These areas usually correspond to the departments of an enterprise (Figure 5.3.2-3).

- Product-oriented enterprise view

The product-oriented enterprise view is a classification of individual product families. A pharmaceutical company, for example, is subdivided into OTC, therapeutics, diagnostics, and injectables. As a rule, the product-oriented view looks at a company from the sales perspective. However, it is wise to ensure in each case that the procurement-based product view is not different. Based on the product lines, business areas are defined that

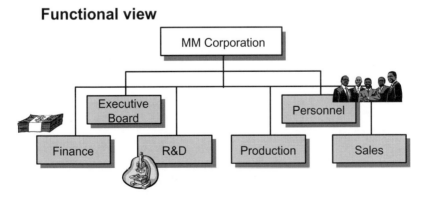

Figure 5.3.2-3:   Functional enterprise view

Product-oriented view

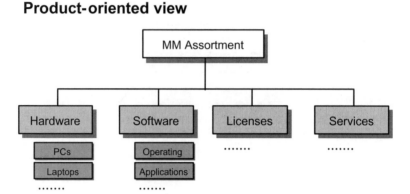

Figure 5.3.2-4:   Product-oriented enterprise view

report results separately per product. These profit and loss accounts are the sales indicators for each product. As a rule, the reporting requirements are sales, turnover, and contribution margin. To build up a product-oriented enterprise view it is usually sufficient to list the hierarchical levels used and support them with corresponding examples. The levels of the hierarchy from top to bottom are total product range, strategic business area, and segment (Figure 5.3.2-4).

• Geographical enterprise view

In this enterprise view, regions are defined according to market orientation aspects. The market structure may be determined by a common language area, a homogeneous customer structure, or certain proposed focus regions. Further levels of focus may be economic regions such as the EU, geographical zones, nations, certain subregions of nations, federal states, or local areas. The regional enterprise view highlights the market structure and then the allocation of companies to certain regions. This view is also sales-oriented and includes reporting requirements such as turnover per region or profit per region. The example shown in Figure 5.3.2-5 is a basic division by continents and states. The levels of the structure from top to bottom are world, regions, and countries.

• Locational view

The locational enterprise view is related to the legal view, as locations may be legally independent entities (Figure 5.3.2-6). Physical locations include production plants, laboratories, warehouses, distribution centers, etc. This example shows the production plant in Berlin, which is a legally independent entity, whereas Munich/Stg. with the location Frankfurt legally belongs to the company Walldorf.

• Enterprise view based on customer groups

An enterprise view based on customer groups is useful for optimizing supply chain management. Customers could be distribution centers or end customers. A pharmaceutical company, for example, supplies hospitals, wholesalers, and doctors (i.e. end customers). The hierarchy is usually structured by customer type, customer

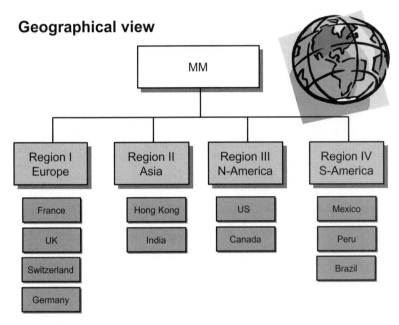

Figure 5.3.2-5:   Geographical enterprise view

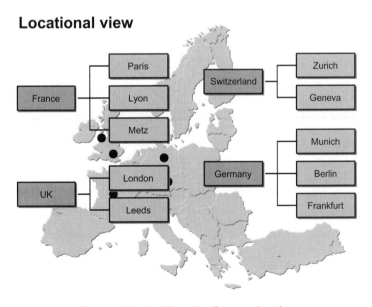

Figure 5.3.2-6:   Locational enterprise view

View based on customer groups

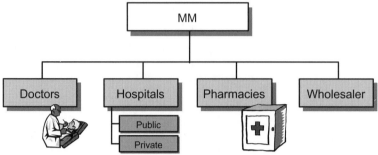

Figure 5.3.2-7:   Enterprise view based on customer groups

View based on distribution channels

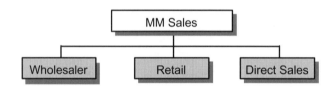

Figure 5.3.2-8:   Enterprise view based on distribution modalities

industries, customer enterprises, and individual customers. Reporting requirements are based on sales, turnover, and contribution margin (Figure 5.3.2-7).

- Enterprise view based on distribution channels

A representation according to distribution channels is not essential but may prove to be useful from a logical and result-oriented point of view. Distribution channels may be divided by types – e.g. direct selling, wholesale, retail, and mail-order selling. The example illustrated in Figure 5.3.2-8 shows another possible method of classification based on distribution modality (rail, truck, etc.). The logical view indicates how the *sales process* will be related to the organizational unit *distribution channel* later on. The result-oriented view compares the efficiency of the distribution modalities mentioned. Reporting requirements are based on the duration of the distribution process, turnover per distribution channel, etc.

5.3.2.2   External and internal reporting requirements

Once the customer has defined the different enterprise views, the consultant is called upon to inquire into the customer's current (actual) reports for each enterprise view. The allocation of enterprise views to the required reports could be documented in a table such as that in Figure 5.3.2-9.

Enterprise view	External/ internal reporting requirements
Legal view	Financial statement, income statement, consolidation
Functional view	Cost center report, profit center report, business area report, internal financial statements and income statements
Product-oriented view	Sales report, revenue report, contribution margin (DB) report
Regional view	Revenue report per region, profitability report per region
Locational view	Activity level of a plant, revenue report per distribution center, profitability analysis
Customer group view	Sales report, revenue report, and DB report per customer
Distribution modality view	Duration of distribution process (tracking), revenue report per distribution modality

Figure 5.3.2-9:   External and internal reporting requirements

5.3.2.3   General description of process areas

In order to be able to map SAP organizational units to different customer enterprise views, the customer's processes first need to be defined at a general level. It is enough to define process areas without analyzing individual process modules as well (Chapter 5.3.3, particularly the section on LEGO process modules). Without the identification of process areas, it is impossible to adequately describe the organizational structure. Conversely, we can assume that a process analysis cannot be performed without the organizational framework conditions. SAP provides several representation models which enable a general description of customer process areas (Figure 5.3.2-10). First, the customer selects a suitable industry model (business solution map) for his enterprise. This model provides an extensive overview of different process chains (lines) in the form of a matrix which has been created specially for one particular industry. Of course, there are also generic process chains such as enterprise management, which is generally valid. In this book, the high tech business solution map is used as an example (Figure 3.4.2-1). If a customer has chosen this solution map, he can adopt individual elements from it for the general business description. The sales & marketing process area indicates that in the next step of the organizational workshop (organizational definition) the organizational units of sales organization, sales area, distribution channel, and division will have to be discussed in detail. Furthermore, we can see from the business solution map that the organization

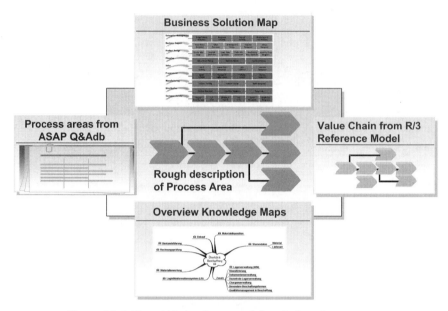

Figure 5.3.2-10:   Aids for the general description of process areas

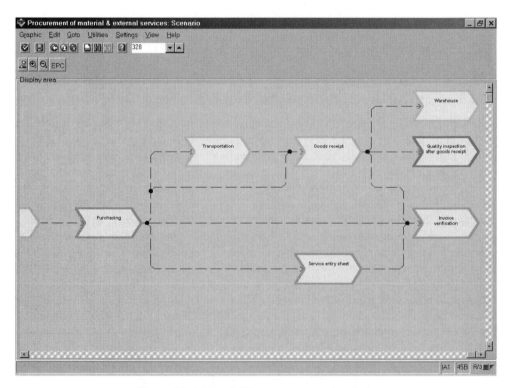

Figure 5.3.2-11:   SAP procurement value chain

includes the area financial accounting. This area is generic and requires the company code and controlling area for the definition of the organizational structure.

Another aid for the general description of customer process areas is the preconfigured value chain of the SAP reference model. This form of representation is familiar to customers and offers the additional advantage of a subsequent mapping of chain elements to SAP process modules, because detailed processes (EPC processes) are stored in the background. The procurement value chain, for example, includes the general processes of RFQ/quote, supplier, outline agreements, supply source, etc. (Figure 5.3.2-11). It helps if customers use SAP process terminology in their general description.

If customers prefer to select process areas from a list, they can refer to the list provided in the ASAP Q&Adb. The example in Figure 5.3.2-12 shows the process areas product development and marketing, sales logistics, revenue and cost controlling, asset management, financial accounting, financial management, customer service, enterprise planning, human resources, business partners, logistics planning, procurement and production, as well as the procurement scenarios on the hierarchical level below.

The *overview knowledge maps* for the individual process areas offer additional assistance. These knowledge maps give a brief overview of the elements contained in the organizational structure and explain the first hierarchical level only. When customers are first confronted with SAP and asked to describe process areas in a general manner during

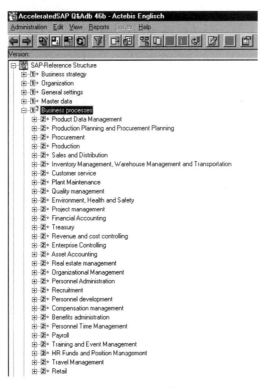

Figure 5.3.2-12:   ASAP Q&Adb – process areas

the organizational workshop, overview knowledge maps can serve as an additional explanation aid. A customer's description may take on a form such as that shown in Figure 5.3.2-13. Each process area is accompanied by a detailed description with a selection of scenarios, as zoomed in for the sales area in the example below.

5.3.2.4   Organizational definition

The fourth step of the organizational workshop includes the main task, i.e. the definition of different organizational scenarios. The aim is to find several organizational models from which you can make a selection. The decision to use one organizational unit and not another is influenced by a number of factors. Organizational knowledge maps are used to show the relevant factors for each SAP organizational unit. Say, for example, you are in a workshop discussing the importance and layout of plants. First of all, you will need an exact definition of the term plant as used in the SAP context. You can then analyze the different influencing factors such as the question of stocks, as shown in Figure 5.3.2-14. This example shows the different options for inventory management for the logical organizational unit plant.

There are several ways of representing organizational units. This means, for example, that you can create different scenarios, each with a different use of the organizational unit

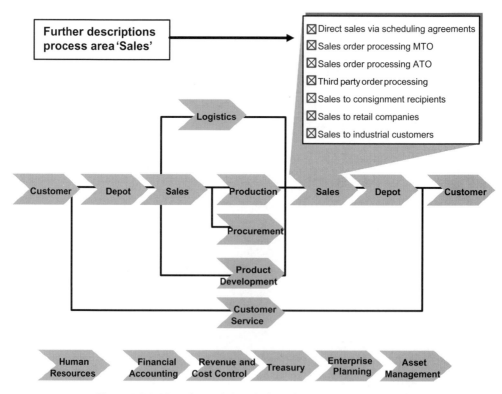

Figure 5.3.2-13:   General description of process areas – example

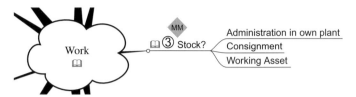

Figure 5.3.2-14:   'Plant' knowledge map

plant. The important thing to remember when designing organizational models is that customer and SAP terminology must be harmonized (Figure 5.3.2-15).

SAP provides two different representation methods for defining several different organizational models. The first method is representation by tiles, where each organizational unit is represented by a *tile* in a three-dimensional graphic. While this technique is visually highly effective, customers tend to identify more easily with the traditional hierarchical view of the organization. We have therefore not included the three-dimensional tile view here but will discuss the various hierarchical organizational models instead. Hierarchical organizational models can be created with traditional graphics tools (see enclosed CD: Micrografix Flow Charter). The aids listed in Figure 5.3.2-16 will then be used to show various analytical steps that need to be performed to find a solution during the organizational workshop.

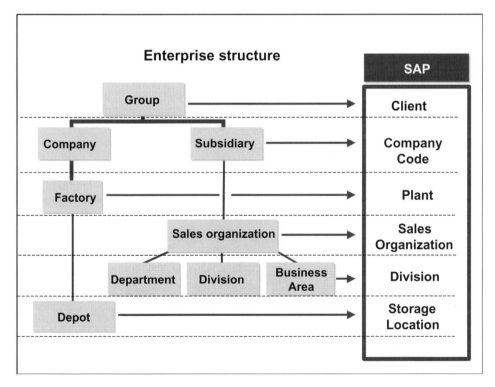

Figure 5.3.2-15:   Different organizational terminology (Source: SAP AG)

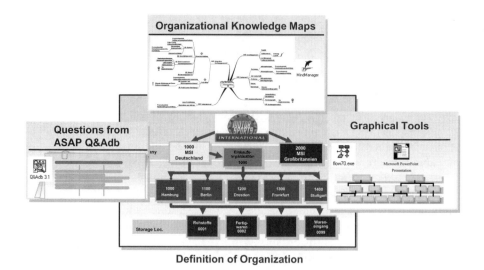

Figure 5.3.2-16:   *Aids for organizational definition*

- **Step 1:** *Determining the company codes and assigning them to a client*

All legal organizational units of an enterprise are subject to financial reporting requirements (tax laws) and therefore require a company code. An international enterprise usually has several company codes that can be assigned to one client. This client then takes the form of a consolidation unit.

- **Step 2:** *Analyzing business areas of a company code*

If an enterprise intends to prepare internal financial statements or income statements, it can define business areas either within one company code or across several company codes. All business areas can be used by all company codes. They represent separate areas of business management within an enterprise and independent accounting units using the US GAAP procedure (Figure 5.3.2-17).

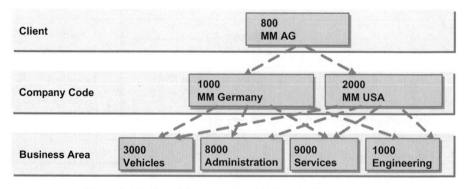

Figure 5.3.2-17:   *Clients, company codes, and business areas*

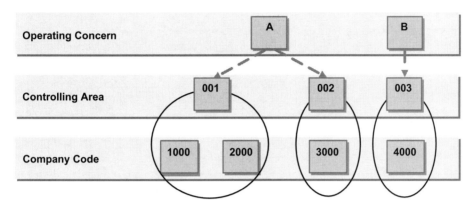

Figure 5.3.2-18:   Controlling area, company code, and operating concern

- **Step 3:** *Analyzing the operating concern, controlling area, and company code*

The focus of controlling largely depends on how the controlling areas within your enterprise are related to your company codes. A controlling area identifies an independent organizational unit for which costs and revenues are recorded. In the organizational workshop, two solutions are usually discussed in this respect – either each controlling area is allocated to exactly one company code, or cost accounting is performed across company codes, i.e. one controlling area is defined for several company codes. Furthermore, an organizational unit *operating concern* needs to be defined for the controlling areas to enable reporting for the profitability analysis. This lets you monitor various market segments of customer-specific business fields and determine their profitability. Several controlling areas can be assigned to one operating concern (Figure 5.3.2-18).

- **Step 4:** *Analyzing the use of profit centers*

Profit centers collect costs and revenues from the corresponding cost centers. The employees responsible for a profit center are assessed based on its cost/revenue result. Profit centers contain a hierarchy of cost centers and may themselves be linked through nodes in a profit center hierarchy (Figure 5.3.2-19).

- **Step 5:** *Analyzing the organizational unit plant used in materials management and its relation to the company code*

The definition of the organizational unit *plant* is of central importance to logistics (materials management, production, sales and distribution, customer service). A plant can be a production facility (e.g. assembly plant, etc.), or it can offer services or store and distribute materials (distribution center). For product costing one *valuation area* must be defined for each plant. The valuation area is the organizational level at which quantity and value-based inventory management takes place. If you are using separate (internal/external) valuation, you will control partial stocks of a material via the movement type (classification key indicating the type of material movement, e.g. goods receipt, stock transfer and goods issue). A plant is assigned to exactly one company code, whereas a company code can comprise several plants. The relationship between the plant

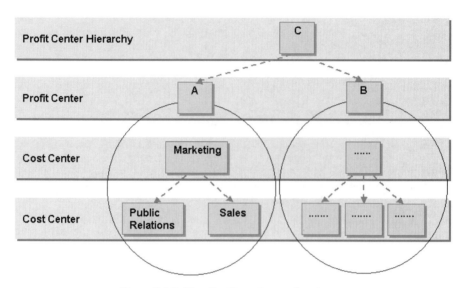

Figure 5.3.2-19:   Profit centers and cost centers

and the company code is similar to the integration interface between materials management and financial accounting (Figure 5.3.2-20).

- **Step 6:** *Analyzing the sales areas used in logistics (sales organization, distribution channel, division)*

The organizational unit sales area is a combination of the organizational units sales organization, distribution channel, and division. Each combination variant has a different combination key, i.e. an additional sales area. Divisions are usually defined for products. For example, you are selling consumer products and capital goods, or, in the case of a motor-vehicle manufacturer, divisions are classified into trucks, passenger cars, etc. It would also be possible to define an individual division for each model. The level of detail of your divisional structure depends on your reporting organization. However, a simple

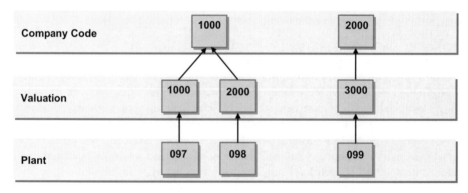

Figure 5.3.2-20:   Plant, valuation area, company code

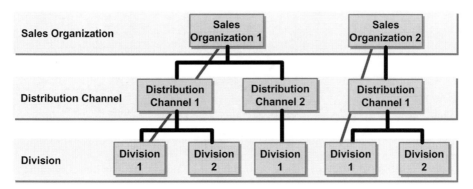

Figure 5.3.2-21:   Sales areas

sales organization structure often has advantages over a complex one, since it has an immediate effect on, for example, order entry and master record maintenance by being more transparent for the user. In Figure 5.3.2-21, five sales areas have been defined for only two physical sales organizations. Each sales organization represents a selling unit in the legal sense (e.g. for product liability, rights of recourse, etc.). In practice, sales organizations are often used to delimit geographical areas. Business cases such as sales order processing are dealt with separately for each sales organization. The sales department relies on different distribution channels to ensure a seamless market supply. The organizational unit distribution channel is also referred to as a distribution lane. Typical channels of distribution include direct sales, wholesale, retail, agency, trade, etc.

- **Step 7:** *Analyzing the relationship between sales organization and plant*

For each sales organization, the plants authorized to sell goods are determined based on the distribution channels, so that one sales organization can sell goods from several different plants. At the same time, a plant can be assigned to several sales organizations, all of which can sell goods from this plant. If, in a direct sale, the sales organization is

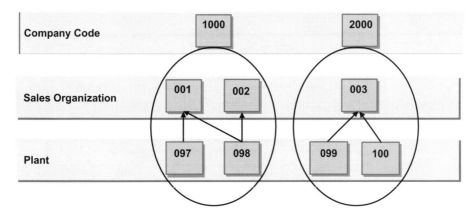

Figure 5.3.2-22:   Sales organization – plant

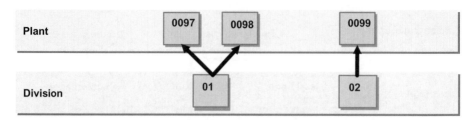

Figure 5.3.2-23:   Plant – division

assigned to a different company code than the plant from which the delivery comes, this is known as intercompany sales (Figure 5.3.2-22).

● **Step 8:** *Analyzing the organizational unit's plant and division*

The organizational unit division can be used to group materials (product groups). Each division can be assigned to several plants taking the relevant product groups into consideration. In addition, customer-specific price agreements and individual terms of payment can be fixed for each division (Figure 5.3.2-23).

● **Step 9:** *Analyzing the organizational structure within a sales area*

The organizational unit sales office represents a sales point (e.g. Denver, Chicago, etc.), where goods are sold locally (geographical aspect). Sales offices are assigned to sales areas and need to be recorded together with the relevant sales area during order entry. Employees of a sales office are entered as sales persons, and then organized into sales groups. These groups are usually classified according to the same criteria as the divisions (Figure 5.3.2-24) (e.g. sales group 001 for the division passenger cars, sales group 002 for the division trucks, etc.).

● **Step 10:** *Analyzing the shipping organization*

Shipping points are defined for planning and handling deliveries to customers. These points are independent organizational units. They are supplied by the delivering plants

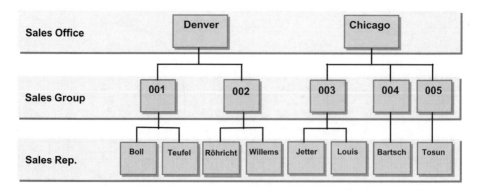

Figure 5.3.2-24:   Sales office, sales groups, sales persons

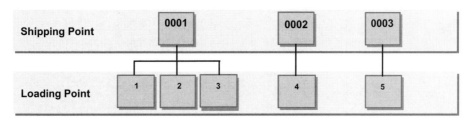

Figure 5.3.2-25:   Shipping point – loading point

and connected to specified loading points. For example, shipping point 0001 consists of ramp 1, ramp 2, and ramp 3, whereas different loading ramps need not necessarily be defined for shipping points 0002 and 0003 (Figure 5.3.2-25).

- **Step 11:** *Analyzing the materials management organizational units – plant and storage location*

Each warehouse is assigned to exactly one plant, whereas a plant can be assigned several warehouses. Storage locations are organizational units which enable you to differentiate between inventories within the same warehouse. Production planning and control (e.g. processes material requirements planning, demand management) usually takes place at plant level. However, planning and production can also be organized at cross-plant level. In materials planning it is also possible to look at inventories per storage location. At any time during the production cycle, you can determine the storage location from where the required materials are to be taken and the finished goods warehouse where goods are to be delivered after production. In practice, a distinction is often made between warehouses for raw materials, semi-finished products, and finished goods (Figure 5.3.2-26).

- **Step 12:** *Analyzing the materials management organizational units plant, purchasing organization, and purchasing group*

The purchasing organization is an organizational unit within materials management that subdivides the enterprise according to purchasing requirements. It procures materials and/or services and negotiates purchasing conditions with suppliers. The assignment to plants is determined by the procurement type. The following types of procurement are possible, either on their own or in combinations: group-oriented procurement (one purchasing organization procures material for all company codes), company-oriented procurement (one purchasing organization procures material for exactly one company code), plant-oriented procurement (one purchasing organization procures material for

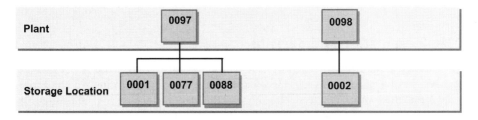

Figure 5.3.2-26:   Plant and storage location

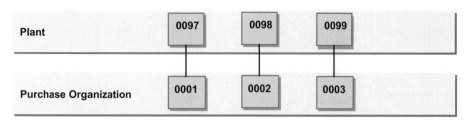

Figure 5.3.2-27:   Purchasing organization (decentralized, per plant)

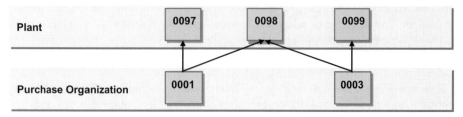

Figure 5.3.2-28:   Purchasing organization (in charge of more than one plant)

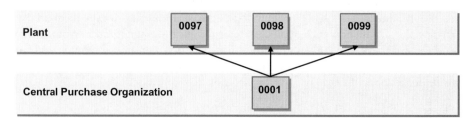

Figure 5.3.2-29:   Central purchasing organization for all plants

exactly one plant) (Figures 5.3.2-27–29). Purchase contracts are usually group- or company-oriented in order to ensure larger purchase quantities. At the level below the purchasing organization, purchasing groups are loosely defined. These groups are not physically connected to the purchasing organization, but a logical link can be established via the authorization concept, where a certain group is authorized to deal with certain objects of the purchasing organization. Purchasing groups are created whenever several buyers are in charge of the same purchasing activities.

5.3.2.5   Presentation and decisions

The easiest way to redefine the organizational structure of an enterprise is to implement a new business application software. Organizational units directly influence the reporting structure and thus enhance transparency within an enterprise. By defining further divisions, for example, you will achieve better sales evaluation results, because divisions are selection criteria in the logistics information system.

The organizational units defined during the analysis workshop are presented to the management using SAP terminology. Only management can decide to adopt the various organization scenarios (structure scenarios) developed in a project. The different scenarios may be portrayed in a *decision portfolio*.

5.3.3   Workshop on the process analysis with knowledge maps

After the global enterprise strategies and goals have been stipulated in a corresponding workshop, and a decision on the future organizational structure has been made based on the mapping of existing organizational structures to SAP organizational units, the same must be done with processes from a BPR point of view. You should always bear in mind that a general process analysis is about identifying, analyzing, and optimizing the processes which exist in an enterprise. In the case of implementing the SAP standard software, the dimensions of mapping and adaptation will have to be added to these

Project Teams (by function) ⇨ Process Areas ⇩	FI	CO	HR	MM	SD	SM	PP	QM	PS	PDM
Enterprise Planning	X	X			X		X			
Sales & Distribution	X	X		X	X	X	X	X	X	X
Product Development/ Marketing	X			X	X	X	X	X	X	X
Logistics Planning		X		X	X	X	X	X	X	X
Production		X	X	X	X	X	X	X	X	X
Asset Accounting	X	X		X	X		X		X	
Revenue and Cost Controlling	X	X	X	X	X	X	X	X	X	X
Financial Accounting	X	X	X	X	X	X				
Finance Management	X	X								
Customer Service	X	X		X	X	X	X	X		X
Procurement	X	X		X	X	X	X		X	X
Human Resources	X	X	X				X			

Figure 5.3.3-1:   Matrix organization and integration points in a process-oriented SAP implementation

tasks. In simple terms, mapping means allocating the requirements of the existing enterprise world, including actual and target views, to the processes of the SAP software. A by-product of adaptation is a detailed description of the processes that are to be supported by, and operated under, SAP in the future. The focus here is on the processes running within the enterprise, a process being " ... a specific ordering of work activities across time and place, with a beginning, an end, and clearly defined inputs and outputs: a structure for action" (Davenport, 1997 p. 5). While in the past, a function- or module-oriented approach was favored in implementation projects, the process-oriented SAP implementation strategy, as described in Chapter 5.2 and detailed in this section, has become ever more popular over the past few years. It is particularly suited to meet the process (re)engineering requirements of an enterprise (Popp, p. 7; Meinhardt and Teufel, p. 15).

You can enhance the benefits of the overall process analysis and the subsequent process-oriented implementation by supporting the project using a project organizational plan which, in business administration, is also called a matrix organization (Wöhe, p. 192) (Figure 5.3.3-1).

In the following, we will describe the topics and procedures involved in the process analysis with knowledge maps workshop (Figure 5.3.3-2).

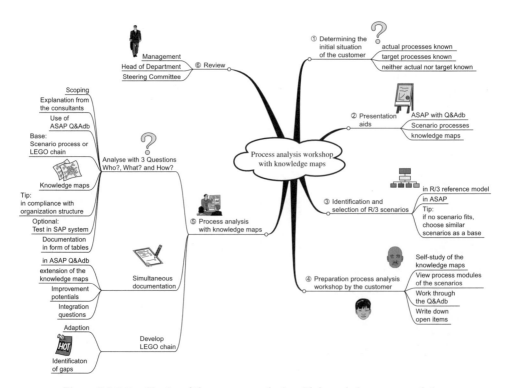

Figure 5.3.3-2:   Topics of the process analysis with knowledge maps workshop

5.3.3.1   Determining the initial situation within the customer enterprise

Before the actual workshop can begin, the current situation of the enterprise with regard to processes must be identified. This includes the question of how the enterprise interprets the concept of processes and how this interpretation has been realized in the corporate philosophy. Another essential question is whether there is an awareness of simply actual processes or also target processes, or neither (see Chapter 5.3.2).

5.3.3.2   Presentation aids

To achieve the process analysis objectives described in Chapter 5.3.1, the aids required for a process analysis with knowledge maps must be introduced and explained. This happens after the enterprise process situation has been identified but before the first workshop begins. This support includes technical presentation aids such as flipcharts, presentation cards, overheads, PCs, etc. as well as the following:

- *Questions from the ASAP Q&Adb*
  The *ASAP Q&Adb* enables a hierarchical display of the SAP reference model, and facilitates the scoping and a description of blueprint-relevant concept decisions (through the customer input template). If the Q&Adb is not available, or the project is not an ASAP project, a spreadsheet or word processing program can be used instead. In ASAP, questions are set up for each process and can be used to support and accelerate the blueprint phase and process analysis.

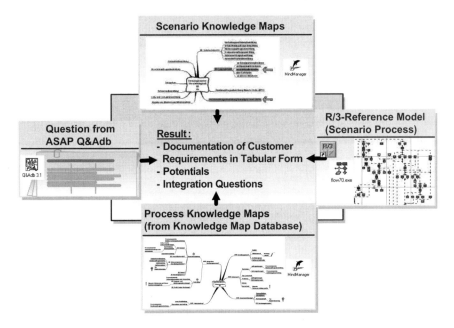

Figure 5.3.3.2-1:   Process analysis components

- *Knowledge maps*
  In addition, or as an alternative, to the ASAP questions, knowledge maps can be used to speed up implementation. Due to their structure and inherent description of business cases and SAP-specific aspects, knowledge maps are ideal for assisting the mapping or adapting processes during the analysis phase.

- *Scenario processes (SAP reference model)*
  The scenario processes from the SAP reference model can be displayed in the SAP system with the business navigator tool as well as with PC solutions such as *Visio*, *Intellicorp*, *ARIS* or *Micrografix Flow Charter* (see enclosed CD). These tools can be used to represent the process chains developed during process analysis in the form of LEGO chain graphics (see Branches ③ and ⑤ in Figure 5.3.3-2), although they may use symbols other than LEGO bricks to visualize process modules (Figure 5.3.3.2-1).

5.3.3.3   Identification and selection (general scoping) of SAP scenarios

Before the actual detailed process analysis with knowledge maps (see branch ⑤ in Figure 5.3.3-2) can start, process areas must be defined at a general level. They form the basis of the subsequent detailed analysis. Usually, these areas are described during the

- *sales phase* (using business solution maps), or the

- *organizational workshop* (Figure 5.3.2-13).

As a rule, feasibility studies are performed in situ as part of the sales activities, which result in a general description of requirements (see also Chapter 3.4). The description of requirements and the use of business solution maps are documented from the **sales view**, not from the **modeling view**. Thus, a detailed terminological definition and exact allocation of requirements to specific enterprise process areas of the SAP reference model is usually not effected. This general identification of requirements, which also serves as the basis for defining the organizational structure (see Chapter 5.3.2), is now used to **select** the relevant SAP scenarios (see Chapter 3.2.3), as described in the following.

We will now discuss, by way of example, some requirements which may result from sales negotiations or be documented during the organizational workshop.

- *Sales*
  - presales activities
  - outline agreements
  - sales order processing with MTO
  - quality management
  - delivery processing
  - etc.

- *Production*
  - materials planning
  - make-to-order production

– goods receipts
– etc.

From the SAP reference model, you can now display the predefined SAP scenarios for these areas and select the most suitable scenarios for your enterprise. Even if you do not find a scenario process that fits your business situation completely, you should try to choose a **similar** scenario as a basis for the subsequent process analysis with knowledge maps. During process analysis, you will have the opportunity to make changes to this scenario by adding any missing process modules. The preconfigured SAP scenario processes enable you to perform a quick analysis and save you having to frequently remodel recurring business processes from scratch over and over again. In our workshop example we have displayed possible sales logistics scenarios in list form, and selected the scenario sales order processing, assembly-to-order, from this list (Figure 5.3.3.2-2). The scenario selection you see here has been taken from the *Micrografix Flow Charter* tool. Of course, these scenario options also exist in the ASAP Q&Adb or in the SAP business navigator. Figure 5.3.3.2-2 shows the optional steps B and C which can be performed to provide a complete LEGO chain as a basis for the process analysis described in Chapter 5.3.3.5. From our practical project experience we recommend preparing a complete LEGO chain, as it reduces the complexity of scenario processes and thus enables a simplified representation. This simplification is achieved by filtering out event symbols from the geometrical routes and taking out functions (B in Figure 5.3.3.2-2). Each function (process module) of the scenario process is portrayed as a brick in the LEGO chain in accordance with the flow logic (C in Figure 5.3.3.2-2).

You will find the complete LEGO chain for the scenario process sales order processing, assembly-to-order, in the SAP Process Library, Book 4, Chapter 5.

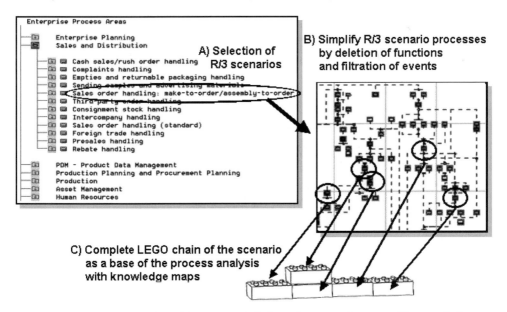

Figure 5.3.3.2-2:   Selected SAP scenario 'sales order processing, assembly-to-order'

5.3.3.4   Preparation of the process analysis workshop by the customer

After SAP scenarios have been identified and selected, the process analysis workshop can begin. The detailed procedure with all individual steps is explained in Chapter 5.3.3.5. To save time and costs on one hand, and to ensure an extensive knowledge transfer in this early phase on the other, project team members should familiarize themselves with the topics to be discussed beforehand. As described in Chapter 1.2, knowledge maps combine business-relevant questions concerning SAP, consultants' tips, documentation, detailed explanations, hints, and integration knowledge. Consequently, knowledge maps are also a means for team members to prepare individually for the workshop, so that the process analysis itself can be performed quickly and efficiently in cooperation with external consultants.

We recommend the following activities during preparation:

- Working through scenario processes/value chains using the plotted/printed documents (wallpaper), the SAP system (if installed), an external visualization or modeling tool, or the Q&Adb structure.

- This involves going through the process modules (with variants if applicable) along the process chains (scenario processes). Each process module has a corresponding SAP knowledge map explaining the content of that process module, the questions that have to be asked to implement it, what else needs to be considered for its implementation, and what is generally recommended by consultants in this context.

- All points that have not been clarified as yet, as well as any questions that may have arisen, should be documented so that they can be solved as efficiently as possible in a target-oriented approach during the process analysis workshop. It is important, however, to document not only open points and questions but also decisions and results that have already been determined. If you need any help in deciding which points are relevant, please refer to Chapter 5.3.1, Point ③, or to the customer input templates of the ASAP Q&Adb (e.g. SAP functional gaps, special requirements, organizational considerations, possible interfaces, etc.).

5.3.3.5   Process analysis with knowledge maps

We have now arrived at the main part of our book. In this section, we will explain how to use knowledge maps to perform a process analysis.

1. *Starting from the scenario process or the complete LEGO chain as a basis*
   If you can, you should plot the complete scenario process and pin it up on a board for the workshop. This enables you to follow the process path with a red line and show the corresponding process modules (functions within the scenario process) for each situation during the workshop. Use a modeling tool when working on your computer; this enables you to navigate through the scenario process in the system as well and to project process symbols onto the wall for the workshop participants. Another alternative which we tried ourselves in a customer project was to take project modules

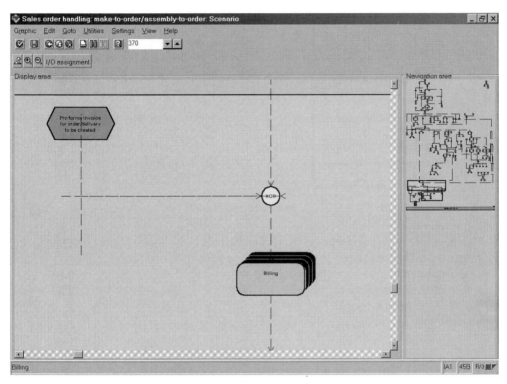

Figure 5.3.3.5-1:   Process module billing
Business Navigator, SAP AG ©

from your PC modeling tool (e.g. *Micrografix Flow Charter*) and put them on cards which we pinned to the board. At the end of our process analysis, the customer-specific process chain (LEGO chain) had been created and everybody had been able to follow the assembly of the LEGO chain step-by-step. Navigating through the scenario process in the SAP system is, of course, also possible with the business navigator tool. However, the SAP system is generally not available during process analysis, as process analysis usually happens very early in the project.

In our example we have chosen the process module **billing** from the scenario process sales order processing, assembly-to-order (Figure 5.3.3.5-1).

2. *Brief explanation of the process module*
The consultant takes the process module billing, writes it on a card, and gives the workshop participants the business definition of this process according to SAP (Figure 5.3.3.5-2). This business explanation at the beginning of the discussion serves to identify and eliminate any terminological differences or misunderstandings with regard to billing between the customer and SAP. The person in charge of writing the transcript of the workshop (a participant who simultaneously records the points discussed using a computer) includes the process module in the documentation.

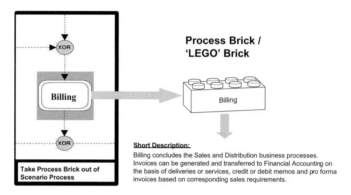

Figure 5.3.3.5-2:   Business explanation of the process module

Documentation in the form of tables has proved very effective in our experience; columns can be used for notes on the following keywords:
- process name and description
- actual/target stipulation
- open points (to be clarified)
- improvement potential
- questions of integration.

Business explanations can also be represented in the root (center) of the knowledge map provided that you are working with the *MindManager* tool and the knowledge map database.

3. *Process analysis with knowledge maps*
   In the following workshop, the individual branches of the knowledge maps will be discussed in detail (Teufel, 1995). The central questions of process analysis are:
   - WHO performs the process?
   - WHAT is actually done?
   - HOW is the process performed?

   You can answer these central questions by referring to the different knowledge maps from the database. The following can be used:
   - WHO: organizational knowledge maps
   - WHAT: process knowledge maps
   - HOW: object knowledge maps.

   In our process analysis, we will focus on the question WHAT and analyze process module knowledge maps. The first branch in our example *billing* contains the question of forms of creation.

   The complete question behind the keyword forms of creation can be found in the text field. It reads as follows:
   - *How do you create billing documents?*
     The knowledge map itself contains four possible solutions to this question which give participants the **knowledge** required to answer this question during the analysis (Figure 5.3.3.5-3).

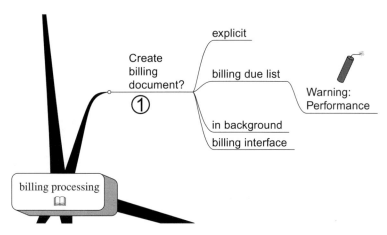

Figure 5.3.3.5-3:   Process analysis with knowledge map – branch 1

The four possible forms of generating a billing document are dealt with in the discussion. Participants will quickly understand that although an explicit generation of billing documents must be possible, it is not practical in everyday use. A controllable generation in the foreground through the billing due list is perceived as desirable. Even though the consultant points out the consequences of performance problems to the workshop participants, the decision (target requirement) is documented as follows (Figure 5.3.3.5-4).

The relevant notes can, of course, be included in the knowledge map, if these are used to document the progress of the overall project. It would be possible, for example, to delete the branches (alternative solutions) that are irrelevant for a particular enterprise. In our concrete case, this would mean deleting the billing document interface, as sales business processes will run exclusively in SAP, i.e. an additional external system will not be used. In the next step of the analysis, the question of billing types must be clarified. The complete question corresponding to this branch is:

- *What types of billing documents do you use?*
  The parameter billing type has been stored in SAP customizing and can be amended by additional entries. The billing knowledge map displays frequent billing types such as invoice, credit/debit memo, proforma billing document, cancellation, as well as the exceptional case of cash sales on the side branches (Figure 5.3.3.5-5).

Process Billing	Target	Open items	Potentials	Integration Questions
Creation	Billing due list in dialog		Yes, no additional entries	

Figure 5.3.3.5-4:   Documentation of the process analysis with knowledge map – branch 1

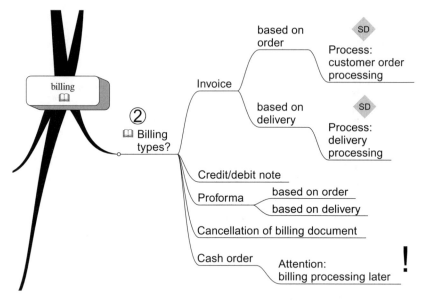

Figure 5.3.3.5-5:   Billing types – branch 2

If an SAP system is available, a **showcase** example can be used in the discussion. However, we would like to make the following recommendation based on our project experience:

No iterative prototyping (testing transactions, displaying customizing tables) during process analysis! This would take too much time and should therefore be done at a later project stage by the project team.

If you want process analysis to be completed in a short time, you should not access the system repeatedly to test transactions or display customizing tables. During the workshop you work with employees who make decisions for different enterprise areas (middle management – such as the head of department, the MRP controller, the finance manager, etc.) and will not have much time for the process analysis. Only in exceptional cases can such a time-consuming, iterative prototyping (applying examples to the SAP system) be helpful (Teufel, 1995), (Keller and Teufel) Should you have to make a detour into the system to agree on a certain point in the discussion, we recommend that you include such a point in the **open points list** of the documentation and leave the actual work in the system for the project team to deal with during the baseline phase of the ASAP roadmap. This makes sense because during the baseline phase at the latest, a **prototype** will be developed by the project team anyway, which will be tested in detail in the system, i.e. mapping target requirements and open points from the process analysis phase. We commend that you test open points on the prototype later, i.e. during the baseline phase of the ASAP roadmap.

The possible billing types proposed in our sample knowledge map require some explanations – these have been stored in the knowledge map as texts beforehand (Figure 5.3.3.5-6).

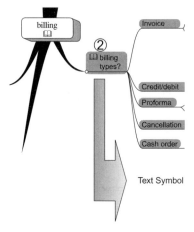

What types of billing document do you use?
For processing different business cases in Sales and Distribution, the system provides a range of billing document types:
-Invoices: The customer is invoiced for deliveries and services carried out on the basis of sale orders. If the customer does not place a complaint, then the transaction is closed from a sales perspective. A difference is made between the delivery-related invoice for goods and the order-related invoice for services.
-Credit and debit memos: Credit memos may be necessary for a number of reasons, e.g. due to defective goods or if the customer was overcharged. A debit memo is needed, on the other hand if the customer was undercharged. Both billing documents refer to order-related billing, i.e., the customer is billed with reference to a credit or debit memo request.
-Pro forma invoices: If you want to process export transactions, you may have to print pro forma invoices. These are used to give the importer or the authorities in the importing country details of the expected delivery. Pro forma invoices can be generated on the basis of sales orders or deliveries.
-Cancellation: To cancel a billing document, you must generate a cancellation document. This cancellation document copies the data from the reference document and transfers an offsetting entry to Financial Accounting. It may be necessary to cancel a billing document for a number of reasons. For example, if you made a mistake in the billing document, or items were posted to the wrong accounts when billing document data was transferred. Cancellation means that the reference document for the billing document (e.g. the delivery) is released again and can subsequently be billed again. Attention: you can no longer cancel an invoice once the open item has been cleared in Financial Accounting.
-Cash sales: For example, if goods are bought at the counter, payment is made as soon as the order has been accepted and the customer receives an invoice. In the system, the sales order and the delivery document are generated in one step. Goods issue is carried out as a separate transaction at a later stage without the customer having to wait. The billing copy is printed in the system based on the sales order. The actual billing document is generated later, after the goods issue has been posted.
The billing type controls the entire billing document. By using control elements in Customizing, you can set billing types so that each have their own range of functions.

Figure 5.3.3.5-6:   Explanatory texts behind branches

During the discussion it very soon becomes clear, for example, that the enterprise needs the billing types listed and intends to use them for delivery as well as sales order-related processes. The knowledge map shows that there is integration with the process modules sales order processing and delivery processing, which will be pinned on the board on separate cards during the workshop. Here they are represented in the form of a LEGO chain (Figure 5.3.3.5-7).

Simultaneous documentation while discussing billing types could assume the following form (Figure 5.3.3.5-8).

The next point of discussion during the process analysis workshop refers to branch 3 of the knowledge map (Figure 5.3.3.5-9). The question addressed here is that of grouping.

• *Is it possible in your enterprise to group several business cases in one billing document?*
SAP enables the grouping of individual sales and distribution documents for invoicing in one billing document (collective invoice), so that the customer receives only one invoice. In our example, the enterprise intends to create one billing document for each sales and distribution document, as we have an assembly-to-order scenario. Besides, the consultant will explain the option of an invoice split which can be defined by certain conditions, such as "based on the material group," and stored in copying control (see the light bulb icon in Figure 5.3.3.5-9). Again, this

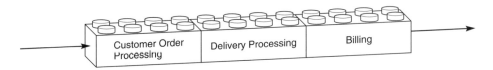

Figure 5.3.3.5-7:   Adapting the LEGO chain during workshops

Process Billing	Target	Open items	Potentials	Integration Questions
Creation	Billing due list in dialog		Yes, no additional entries	
Billing types	Invoice Credit/debit note Cancellation Cash sales possible	Necessity of proforma invoice must be checked		Customer order processing, delivery processing

Figure 5.3.3.5-8:   Notes on the process analysis with knowledge maps – branch 2

does not apply to the enterprise in our example, so that this side branch can be deleted from the knowledge map as well.

During analysis with knowledge maps, interdependencies may occur, visualized by connection arrows. In our example, there is a connection between collective invoices and invoice dates (Figure 5.3.3.5-9).

We are now embarking on the most interesting part of our billing process analysis, i.e. integration of sales and distribution with accounting. It makes sense to analyze integration with financial accounting (FI) first. Here, the consultant should draw attention to SAP's automatic account determination.

- *To which accounts in financial accounting is the billing document posted?*
Automatic account determination addresses the G/L accounts, the various types of which are displayed on the side branches revenue, freight, accruals, etc. (Figure 5.3.3.5-11). A prerequisite of automatic account determination is the existence of the process module G/L account processing.

Account determination can be controlled by parameters in material master processing (account assignment group "material") and customer master processing (account assignment group "customer") and in the individual condition types (customizing). Furthermore, billing in sales and distribution automatically triggers customer invoice processing in FI. These process modules are copied onto cards and pinned on the board for the workshop. They complement the LEGO chain, which is the **keynote** of our process analysis (Figure 5.3.3.5-11). The process module customer rebate agreements has been included in the LEGO chain as an option, as

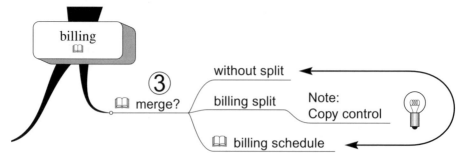

Figure 5.3.3.5-9:   Process analysis with knowledge map – branch 3

Process Billing	Target	Open items	Potentials	Integration Questions
Creation	Billing due list in dialog		Yes, no additional entries	
Billing types	Invoice Credit/Debit note Cancellation Cash sales possible	Necessity of proforma invoice must be checked		Customer order processing, Delivery processing
Merge	Split per delivery			Delivery processing

Figure 5.3.3.5-10:   Notes on the process analysis with knowledge map – branch 3

the enterprise in our example is currently not using rebate processing but is thinking about using it in the future to reinforce customer retention. In connection with the analysis of branch 2, billing types, the system finds a **clearing account** for cash sales but not for standing orders. While the option of cash sales has been included (Figure 5.3.3.5-8), it is an exception and has therefore not been highlighted in the knowledge map (Figure 5.3.3.5-12).

Financial accounting business areas can be used for the billing process if desired (Figure 5.3.3.5-13). This enables business area account assignment via the sales area and the company code. This means that a business area needs to be determined in the billing process. The corresponding question from the knowledge map reads:

• *Do business areas need to be determined for your sales and distribution business cases?*

Business area account assignment is not envisaged for our process analysis and thus is not highlighted in the knowledge map nor listed as a target requirement in the simultaneous documentation.

If you take a closer look at the knowledge map (Figure 5.3.3-2), you will see a side branch with the issues of installments and posting block. In the process analysis

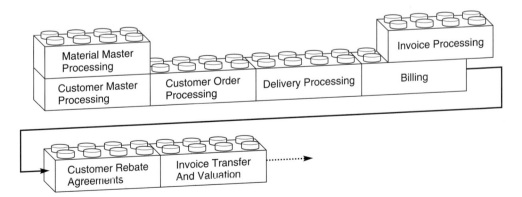

Figure 5.3.3.5-11:   Complementing the sales logistics LEGO chain

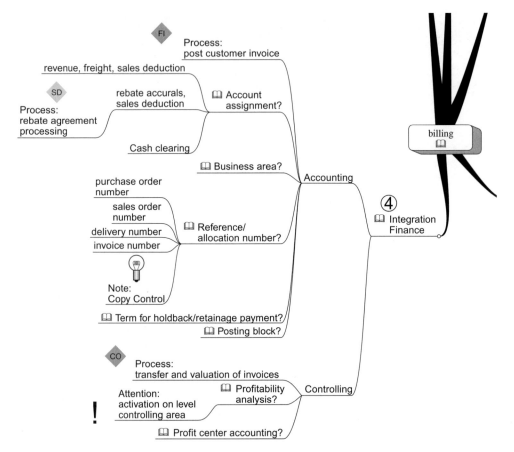

Figure 5.3.3.5-12:   Process analysis with knowledge map – branch 4

discussion, decision makers are called upon to say whether installment payment should generally be permitted.

- To what extent do you make agreements with customers on using installment payments?
- Should billing documents be released explicitly each time for financial accounting or posted directly?
  A posting block can be used to check the billing document before it is transferred to financial accounting. In our example, this is omitted and documented accordingly in the workshop documentation (Figure 5.3.3.5-13).

After giving due consideration to financial accounting aspects, questions of controlling are now dealt with. If, for example, integration with the profitability analysis (CO-PA for short) is desired, the process module billing document transfer and valuation must be triggered by the controlling area. In the process analysis workshop, this raises the question: "Do billing documents need to be transferred to the profitability analysis?"

Process Billing	Target	Open items	Potentials	Integration Questions
Creation	Billing due list in dialog		Yes, no additional entries	
Billing types	Invoice Credit/debit note Cancellation Cash sales possible	Necessity of proforma invoice must be checked		Customer order processing, delivery processing
Merge	Split per delivery			Delivery processing
Integration finance	No cash clearing, No determination of business areas, allocation no. – invoice number	Profit center accounting is subject for steering committee		Customer master proc, material master proc, invoice transfer and valuation, invoice processing
Invoice amount	Copy prices from order			

Figure 5.3.3.5-13:   Notes on the process analysis with knowledge map – branches 4 and 5

A document can only be created by billing in the profitability analysis if the CO-PA is active for the controlling area of the invoicing company code (Figure 5.3.3.5-14). All characteristics defined in the profitability analysis and contained in the billing document are transferred from the document to the profitability analysis line item together with the customer number and item number. In the discussion, middle management favored this integration and harmonized it with the corporate goals from the target/strategy workshop described in Chapter 5.3.1. For the project, this means that the areas of sales and financial accounting (particularly CO-PA), including all value fields and characteristics, need to be harmonized.

As the new organizational structure of profit centers has not been established in the analyzing enterprise, participants cannot decide on it in the discussion.

• *Do billing documents need to be transferred to profit center accounting?*

The issue of the profit center structure is documented as an **open item** and submitted to the decision committee (review). In the steering committee, the topic is presented to top management (see Chapter 5.3.3.6).

The process analysis of the process module billing is concluded with the last question represented on branch 5. This question refers to the billing document amount. It reads as follows:

• *How is the billing document amount to be determined?*

You may either transfer the price confirmed in the sales order directly to the billing document as is it, or calculate a new price at the time of invoicing. Workshop

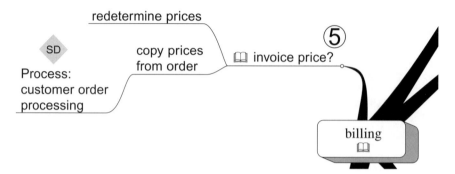

Figure 5.3.3.5-14:   Process analysis with knowledge map – branch 5

participants decide, in line with the corporate sales policy, not to change the price confirmed in a sales order and thus not to determine a new price. Therefore, new pricing is not highlighted in the knowledge map and is permitted only in exceptional cases of explicit billing (Figures 5.3.3.5-14 and 5.3.3.5-13).

5.3.3.6   Review of results

The most important results from the individual process analyses are illustrated on management slides in condensed form and distributed to the members of the steering committee. This committee plays an essential role in informing top management immediately and, even more importantly, in presenting certain open points on which participants of the process analysis did not have the authority to decide. The project manager needs to obtain these decisions from the top management. This requires presenting sound and well-structured information on the topics in question, e.g.

Process Area: Sales

		Decision/Info
1.	No permit procedure for conditions in SAP, but organizational process	Decision
2.	Configuration of assortments as an aid for order entry	Information
3.	Realize and evaluate system opportunities of promotions, including mailings	Information
4.	Central processing of serial numbers in the production area	Information
5.	Common regulation in the context of preference calculation	Information
6.	Automation of purchase processing to the sales companies via cross company purchase orders	Information

---

Figure 5.3.3.6-1:   Decision slide

structured by process modules. Important matters can also be presented to the management for information only, i.e. to review the process analysis. In Figure 5.3.3.6-1, a practical example of improvement potential and open points is displayed for the process area sales logistics.

6 Knowledge management

6.1 Basics

Chapter 1.1.6 generally described and delimited the topic of knowledge and knowledge management and its close relationship with organizational learning. It also showed the enormous importance of this still relatively young management concept. As knowledge management is an extensive concept, which includes all the knowledge sources and processes of an enterprise, we will restrict ourselves in view of the focus of this book (process analysis/business engineering) to expand on the knowledge of processes which can be gained from management analysis.

Within the overall context of knowledge management (Figure 1.1.6-1) our thoughts and suggestions regarding knowledge management with master knowledge maps will only cover the field of organizational process knowledge. As both explicit and implicit knowledge is used or disclosed in process analysis workshops, both types of knowledge are included in our observations (Figure 6.1-1).

As the new millennium approached, we could see that it was not just a case of numbers changing from 1000 to 2000, but that the whole enterprise environment was being affected by continuous changes occurring in the market, increasing globalization, making competition more fierce and, particularly, bringing rapid development in the IT world. This demanded maximum efficiency and flexibility in an enterprise and thus the use of extensive and flexible IT solutions to manage business and processes and the collection, creation, maintenance, and distribution of information across all areas, ranging from the customer through the products to the processes.

Here, and also in the conceptual roots of knowledge management, the management of process knowledge reveals its essential importance (Figure 6.1-2). Scheer shares the opinion that the knowledge and management of business processes are essential prerequisites for targeted knowledge management, which can be supported by a **process warehouse** (Scheer, 1998a, p. 63 and p. 162). We use the knowledge map technique to manage this process knowledge. To this end, we will expand the knowledge maps presented in previous chapters to become master knowledge maps. Their construction is detailed in Chapter 6.2 where the complete knowledge integration of all components involved in process knowledge is described. In this context it is irrelevant which software is used in the realization of master knowledge maps, e.g. linking Office products with hyperlinks or special MindMap software. We will concentrate primarily on the content and visualized link to a central object, i.e. the process. In doing so, the impact of this innovative, intuitive, and easily comprehensible method should become apparent. If

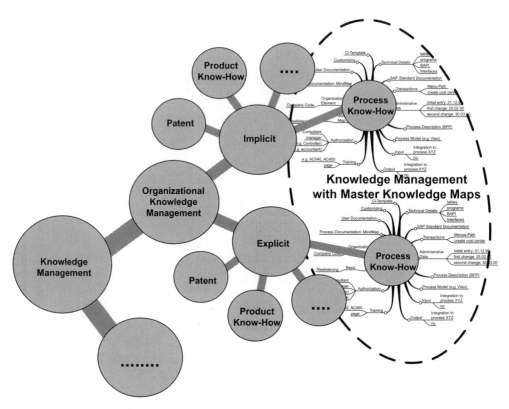

Figure 6.1-1:   *Position of process knowledge management with master knowledge maps in the overall context of knowledge management*

several master knowledge maps are linked, the result is a knowledge warehouse which is responsible for the following:

- It serves as a commonly accessible source of information.

- It guarantees the consistent management of knowledge (version management, translation, localization, etc.).

- It ensures that objects are not redundant.

- It enables access to all types of information from anywhere in the world.

What knowledge management needs to offer to fulfill all these requirements is explained in a **knowledge transfer cycle**. This describes the flow of a knowledge management process for the generation or transformation (of implicit and explicit knowledge), storage, distribution, and application of the knowledge available in an enterprise (Figure 6.1-3).

What does each individual step mean if we consider process knowledge in connection with the process analysis and the subsequent life cycle of the R/3 system?

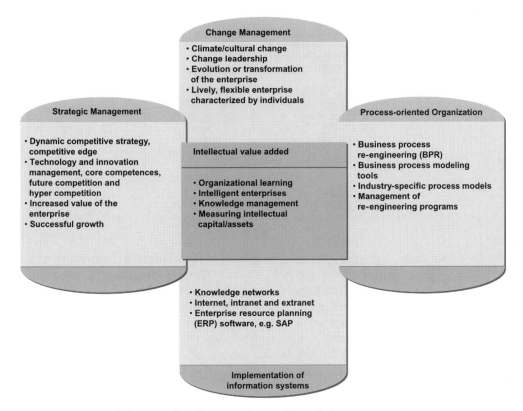

Figure 6.1-2:   Conceptual roots of knowledge management
Servatius, 1998, p. 340

- *Generation*
  Within the framework of process analysis or business engineering, various people from different backgrounds collaborate, e.g. enterprise consultants, users, IT employees, managers, etc. The current situation is briefly discussed before turning to the target processes adapted to the R/3 system. Existing and documented material is generally used in these discussions which may stem from within the enterprise, e.g. process flows, reports, or job descriptions. It could also be documented SAP knowledge in the form of SAP standard documentation, process descriptions (ASAP business process procedures), training material, etc. In addition, and this is an important by-product, a lot of implicit knowledge emerges in the course of the discussions. As the project develops, and over the entire life cycle of the R/3 system, additional material is produced, e.g. documentation of customizing settings, test procedures, or cases. All this falls under the category of generation.

- *Documentation*
  Existing knowledge (material), both implicit (tacit) and explicit (documented), must first be collected, documented, and stored in one central place. This step is of essential

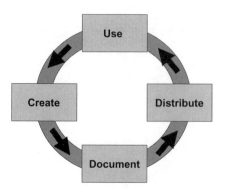

Figure 6.1-3:   Knowledge transfer cycle
Source: Cohen et al., p. 13

importance to the whole process of knowledge management. This is particularly true with regard to implicit knowledge as it is very difficult to transform it into explicit knowledge. However, there will never be a better time than during process analysis and the subsequent activities in connection with R/3 implementation. In this context, Cohen *et al.* write, "The aim of codification – capturing knowledge in a documented or formalized process – is to make local and often tacit (or hidden) knowledge explicit and available for worldwide distribution" (Cohen *et al.*, p. 14).

- *Distribution*
  However, merely capturing knowledge is not enough. To become organizational learning, knowledge has to be accessible to the entire organization and distributed proactively. How this is carried out depends, to a great extent, on the corporate policy and on the maturity of the IT landscape. Nowadays, groupware, or internet or intranet, are used primarily. All employees should not, or may not, have access to the same information, and so an authorization mechanism has to be developed as part of the authorization concept. The emphasis here must be on the world-wide availability and distribution of knowledge.

- *Use*
  Knowledge which is not used is not productive (Cohen *et al.*, p. 14) and has no social or economic value. This means that it is of tremendous importance that generated, stored, and distributed knowledge is also used. This is an absolute necessity for **organizational learning**. Supporting it is part of corporate culture. Its success depends, to a great degree, on the competence of managers and also on the willingness of employees: "… knowledge can be bought or rented, but learning is a process that must be developed and supported" (Cohen *et al.*, p. 15). One tried and tested method to increase willingness is the training of employees. Ultimately, not only the employee profits from good training but also the enterprise as a whole: "For employers, the value of training ultimately lies in the bottom line. Greater productivity, higher quality, better customer service, positive employee relations and lower costs are among hundreds of factors that typically contribute to higher profits" (Hackett, p. 17). As

described, knowledge can be used both proactively and reactively. Knowledge is used proactively by the process-oriented training of employees; reactive use is when the employee can access specific information needed regarding a certain topic.

6.2   The master knowledge map

During the process analysis within the framework of the feasibility study, during the creation of a target concept, during the ongoing process of the entire implementation project, and also during the entire R/3 life cycle, a large amount of knowledge is generated, transformed from implicit to explicit knowledge, and documented. The question is how to document, organize, and distribute this knowledge in a process-oriented way.

   We must remember that each object (as we will call them for now) contains a variety of materials and documents:

- R/3 knowledge maps

- protocol of the process analysis or the ASAP CI template

- training material

- test cases and descriptions

- authorizations and job descriptions, etc.

We must first take a look at what a master knowledge map is and what it has to do with the documentation and distribution of process knowledge. A master knowledge map is the consequent development of the knowledge map into an integrated process knowledge **warehouse** (see Chapter 6.1) along the process chain (LEGO chain) of the enterprise. All the essential information which generally emerges during the course of the R/3 projects, and also from individual process modules in the enterprise, can be seen in Figure 6.2-1 and is explained in Chapters 6.2.1 to 6.2.9. We do not claim to have included everything. If your enterprise has other elements which could be assigned to a process module, this naturally has to be done. Figure 6.2-2 shows how this documentation is carried out in a process-oriented way, as a master knowledge map for each process module links together all the elements which are necessary for its description, explanation, documentation, training, etc. All the descriptions in this chapter refer to a billing process module.

   The process knowledge presented and documented in this way can be used as follows.

- As a general and globally accessible source of information.

- For consistent knowledge management by version management (i.e. changes are documented). In addition, this information can be translated and localized (i.e. in an international case, country-specific information can be added, or changes made to existing information).

- As documentation.

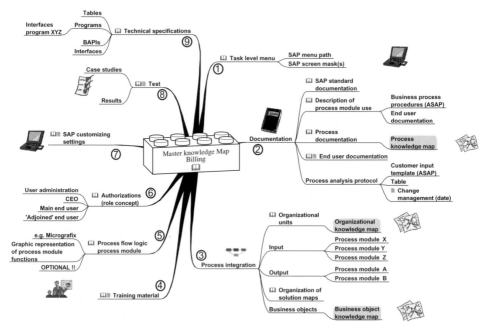

Figure 6.2-1:   Master knowledge map

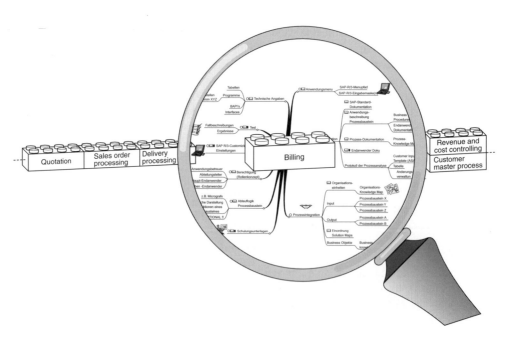

Figure 6.2-2:   Section of a process chain of master knowledge maps

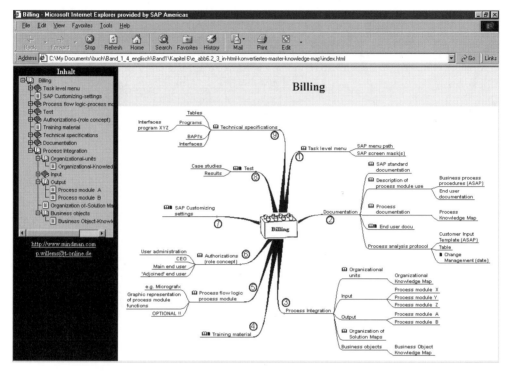

Figure 6.2-3:   Web master knowledge map converted to HTML

- For proactive information requirements – if, for example, an employee wants to find out about a particular process before carrying it out.

- For process-oriented training, etc.

A large number of these tasks can be aided by placing the master knowledge map in the company-internal intranet. Depending on which software you used to create the master knowledge map, you may have to convert it to HTML format. This gives every employee the information needed for individual requirements and level of training. This activity paves the main part of the way for effective and efficient **organizational learning** (Cohen *et al.*, p. 15). Also, please refer to the descriptions in Chapter 6.3.

6.2.1   From master knowledge map to task level menu

A process module can generally be assigned several concrete activities in the task level menu (Figure 6.2.1-1). For those who are interested, there are three essential pieces of information:

- the specific menu path

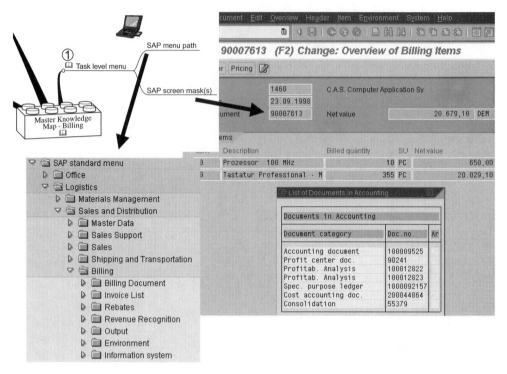

Figure 6.2.1-1:   From master knowledge map to task level menu

- the appearance, and possibly the description, of the input mask (this description may also be included in the end user documentation, e.g. in the ASAP business process procedure)

- the transaction, if necessary.

6.2.2   From master knowledge map to documentation

To ensure comprehensive process documentation, all the necessary documentation elements which describe a process module, and can thus be linked to it, must be assigned to that process module, taking the different enterprise levels into consideration (Figure 6.2.2-1).

This could include the most diverse documentation elements, such as:

- SAP R/3 standard documentation

- process documentation in the form of knowledge maps

- application and procedure descriptions or instructions for the process module in the form of end user descriptions or business process procedures (ASAP)

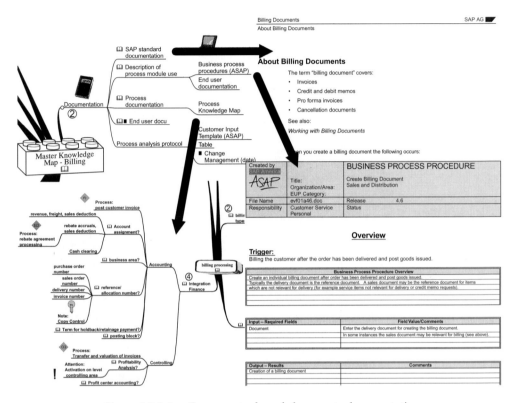

Figure 6.2.2-1:   From master knowledge map to documentation

- protocol of the process analysis in the form of the protocol table we recommend (see Figure 5.3.3.5-4), of the customer input templates (ASAP) and a "change history"

- documentation of customizing settings (see Chapter 6.2.7).

6.2.3   From master knowledge map to process integration

The main characteristic of process analysis and process-oriented knowledge management is integration. It is therefore necessary to explicitly prepare and document it. An example of the form this documentation could take can be seen in Figure 6.2.2-1. It is important to note, however, that this example refers specifically to the description of an individual process module. In master knowledge maps and process integration, each integrated process module is explicitly illustrated with all its links. This makes it possible to go directly and immediately from the process module to the units that adjoin it. Thus, users are able to determine immediately which **units** are integrated with (i.e. connected by links to) the process module. Integration includes the following.

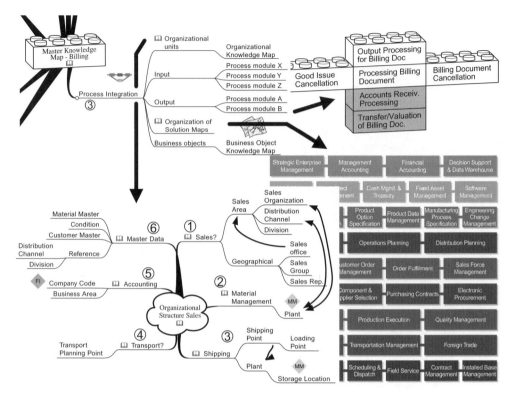

Figure 6.2.3-1:   From master knowledge map to process integration

- *The relationship with organizational units*
  When a process is carried out in the R/3 system, it usually affects several organizational units. These relationships should be recorded per process module.

- *Input process relationships*
  Apart from the start process module of a process chain (LEGO chain), each process module of a (scenario) process is preceded by one or more upstream processes (input). This can be seen by looking at the complete process chain to which the process module belongs. The environment of the process module which we look at must be highlighted so that the user becomes aware of the upstream processes affecting the flow of the current process module in the course of the entire process chain.

- *Output process relationships*
  Apart from the end process module, each process module in the chain also has one or more "successor" modules. The same applies here as for the "predecessor" processes, as it is of utmost importance that the user is aware of the effect a change in the current process module would have on subsequent/downstream modules.

- *Relationship with business objects*
  The same applies to business objects as to organizational units, i.e. more than one business object is generally involved in the execution of a process. The transaction data

of these objects is changed with the updating of a specific business situation. For this reason, business objects affected by a process module should also be assigned to it, although in our opinion this is not absolutely necessary.

- *Relationship with SAP solution maps*
  In addition, the individual process modules can be linked to solution maps as these are used to document the **main processes** of a specific industry. Each main process of a solution map is supplemented by information about which features are available in standard R/3, other SAP products or products from certified SAP partners, or when such features will become available. This information is particularly important with regard to the industry-specific characteristics of certain process modules and processes.

6.2.4   From master knowledge map to training material

For every application of the R/3 system there is level 2 and level 3 training. Level 2 training offers an overview of the overall applications (e.g. SD, CO, PP) and how they are integrated, while level 3 training goes into detail on the functionality of an application regarding customizing and the task level menu. This training is available either at an SAP training center or on the customer's premises. Customers can access the training material

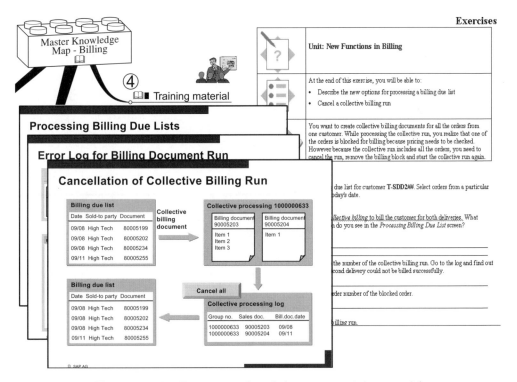

Figure 6.2.4-1:   From master knowledge map to training material

by purchasing the SAP InfoDB (information database). In most cases, transparencies can be assigned to a specific process module according to their level of detail. This, together with process-oriented documentation, enables targetted and process-oriented training for end users (Figure 6.2.4-1).

6.2.5   From master knowledge map to process flow logic

For each process module there are process EPCs (see Chapter 3.2) directly in the R/3 system. They may be represented either with the R/3 reference model or with well-known modeling tools (*Micrografix, ARIS, Intellicorp*). They show, using functions and events, which functions take place in what chronological order during the execution of a specific process module, which generally reflects a transaction (e.g. billing).

The case described here does not deal with **scenario** EPCs but with **process module** EPCs. In our experience, processes are generally not portrayed or processed for business engineering at this level, and it is not recommended. There are, of course, exceptions, e.g. the process module *sales order processing*. If, in your enterprise, you want to model processes at this level of detail, this process model can, and should, be linked to the process module (Figure 6.2.5-1).

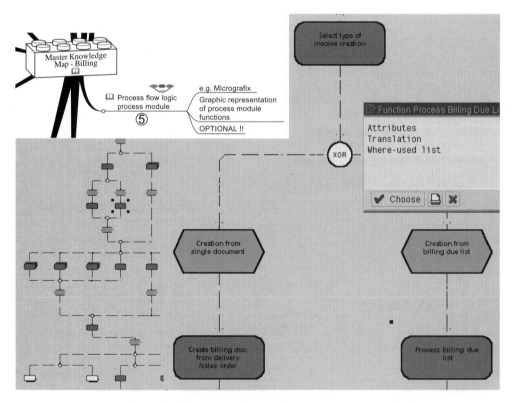

Figure 6.2.5-1:   From master knowledge map to process flow logic

6.2.6 From master knowledge map to authorizations

Another important link to the process module, which cannot be ignored, is the assignment of roles and their authorizations. A specific process module will usually be executed by more than one person and at different locations. These people will not necessarily have the same, or even similar, functions within the enterprise but still process the same module as part of their daily/periodical work. One user will be allowed to perform certain tasks within the system according to his role, and the other will not (e.g. a financial accountant can post documents and view them in the system, whereas a controller will often have to verify data in the system as far back as the original document level but is still not able to post documents in financial accounting). For this reason, a process module is assigned all the roles which are authorized to execute it with applicable restrictions. This could mean purely the assignment of roles but it could also be a concrete description of authorizations, e.g. using the profile in the authorization generator of the R/3 system. Examples of roles (without function assignment) are chief executive officer, department manager, user administration expert, IT user administration, end user (main status), end user (adjoined status), etc. (Figure 6.2.6-1).

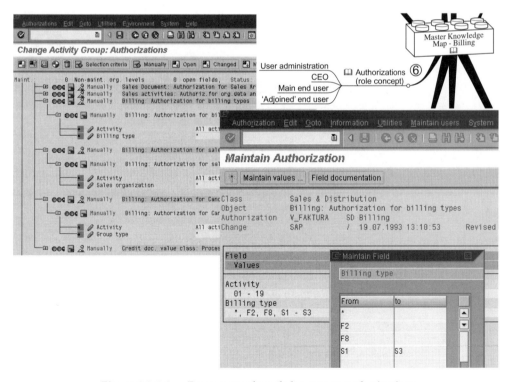

Figure 6.2.6-1:   From master knowledge map to authorizations

6.2.7   From master knowledge map to R/3 customizing

After the enterprise processes have been mapped to R/3 processes in the process analysis, mapping to R/3 functionality has to be carried out as part of the baseline and final configuration or prototyping. The R/3 system is parameterized as part of customizing, i.e. the R/3 system, which is architecturally designed so that it can be parameterized, is customized (i.e. adjusted) to the specific demands of the customer by setting **switches**. No additional programming is necessary. The implementation guide is used for customizing. This is also a form of documentation as these settings are available and can be accessed at all times within the system. In addition, the reason for selecting these and not other settings must be justified and documented. This can be done in different places, e.g. with the documentation options of the IMG itself (project administration), as part of the business process masterlist when using the ASAP procedure, in Office products, etc. Regardless of how and where the documentation of specific system settings takes place, all the locations which describe system settings should be assigned to the corresponding process module. This ensures the comprehensive documentation described in Chapter 6.2.2 (Figure 6.2.7-1).

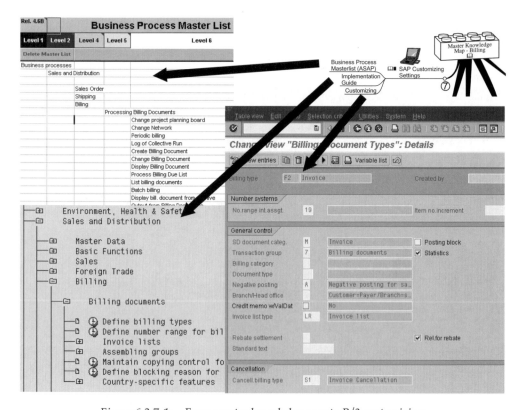

Figure 6.2.7-1:   From master knowledge map to R/3 customizing

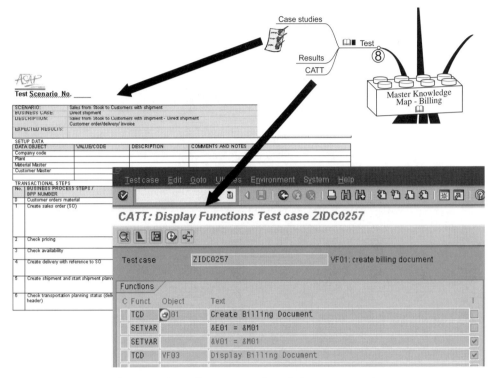

Figure 6.2.8-1:   From master knowledge map to testing

6.2.8   From master knowledge map to testing

Performing extensive tests, especially the integration tests, is an essential step in an implementation project. To this end, comprehensive test procedures and descriptions are usually created or, as part of ASAP, ready test procedures are used. The results of the tests should also be documented. However, along with the integration test, stress and throughput tests are also very important. These simulate how the R/3 system behaves in a live situation, e.g. whether performance problems arise. Aids are often used for carrying out tests – for example *Computer Aided Test Tool* (CATT) or *Autotester*. These are able to create mass data which they input to the system again and again in order to simulate the required live environment. The description of these test procedures, as well as the results of the tests and the example data created (e.g. CATTs), is then assigned to the corresponding process module and thus enables process-oriented administration (Figure 6.2.8-1).

6.2.9   From master knowledge map to technical specifications

Each process module is based on transactions and thus, from a technical point of view, ABAP/4 programs, databases, database views, and function modules. It is generally

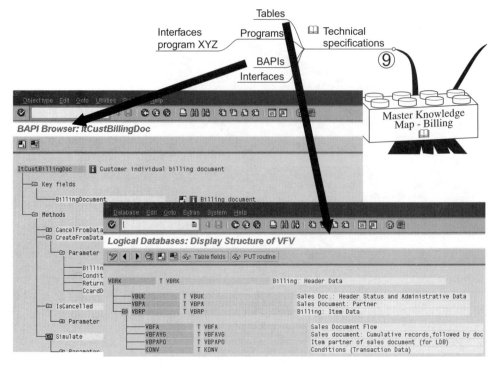

Figure 6.2.9-1:   From master knowledge map to technical specifications

necessary to identify and document these technical foundations if enterprise-specific programs are to be written. This could be necessary for a number of reasons.

- Certain enterprise-specific process flows are not supported in the standard R/3 system and must be programmed individually in the form of additional programs.

- The standard functionality of the R/3 system is not sufficient to represent enterprise-specific functionality in detail. However, SAP offers the option of programming such functionality yourself using predesigned interfaces (user exits).

- If a company's existing legacy systems are not all replaced by the R/3 system, thus requiring interfaces with the R/3 system for data exchange, ABAP/4 programming is carried out.

In all cases, the specifications of program structure and program logic, and the program documentation, should be assigned to the corresponding process module (Figure 6.2.9-1).

6.3   Master knowledge maps for uniform enterprise documentation

In the previous chapter, master knowledge maps were described per process module. As is evident from the process library, each chapter contains the same **elements**. These elements are as follows:

- the overview knowledge map
- the organization knowledge map
- the business object knowledge map
- the scenario knowledge map
- the process knowledge maps

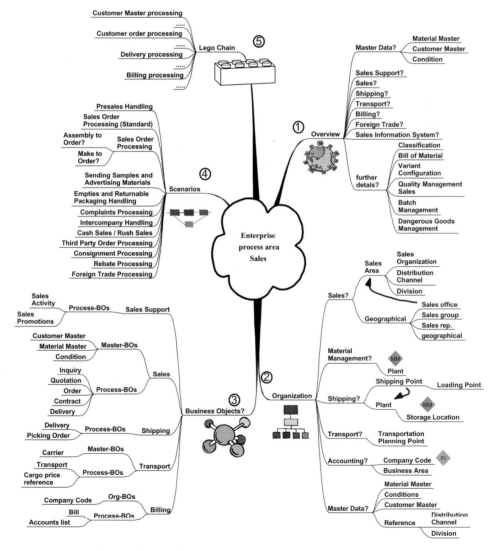

Figure 6.3-1:   Enterprise process area master knowledge map

- possibly other descriptions, e.g. in the process area revenue and cost controlling (SAP Process Library, Book 3, Chapter 6.4).

As is the case for process knowledge maps, all other types of knowledge map can also be extended to form master knowledge maps containing the corresponding links. If all the master knowledge maps per enterprise process area are joined together, it forms an enterprise process area master knowledge map. This has the structure shown in Figure 6.3-1. It is evident that it combines all the elements needed for a complete and overall description of an enterprise process area.

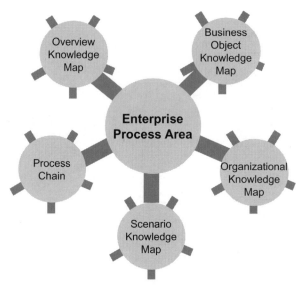

Figure 6.3-2:   Enterprise process area master knowledge map in molecular form

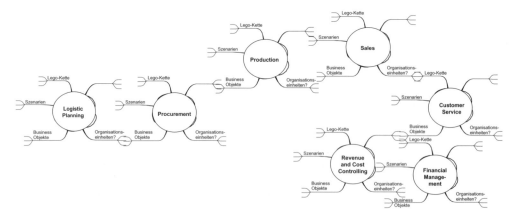

Figure 6.3-3:   Population of self-similar description structures – in knowledge map form

The result is a comprehensive and integrated knowledge management which branches through the corresponding IT, from the starting point, i.e. the root of the process area master knowledge map, to each individual branch. The end of each branch is linked to a further master knowledge map (Figure 6.3-2). Starting from the root of the master knowledge map, branches lead to additional information that can, or should, be assigned to the corresponding master knowledge map. This enables a drill down through all of the knowledge which can be assigned to an enterprise process area, starting at a very high level down to detailed information. This type of documentation, unlike other forms, is not hierarchical but is dynamically structured and can easily be compared to "creative chaos."

The description above refers to an enterprise process area. However, several enterprise process areas are used in the R/3 system to portray the business demands of an enterprise. If such a process area master knowledge map were to be created for each process area, it would become apparent that the structures constantly repeat themselves. From the chaos theory point of view, this is known as **self-similar structures**.

If, as a consequential next step, we were to place all the enterprise process area master knowledge maps next to each other [which can be carried out along a very basic value chain (Figure 6.3-3)], a population of self-similar description structures would be formed. This can result in certain processes **attracting** one another (i.e. showing integration) or else **repelling** each other (i.e. not showing integration). This population of self-similar description structures enables a comprehensive and complete description of the entire enterprise integrating all user departments beyond department boundaries, as shown in Figure 6.3-3.

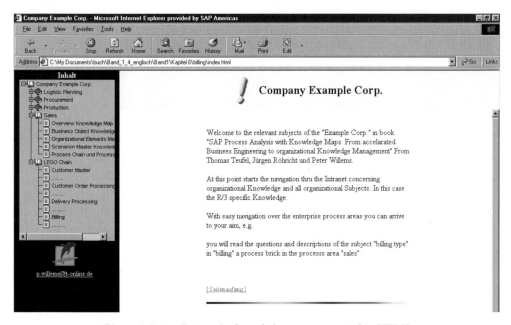

Figure 6.3-4:   Enterprise knowledge map converted to HTML

Supported by the corresponding software, an enterprise knowledge map converted to HTML could look something like Figure 6.3-4. All the process areas essential for the enterprise are contained in the left navigation bar of the web browser. As on the internet or intranet, users can navigate through the **chaotic** structure to find whatever information they require.

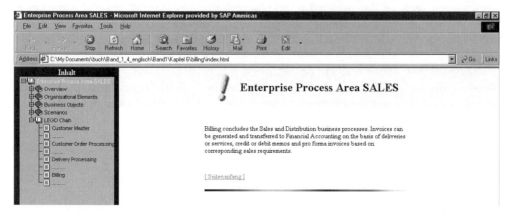

Figure 6.3-5:   Process area knowledge map converted to HTML

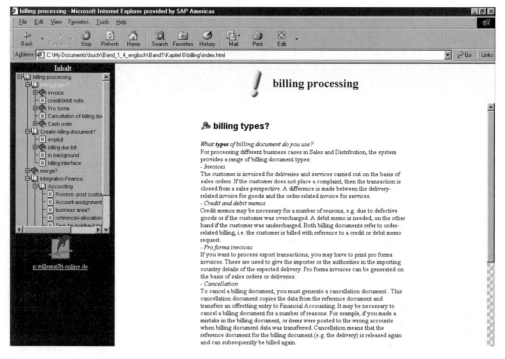

Figure 6.3-6:   Process knowledge map converted to HTML

If you are interested, say, in the billing process module, which is in the **category** process chain for the enterprise process area sales and distribution, you can drill down until you reach the information you are looking for.

In this case, you would start from the enterprise knowledge map webpage, as shown in Figure 6.3-4, and branch to the enterprise process area sales and distribution. Once on the sales and distribution webpage (Figure 6.3-5), you select the category process chain. Here you can choose the information you require (the process module billing).

As you are interested in specific information, e.g. what **billing type** means and which types there are, you can easily navigate to the highest level of detail and display this information (Figure 6.3-6).

7 Knowledge map database

The knowledge map database contains knowledge maps from seven enterprise process areas. In this chapter we will discuss one example for each process area. You can find the complete database in Books 2 to 4 of the SAP Process Library or order the CD under www.knowledgemap.de.

7.1 Financial accounting – example: customer dunning notice

The process module **dunning notice** is an important means of claiming open items from business partners falling behind on payments. How, and how emphatically, this is done can be determined in the dunning program settings. You can make different settings for different business partners as required. If one of your best customers is in arrears, you will probably just send a friendly reminder, whereas you will send a customer who has repeatedly defaulted on payment in the past a dunning notice of some severity, depending on the dunning level. You can make these detailed settings in various dunning procedures and assign them to different business partners.

The following procedure is recommended for the dunning run:

- *Dunning proposal*
  The dunning program identifies the items to be dunned per dunning level depending on predefined settings. The items proposed by the system can then be modified. For example, you can change dunning levels or block certain items for the dunning run. In addition a log is created that can be displayed in short or long form according to your settings. An exception list provides quick information on items not included in the dunning notice and the reasons for excluding them.

- *Dunning notice printout*
  The processed dunning items are printed out in the dunning letter. With the printout of the dunning notice, relevant values, such as dunning level and date, will be entered into the corresponding items and the business partner account.

Each of the major branches, 1–6, will be discussed in the six sections which follow. The items printed in bold in the subheadings relate to procedures in the knowledge map in Figure 7.1-1.

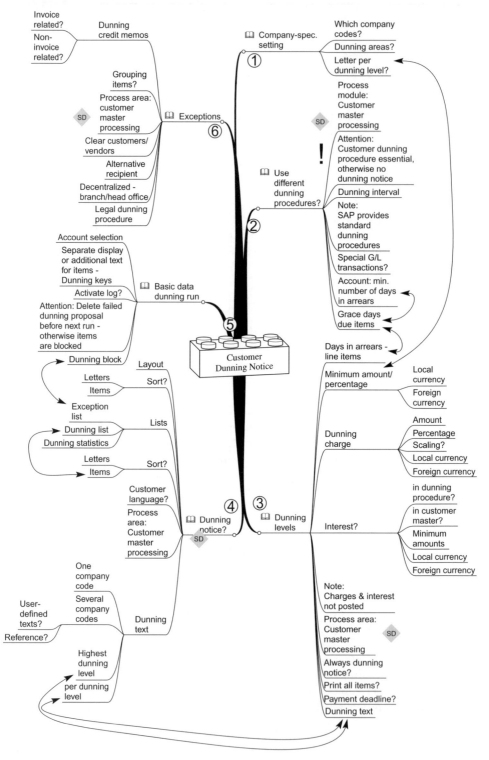

Figure 7.1.-1:   *Process knowledge map – dunning notice*

7.1.1   How is your dunning run organized? (*company-specific settings*)

- *Does your enterprise consist of several legally independent companies (**company codes**)?*
  In this case, you need to decide which company codes are to be included in the dunning process. This is defined just once in the dunning program in the enterprise-specific settings.

- *Are you using divisions and do you intend to apply dunning at this organizational level (**dunning areas**)? Or do you intend to assign dunning responsibilities per distribution channel, sales organization, or business area?*
  If the answer to one of these questions is yes, dunning areas are worth using. Dunning areas enable you to organize dunning notices one organizational level below the company code. If, for example, your enterprise has two divisions, electronic and mechanical products, customers in these areas may be dunned in different ways. It is also possible for a customer to buy products from both divisions and be dunned by both dunning areas. Moreover, the following two options should be considered.

  - *Dunning areas with different dunning procedures*
    If you use different dunning intervals for both divisions, different dunning procedures must be stored for each dunning area in the customer master record.

  - *The same dunning procedure for several dunning areas*
    If you are using the same basic data (e.g. dunning intervals) for different dunning areas but would like to organize dunning into separate areas, you need to define the dunning procedure centrally in the customer master record. You therefore need to state the relevant dunning area in the document. If the information in the document comes from upstream areas, such as sales and distribution or purchasing, the system can automatically derive the corresponding dunning area so long as you have defined the relevant derivation rules.

- *Do you generally intend to send different **dunning notices** for different **dunning levels**?*
  If you have opted for this alternative, you should take a few framework conditions into account. The minimum amounts or percentage rates apply to all dunning levels, i.e. if these thresholds are not exceeded, no dunning notice is created at that level. Furthermore, dunning items are not added to the next dunning level below. The "dun all items" characteristic does not make sense combined with the abovementioned characteristic "dunning notice per level." A reasonable allocation of items not yet overdue to a dunning notice or level would be impossible.

7.1.2   How do you intend to control your dunning runs? (*dunning procedure*)

- *What **dunning interval** do you intend to use per dunning procedure? How many **dunning levels** should your procedure have? Will you grant your customers **grace days**?*
  All this basic data is defined per dunning procedure which, in turn, must be linked to the customer master record. The system stores the highest dunning level and the date

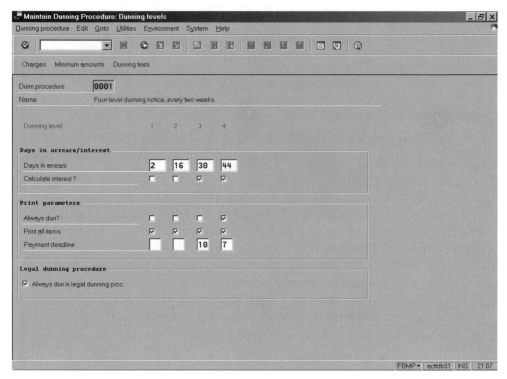

Figure 7.1.2-1:   EnjoySAP screen for customer dunning notice – customizing

of the last dunning run in the master record. On the basis of the dunning date together with the dunning interval defined in the dunning procedure, the dunning program determines whether or not an account is to be dunned.

- *Do you intend to grant **grace periods** for your dunning notices to allow for processing times and/or bank clearing delays?*
  Based on the issue date and payment term entered for the item, the dunning program determines overdue items. You can extend this term by entering more grace days for an item. Alternatively, you may enter minimum days in arrears for the account. The dunning program compares these minimum days with the days in arrears of the longest overdue item. If the number of days for that item is greater than or equal to the minimum days in arrears, the account is dunned.

- *Do you intend to include special business transactions such as down payments, guarantees of payment, etc. in your dunning procedure? (**special G/L transactions**)*
  You can assign to the dunning procedure any special G/L transactions you would like to consider in your dunning run.

7.1.3   How do you intend to handle the individual *dunning levels?*

- *How many **dunning levels** would you like to use in your dunning procedure?*
  You must use at least one and may use a maximum of nine dunning levels. Dunning procedures containing only one level are considered as payment reminders. You may want to use them for important customers. An open item is assigned to a dunning level as soon as the number of days in arrears equals or exceeds the number defined for that level. The dunning notice printout contains the item and the relevant dunning level. In addition, the dunning level is documented in the item itself, and the highest dunning level for all items belonging to that customer is entered in the customer's account. The highest dunning level usually determines the text of the dunning notice. Alternatively, you can send a different dunning letter for each level. The days in arrears per dunning level are proposed automatically by the system (by default). At dunning level one, they are determined by the grace days of the line items; for all further dunning levels, dunning intervals are added to the days of the previous level.

- *Would you like to define a **payment deadline** as from a particular dunning level?*
  You can print out a payment deadline. The dunning program adds the number of days entered for the payment deadline to the issue date and states this date in the dunning letter. In addition, a link with a public holiday calendar can be set to ensure that this date does not fall on a weekend or public holiday. In this case, the dunning program automatically selects the next working day.

- *Would you like to avoid triggering high dunning levels for minor amounts? (**minimum amounts, percentage rates**)*
  You can set a minimum amount and a minimum percentage rate for each dunning level. The system compares the minimum amount with the amount of all items. Moreover, the amount is checked against the total of open items for the account and compared with the minimum percentage rate. If the amount is less than the minimum percentage rate, the conditions for the dunning level are not fulfilled.

- *Would you like to include the account in dunning runs irrespective of any changes in the dunning situation? (**always dunning notice**)*
  You can make this setting in the option "Always dunning notice." This is recommended for single-level dunning procedures such as payment reminders.

- *Would you like to print out not only open due items but all items of a specific account? (**print all items**)*
  This setting can also be made during fine tuning of the dunning program.

- *Would you like to calculate **dunning charges** and **interest**?*
  You can stipulate charges per dunning level, dunning procedure, and currency. You can either use a fixed amount or a percentage rate. If you wish, you can even stagger these charges depending on the dunning amounts. Charges are calculated per currency. If the dunning program cannot find an entry for charges, no charges will be displayed in the dunning notice. In addition, you can calculate interest in the relevant

currency per dunning level or dunning procedure. Interest can be calculated in local or foreign currency based on a minimum amount. If the program does not find an entry for foreign currency, the local currency applies. The interest indicator for the dunning program may be entered either in the customer master or the dunning procedure. If entries exist for both, the dunning program selects the master record entry. Interest rates are calculated for each interest indicator based on the date.

7.1.4   What are your *dunning notices* going to look like?

- *Would you like to **sort** your notices (e.g. by zip code) in order to be eligible for a special post office discount for presorted letters? Or would you like to sort items in the dunning letter by specific criteria?*
  You can set your individual sort criteria for both dunning notices and dunning list.

- *Your enterprise comprises several company codes, but you would like to use a standard form for your dunning notices. (**dunning text**)*
  You can determine this by making reference to the corresponding form of the relevant company code in the company code-specific settings.

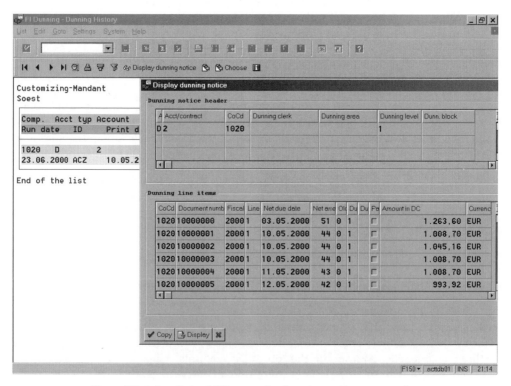

Figure 7.1.4-1:   EnjoySAP screen for dunning notice – processing

- *Would you like to define different **texts** of varying severity for different **dunning levels**?*
  In the SAP system, you can define texts per dunning level. A maximum of nine levels is permissible, and you must use at least one level (see Chapter 7.1.3).

7.1.5   Which items are to be considered in the dunning run? (*basic data, dunning run*)

Before starting the dunning run, you define certain basic data, such as account selection and issue date. An additional log can be activated as required and provides valuable information. If, for example, a dunning notice cannot be executed because the address does not contain a street name, this exceptional situation is displayed in the exception list as well as in the additional log, if this is activated. By defining additional dunning keys for specific items, you can determine that an item is to be dunned only up to a certain level, or that certain items are to be displayed separately and accompanied by some text in the dunning notice. By entering a dunning block, you can exclude certain customers or customer items from dunning. Dunning blocks are defined with different texts.

7.1.6   Are there any specific business transactions in your enterprise that need to be considered in the dunning procedure?

The following questions will throw some light on the large number of different methods for dealing with business cases.

- *How are **credit memos** posted/treated with regard to due dates or offsetting against invoice items?*
  A credit memo normally falls due immediately unless you have created an invoice-related credit memo, in which case the terms of payment of the invoice apply. For invoice-related credit memos, the SAP system transfers the dunning level of the relevant invoice to the corresponding credit memo. For non-invoice-related procedures, the program automatically selects the highest dunning level of the account to set off the credit memo against the longest standing dunning items.

- *Would you like to group certain items in the dunning notice? (**grouping items**)*
  This requires the definition of grouping keys, i.e. grouping criteria for items. In addition, the grouping key must be entered in the customer master record. Dunning run items featuring the same characteristics will then be grouped.

- *Would you like to forward an internal notification to the legal department or lawyer as soon as the highest dunning level is reached? (**legal dunning procedure**)*
  The internal notification can be generated just before the highest dunning level, if an entry is made to that effect. If the legal department initiates a legal dunning procedure, the initiation date must be entered in the customer master record. If a new due item comes up after considering the dunning interval, the legal department will be notified by an internal notification.

- *Do you have any customers with a **branch/head office structure**? Who is to receive the dunning notice?*
  As a rule, a head office settles invoices and thus also receives any dunning notices and other correspondence. If you wish, you can change this by entering the indicator decentralized processing in the customer master record. In this case, the dunning notice (etc.) will be sent to the branch office.

- *Does your enterprise have one-only customers for whom it is not worth creating a special master record but to whom you want to send dunning notices?*
  In this case, you need to consider the following. The SAP system groups all items which contain the same address. Dunning data is maintained in the items.

- *Would you like to dun **customer credit memos**?*
  Or do you have customers who are vendors at the same time, resulting in an overall debit balance that needs to be dunned? You can also dun vendors with a debit balance. For business partners who are both customers and vendors you can determine whether a dunning notice should be sent based on the total sum of all accounts.

7.2   Revenue and cost controlling – example: sales planning

Sales planning refers to the planning of the business output volume (products, services, etc.) you intend to sell on the market within a certain period, taking into consideration the production capacities and the market demand. While revenue planning is not explicitly mentioned in the name of this process, it forms part of it, i.e. how much revenue (= sales volume × price) can be achieved on the market within the period described above. Depending on the planning philosophy, this planning is carried out between once a year and once a week and also differs in duration (Figure 7.2-1).

7.2.1 Do you plan your sales and revenue in the profitability analysis (CO-PA)?

In the SAP system you can carry out sales planning in the LIS (logistics information system) of the enterprise process area, sales and distribution, or in CO-PA (Figure 7.2-2).

Note: If you are working with the LIS in logistics, you have the option of transferring all planned figures and data from LIS to CO-PA and vice versa.

Regarding ①: *Would you like to extend/**develop** your sales and revenue planning into **profit planning**?*

If you plan to extend sales and revenue planning in your enterprise into profit or contribution margin planning, the only sensible way to do so is by using CO-PA, not the

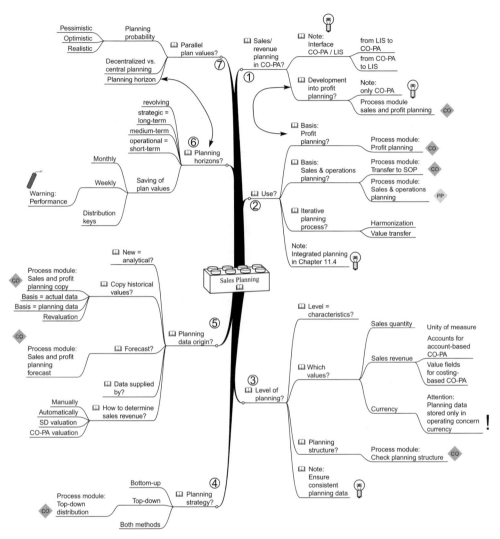

Figure 7.2-1:   Process knowledge map – sales planning

LIS. There are several reasons for this:

- Integration with the total value flow and revenue and cost controlling processes.

- Certain data are not available in the LIS.

- Higher level of detail in CO-PA.

- Planning in CO-PA is more flexible than in the LIS.

For detailed explanations regarding profit planning see process module *profit planning*.

Figure 7.2-2:   EnjoySAP screen for sales planning

7.2.2 Will your sales and revenue plan be used in other functional areas such as production?

The overall business planning process consists of several parts (sales plan, revenue plan, demand program plan, cost plan, financial budget, profit plan, etc.). A distinction is made between strategic and operational planning, planning according to planning horizons, and planning scope (total and partial planning). Apart from the technical aspects offered by SAP, the planning process usually contains several iterative loops between the individual plans which are repeated until all plans have been harmonized. Please specify whether or not, and if so where and how, you intend to reuse the sales and profit plan in your enterprise (Figure 7.2-3).

Note: Integrated planning in the SAP system is described in the SAP Process Library, Finance and Controlling, Chapter 6.4.5, Integrated Planning. Please note that this description only deals with integration in terms of what is technically feasible.

Regarding ②: *Is your sales and revenue plan going to be expanded and developed into **profit planning**?*

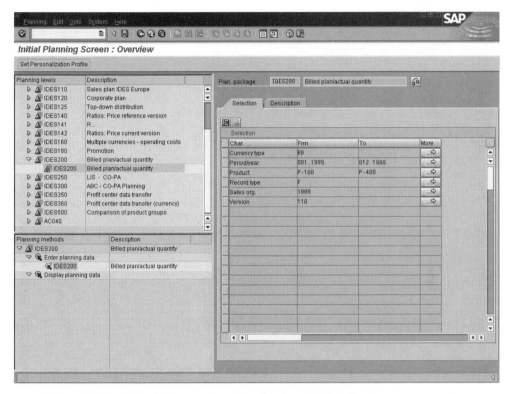

Figure 7.2-3:   EnjoySAP screen for sales planning – initial planning screen overview

If you intend to expand your sales and revenue plan into a profit or contribution margin plan, you need to include, besides sales and revenue figures, the cost of production, general administration, and operation. This expansion may be done manually or automatically (see process module *profit planning*).

Regarding ②: *Is your sales plan going to be the **basis of sales and operations planning**?*

The first draft of the sales plan usually states the production quantity that can ideally be sold on the market and which has been determined by means of market research or forecasts. Based on this draft, sales and operations planning (PP-SOP) can be performed. The sales and operations plan is usually created without bills of material or task lists. It serves to collect general production planning data and to harmonize the sales plan and the production plan. In the process, production capacity is assessed, i.e. is there sufficient/too little/too much production capacity? *Note:* If you intend to automatically transfer sales planning data to sales and operations planning, see process module *transfer sales quantities to SOP*.

Regarding ②: *Does an **iterative planning process** exist in your enterprise, and do you specify it?*

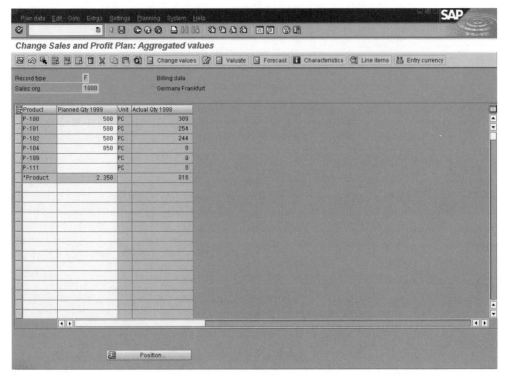

Figure 7.2-4: EnjoySAP screen for sales planning – aggregated values

If concrete planning cycles are used in your enterprise in the framework of an iterative planning process (manual or automatic), you should discuss how sales planning communicates and is harmonized with other plans.

7.2.3 At what level do you plan specific values for sales and revenue planning?

Planning values can be entered in different profitability segments and with different dependencies between these segments. The values planned in the concrete case differ from one enterprise to the next (Figure 7.2-4).

Regarding ③: *In what **profitability segment**, i.e. for which characteristics, do you intend to enter planning data?*

In CO-PA you can enter planning data in profitability segments of various interdependencies which you are free to define, e.g. for products, product groups, product and customer groups, product and country groups, etc.

Regarding ③: ***Which values*** *do you plan?*

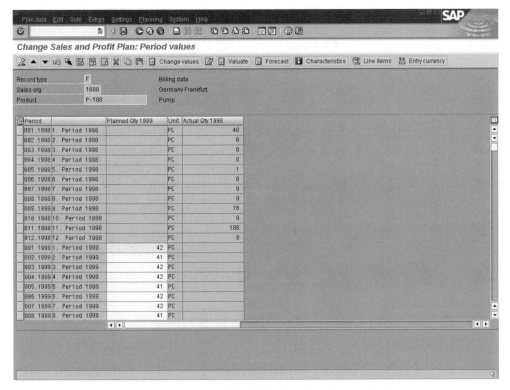

Figure 7.2-5:   EnjoySAP screen for sales planning – period values

You may freely define the level of detail of your sales and revenue planning figures (Figure 7.2-5). For example, sales may be broken down into gross and net sales. In addition, the unit of measure must be specified. For revenues, the level of detail must also be defined, as there is a range of different values, particularly in the area of sales deductions. Moreover, you need to determine the currency you intend to use for planning. Note that in account-based profitability analysis you can plan sales data at account level only.

Note: Planning data is only stored in the currency or currencies of the operating concern (costing-based CO-PA).

Regarding ③: *Should planning levels be based on a certain **structure** that you will define and that they can be checked against?*

Frequently, not all characteristics available for evaluation can or should be used as planning levels. Moreover, it is often necessary for planning levels to adhere to a specific structure. For this purpose, you may define your own structure and check planned values against it (see process module *plan structure check*).

Note: While you may freely choose planning levels in CO-PA, it is not necessary to have an integrated planning level. The system's inherent bottom-up summarization guarantees the consistency of plan values entered for profitability segments at all levels. If, for example, you are planning a product–customer combination and, in another planning session, a customer–country combination, the previously planned values are taken into account and displayed.

7.2.4   Do you pursue a top-down or bottom-up strategy in your sales and revenue planning?

You need to determine whether you intend to use top-down or bottom-up strategies, or a combination of both, for planning. In CO-PA you are able to realize all the above-mentioned options. Bottom-up summarization is always provided by the system, i.e. you can enter plan values at a detailed level, which are then aggregated at a higher level. Top-down distribution is also possible, i.e. you plan data at a high level, and the system automatically distributes it to more detailed levels below according to rules that you are able to define (see process module *top-down distribution*). You can also use a combination of both procedures. This makes it possible to use either decentralized or central planning or a combination of both.

7.2.5   Where does your planning data come from (planning data origin), i.e. do you use analytical planning, planning based on historical values, or mathematical forecast models?

Planning can usually be performed in a number of ways. Therefore, the origin of the plan values must be specified.

Regarding ⑤: *Do you use a **new**, i.e. **analytical** planning for each period?*

In this case, planning data is not based on historical values, but new figures are used for each period (year, month, week) based on, for example, market research results, data provided by sales representatives.

Regarding ⑤: *Are your current plan values based on **historical values** which are **copied** and adapted to the relevant planning period(s)?*

If you are using this method, you will be able to copy historical values to the planning period according to the freely definable rules at your disposal and then adapt them to expected market developments. Actual data or existing planning data can be used as a basis. These values can be adapted either automatically (*revaluation* functionality) or manually by direct modification (see process module *sales and profit planning copy*).

Regarding ⑤: *Are current plan values based on historical values which are **forecast** for the planning period(s) using mathematical models?*

Many enterprises use mathematical probability models to support planning, e.g. first-order exponential smoothing. In this method, historical values are extrapolated to the future and transferred to planning as forecast values (see process module *sales and profit planning forecast*).

Regarding ⑤: *Where does the relevant data come from, i.e.* **which function provides the data**?

Depending on the organizational structure of your enterprise, there are a number of possible scenarios for procuring relevant planning data. First of all you need to clarify whether controllers have the data at hand or can at least find and process it easily, or if they rely on input from other departments in your enterprise, e.g. direct sales.

Regarding ⑤: *How is the* **sales revenue** *to be* **determined**?

In contrast to sales quantities, sales revenues can be planned in several different ways. When planning is from scratch, sales quantities are always planned first. Revenues, which are directly related to sales quantities, can then be planned as follows:

- Plan sales revenue and sales quantity together in the same planning session.

- Determine the sales revenue automatically, as there will be a price list for most articles in sales and distribution, which can be used to valuate the sales quantity. The sales and distribution pricing procedure is used for valuation!

- Determine the sales revenue automatically by using the internal CO-PA rules.

7.2.6   For which planning horizon(s) do you plan sales and revenue figures?

In CO-PA, you are free to define planning periods, using weeks, months, or years. You may also plan across years, i.e. revolving planning is possible. Plan values are always saved per month or per week (if defined in the operating concern).

Warning: If you save each week, performance may be impaired due to large data quantities.

In some cases you may not want to plan data for certain periods (e.g. months) directly but for the entire business year. These annual values can be automatically distributed over the months by using the existing distribution keys or by creating your own.

7.2.7   Do you need to maintain several parallel planning data sets for one and the same profitability segment?

Should it become necessary to store several parallel plan values for the same profitability segment (e.g. Product X and Customer Group 1), this can be done at any time by maintaining plan versions. Reasons for maintaining several values include:

- Planning probability: you can always perform optimistic, pessimistic, and realistic planning.

- Planning horizon: you can distinguish between strategic planning, i.e. where plan values are determined in advance for several years, which reduces planning security, and operational planning, i.e. where you plan a specific business year, for example, which increases planning security.

- Decentralized planning and central planning: decentralized planning is performed directly by sales staff. These planning values are then compared with your own planning values.

7.3   Logistics planning – example: demand management

Demand management determines the requirements date and quantity for planned assemblies, and specifies the strategy for planning finished products. Demand management is the link between planning at the highest level (sales and operations planning) and the planning level of materials and master production scheduling. The requirements dates and quantities are determined for planned materials. Demand management supplies the demand program with independent requirements and it distinguishes between planned requirements and customer requirements. Planned requirements consist of exactly one planned quantity with a due date, or a number of planned requirement schedules (planned quantity divided over a time interval). The receipt of sales orders leads to consumption, and thus the reduction of the planned independent requirements.

Figures 7.3-1 and 7.3-2 show process knowledge maps for demand management. They are discussed through their main branches, 1–8, in the sections which follow.

1. *Which **starting point** do you choose for demand management?*
   Planned independent requirements can be transferred from the preceding plan processes as a starting point (see SAP Process Library, Book 3, Chapter 5.5.2.) There are three display options for the maintenance of planned requirements: planning tables, BOM items, and schedule lines. The planning table is the instrument most commonly used in practice (see branch ⑤ in Figure 7.3-2). Note the relationship to *material* or *product group*.

2. *What **planning strategy** do you use?*
   A planning strategy specifies the planning procedure. In the standard SAP system, you can choose from a selection of strategies or combine more than one. For example, you can plan an assembly with the planning at assembly level strategy, which will later evolve into the finished product with the planning with final assembly strategy. The different demand management planning strategies are specified on the basis of the entries made in the material master. The planning strategies are combined with the requirement types, which from a technical point of view are texts representing the planning strategy in demand management. The requirements type is controlled by the requirements class. The requirements class contains all the control parameters needed for demand management. The most important strategies are briefly described in the following.

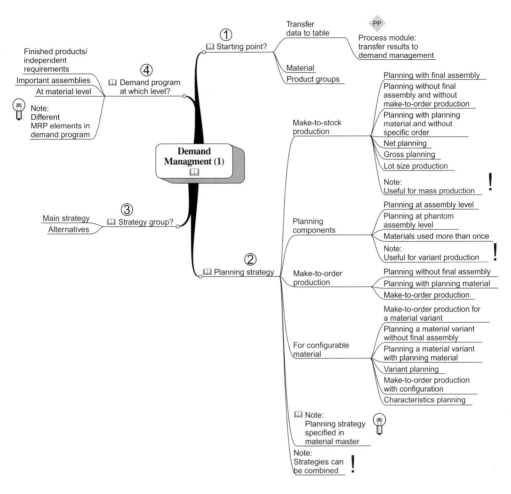

Figure 7.3-1:   Process knowledge map – demand management (1)

- *Make-to-stock production strategies*

  The use of make-to-stock production requires **mass production**, for which consumption of sales orders is not worthwhile. Instead, attention is paid to ensure that the **sales forecasts** are as correct as possible. The sales forecast is announced as planned independent requirements to production. In this case the planned independent requirements are relevant for the production process. Any sales orders which are known at this time are checked in, but only considered in terms of information as registered goods are sold ex-warehouse. The make-to-stock production can be executed either as **gross** or **net requirements planning**. In gross requirements planning, no comparison is made between the warehouse stock and the requirements, whereas net requirements planning compares receipts and issues

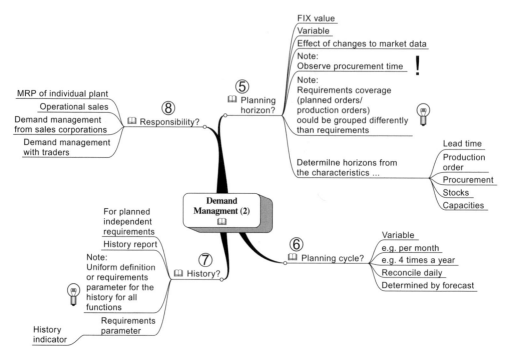

Figure 7.3-2:   *Process knowledge map – demand management (2)*

for a certain deadline. Planned independent requirements are reduced at the time of goods receipt. A consumption period also enables planned sales orders to reduce the planned independent requirements. However, generally issuing goods for a particular sales order will also reduce this sales order. The knowledge map includes a note saying that make-to-order production makes sense for mass production. **Lot size production** on the other hand also enables smaller requirements to be processed ex-warehouse. Production by lot size combines several lots (sales requirements) for a certain deadline (creation of lot sizes from a production-based point of view). With the planning with final assembly strategy, as opposed to make-to-order production, you can achieve a consumption of received sales orders. Thus, you are shown the current requirements situation and can respond flexibly to customer needs. In real life, this strategy is used to plan independent requirements, and the receipt of sales orders triggers final assembly. If your requirements should unexpectedly exceed your planned independent requirements, you can level out these fluctuations by increasing the production quantities in the demand program. A disadvantage of the planning with final assembly strategy is an increase in stock levels if the planned independent requirement quantities are not used up. Planning without final assembly is useful on the other hand if the actual value-added stage is the final assembly and you want to wait until the relevant sales orders have come in. As long as no sales orders arrive, the components or assemblies are kept in storage. The advantage of this planning type is that the planned orders are created with the order type "Plng", i.e. these planned orders can be realized (see process module SAP Process Library, Book 3, Chapter 5.5.6) only after a sales order has been received. Another make-to-stock production strategy is planning with planning material, which can be used for bills of materials (BOMs) with variants and non-variable parts. The special feature here is that planning material passes on dependent requirements for the non-variable parts from the finished product. Using this strategy, you can plan non-variable parts for several finished products. You must create an independent material master record for the planning material.

- *Planning component strategies*
  The planning at assembly level strategy is useful if you use variant production and find it difficult to plan the independent requirements for several variants. In this case you plan joint assemblies for which you can make more accurate requirements forecasts (Figure 7.3-3). With the demand management process you plan independent requirements but no dependent requirements, so that the assemblies in this case are the planned independent requirements. By planning, you trigger the production of assemblies. Sales orders requiring a certain variant as the finished product do not have to exist at the time of planning and production. With the

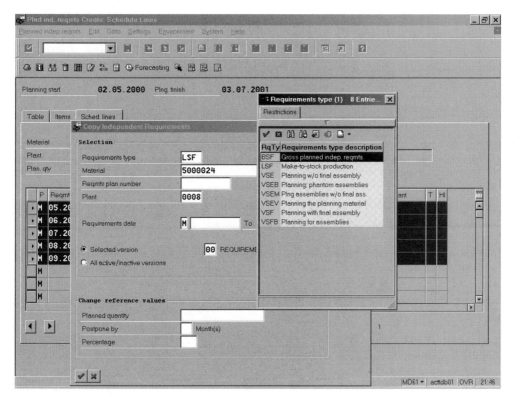

Figure 7.3-3:   EnjoySAP screen for demand planning – requirement type (planning strategy)
Source: SAP AG

receipt of the sales orders, the bill of materials explodes and the dependent requirements which result are consumed by planned primary requirements at assembly level. For consumption to take place, you must set the **consumption indicator** in demand management. Another strategy is planning at phantom assembly level which allows individual components to be grouped to form phantom components. This is a useful strategy if you want to group similar components and plan them together.

- *Make-to-order production strategies*
  The name of the "make-to-order production strategy" already indicates the aim of this planning form – to produce a product specially for a certain customer. Each product is produced only once. Naturally, similar products will be produced on occasions, but each product is made to order. Sales orders are planned directly as requirements for production. Storage is usually unnecessary. You can decide to what extent the BOM should be exploded and what planning is necessary for assemblies. Note that there is an integration interface with CO (controlling) because production and procurement costs are settled directly to the sales order. In an analysis, you can view a direct planned/actual costs comparison.

- *Strategies for configurable material*
  Even when configurable material is used, it can happen that individual configurations occur on a more regular basis, making it useful to plan these configurations. To do so you must create a material master record for configurations which occur regularly. When a sales order is entered, these configurations can easily be changed.

3. *Do you use a **strategy group**?*
   A strategy group can come in useful if you want to use more than one strategy, as described in branch ②. The material or product group can be planned with several planning strategies, although you have to define a main and an alternative strategy. In the material master record you maintain the strategy group which then enables the right requirements type to be automatically determined at the right time. You could also assign the strategy group to the organizational unit material requirements planning (MRP). In this case, you add the MRP group to the material master record. Maintaining the master data of the strategy group or the MRP group renders entering the requirements type in demand management superfluous. The control parameters for planning with valid requirement types are proposed via the strategy group.

4. *At which level do you want to create the **demand program**?*
   Depending on the planning strategy (branch ②), you define the level at which you wish to create the demand program. You generally plan independent requirements in demand management and you must thus define the level at which you want to plan; e.g. if you want to plan at assembly level, you will also define the planned independent requirements at this level. The demand program is created in the form of planned independent requirements. Choose the correct designations of the different MRP elements which are displayed in the current requirements and stock list following demand management (Figure 7.3-4).

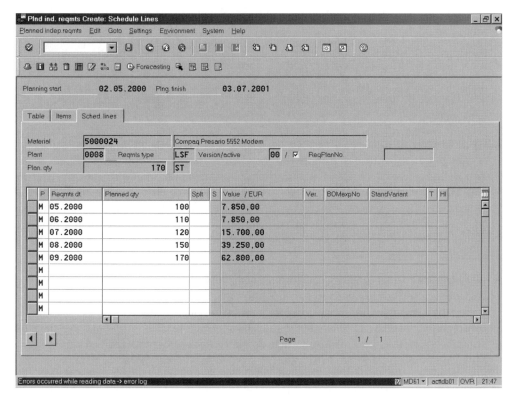

Figure 7.3-4:   EnjoySAP screen for demand management
Source: SAP AG

For example, the MRP element **planning requirements** is indicated for a planned independent requirement, while for external procurement the MRP element **purchase requisition** is used. In the process analysis, we therefore recommend that you analyze MRP elements defined in the standard SAP system to determine requirements.

5. *How do you define the **planning horizon**?*
   The planning horizon (planning period) is unlimited. If you have already specified a period by transferring results to demand management, the planning horizon is transferred from the preceding process sales and operations planning. If you did not enter a period during transfer, the entire period with the reference requirements quantity is transferred. You can define the planning periods in more detail at a later point in demand management. For example, you may change the sales plan which is divided into monthly periods to weeks or days. Of course, a division is useful only if you take into account the characteristics production order, procurement time, lead time, etc. The time divisions refer to a material (independent requirements) or a product group. You can also specify the planning horizon as a fixed value in customizing. Or you can specify a planning horizon for a planning type. A planning type is based on an information structure. This could be a standard information

structure or one structure that you have defined yourself. This gives you almost unlimited possibilities regarding dates that can be planned.

6. *Which **planning cycle** do you define?*
Demand management as a planning process is situated between rough-cut planning sales and operations planning (SOP) and detailed planning (MRP). It is therefore very important that you bring the planning cycle (per month, quarter, etc.) into line with SOP and MRP.

7. *Which standard **history** evaluations can you call up for demand management?*
A change history with descriptions can be created for the demand management plan. You define a history indicator within the requirements parameter to control whether you want to create a **history** or an **original plan** (the first version of a planned independent requirement, which you can use as a template). A change history is useful because the demand program is often planned over a long period following demand management, and several changes could occur within this time period which would be recorded in a change history.

8. *Who is **responsible** for demand management in the enterprise?*
The areas of responsibility shown in the knowledge map are taken as examples from a project, i.e. in this case, demand management would include operative sales, sales corporations, and traders in the distribution network. The sales and distribution organizational units had to supply their demand management forecasts. Generally the MRP (organizational unit: MRP group) of the individual plant is responsible for demand management.

7.4   Production – example: production order processing

Production orders are an essential component of the production planning system. This system is a fully integrated component of the SAP logistics system. It contains, among others, interfaces with the process areas sales logistics, procurement, and revenue and cost controlling. Within an enterprise, internal services are processed by means of orders. A production order specifies which material is to be produced where, when, and how. In addition, it stipulates which resources (capacity) are to be used, and how the order costs are to be allocated. As soon as a planned order or an internal request comes up from preceding planning levels (MRP), shop floor control transfers the existing information and adds pertinent data to the order to ensure complete order processing. Production orders are used to control and monitor production within a company and also as a controlling instrument in cost accounting. Figure 7.4-1 is the subject of the following discussion.

1. *Which **requirements** must be met for production to proceed?*
Operations can proceed when either the individual processes or the entire order have been released and the working documents have been made available. As described in the previous chapter for branch ① (see SAP Process Library, Book 3), individual

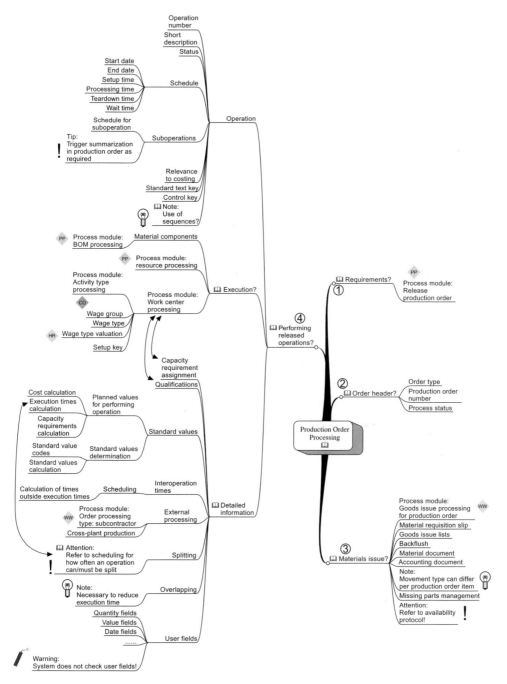

Figure 7.4-1:   Process knowledge map – production order processing

processes may have been released, even if the production order status has been flagged as only partially released. Once you have released a production order, the system automatically sets the system status to "released" accordingly. You cannot change the system status unless you carry out a process which results in a change to the system status.

2. *Which important information from the **order header** do you require for processing?*
   A unique **order number** is very important for production and controlling. This is found in the order header and is assigned to the **order type**. A number range with interval is assigned by means of the order type with the number range group (see branch ② – Control within the process module 7.5.6 SAP Process Library, Book 3). The **status** in the order header documents the current production status. The status changes depending on which processes have been performed. You cannot change the status, i.e. the status cannot be deleted or changed directly (Figure 7.4-2).

3. *How is **goods withdrawal** processed for production?*
   For production to begin, the essential material components must be made available. This happens with the physical issue of goods from the warehouse, although the material has been reserved since the time of opening. When material components are withdrawn, the values in the order are updated as actual costs by cost type (see

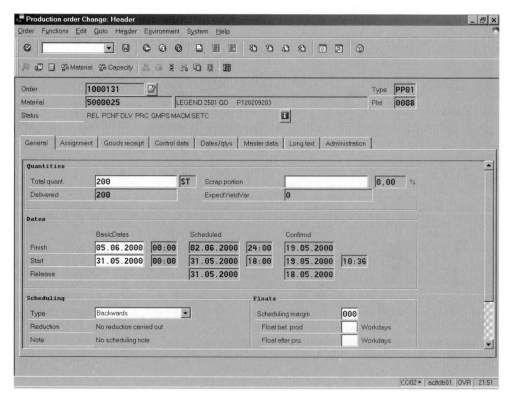

Figure 7.4-2:   EnjoySAP screen for production order processing – header date

Figure 5.5.7-1 branch ①, SAP Process Library, Book 3). The actual costs entered here are used at a later stage for comparison with the planned costs of the production order preliminary costing (Figure 7.4-3).

Material withdrawal can be either planned or unplanned. To withdraw materials for production orders, material requisition slips, goods issue lists, or similar documents are required. Planned material withdrawals are possible only for stocked components and thus not suitable for backflush items. In backflush, material withdrawal is automatically posted when an operation is confirmed (see also the process module *production order confirmation*). Two documents are created each time stock is moved: the material document and the accounting document.

The material document describes the movement of goods from an inventory management aspect and the accounting document from a financial perspective (posting to accounts), always creating a link to a company code. For this reason, it is also possible to have more than one accounting document.

If you issue goods that have been reserved for a production order, this is a planned movement of goods, as mentioned above. Note that movement type can be different for each production order item.

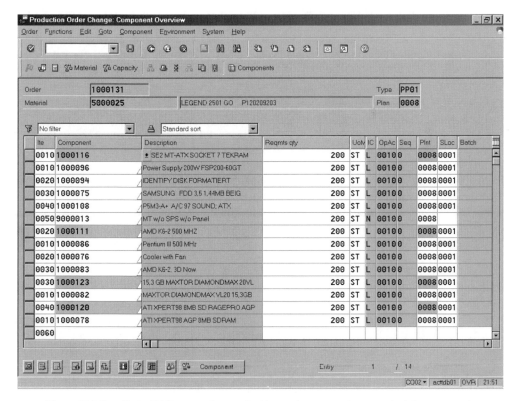

Figure 7.4-3:   EnjoySAP screen for production order processing – material components

The movement type determines the rules for updating the quantity fields and allocating the G/L accounts (automatic account determination) (see Figure 6.5.6-1, SAP Process Library, Book 3).

If the availability check determines missing parts (see branch ② of SAP Process Library, Book 3) material components may not be available for withdrawal for the production order on the calculated requirements date. The **availability protocol** with an overview of the missing parts shows which materials are concerned. In the missing parts overview, you can, for example, change the requirements quantity, determine a different storage location for withdrawing the material, etc.

4. *What information is available while **released operations** are being carried out?*
An **operation** is the description of a production order activity. The operation overview screen lists the scheduled operations which are transferred from routing while the production order is created. Important information is supplied for each operation item, such as the operation number, short description, work center, control key, operation status, schedule (start and end date). An operation is only authorized if it is permitted by at least one status, or if no status prohibits it. The status provides important information regarding the state of production. If the situation changes, a change document is created (protocol). You can list these documents, for example chronologically. The information enables you to understand why a certain operation was permitted or prohibited at a certain point in time. The system lists each status that had an influence on the operation.

The scheduling of an operation (start and end dates, setup time, processing time, teardown time and wait time) depends on the control key (see branch ④ in Figure 7.5.6-2 SAP Process Library, Book 3). Scheduling determines the duration and the earliest and latest date, with time of day, for each operation. The wait time is not considered in the earliest date and time. When determining the latest date and time, the system assumes that the normal waiting time applies. If the control key specifies that an operation is for external processing, the system includes the number of delivery days. Suboperations are given a start and end date depending on the operation reference date. The reference date could be the start date for setting up or the end of processing. In addition, you can collate the default values (values for carrying out the operation) of suboperations to the main operations in the production order. Note that you can trigger the **collation** of default values in the production order.

Other important data concerning the operation are the relevant costing indicator, the standard text key, and the control key, which are described briefly:

- *Relevant costing indicator*: indicates what percentage of activities performed in the operation is relevant to costing. This key is only taken into account if the control key indicates the operation as costing-relevant.

- *Standard text key*: frequently used descriptions of procedures (e.g. lathing or milling) are assigned to this. If a standard text key is entered for an operation, an operation description is assigned to it. You can use this operation description as a template to create your own text.

- *Control key*: specifies which business operations should be carried out for the object of a plan or an order (e.g. scheduling or costing). Control keys are used in different

Control Key	Description	Confirmation
PP01	In-house production	Required
PP02	External production	Milestone confirmation
PP03	In-house production. Display and print only	Confirmation not necessary but possible
PP04	In-house production without confirmation	None

Figure 7.4-4:   Examples of standard control keys for operations

modules and components. Figure 7.4-4 shows to which objects they can be assigned in these areas.

The operations involved in a production order can be brought together in **sequences**, i.e. you create network structures, the nodes of which are linked by upstream and downstream relationships. There are three types of sequences.

- *Standard sequence*
  If you intend to group operations as sequences you need a standard sequence. The first sequence of operations in the production order is known as the standard sequence. The operations of this standard sequence run sequentially. If you intend to use further sequences, you can replace parts of the standard sequence with alternative sequences, or define parallel sequences.

- *Alternative sequence*
  You can replace the standard sequence with an alternative sequence. The order type parameters can be set in customizing and receive an indicator denoting the exchange between standard and alternative sequence. The alternative sequence must be able to branch from and return to the standard sequence. The standard sequence can be replaced by an alternative sequence and vice versa until the operations are released.

- *Parallel sequence*
  The parallel sequence enables the independent parallel processing of operations. It runs parallel to the standard sequence operations. The start of the parallel sequence results from the start of the branch operation from the standard sequence. The end is defined by the return to the standard sequence. Parallel sequences reduce lead times, creating buffer times.

Which requirements must exist for an operation to qualify for **execution**? If the material components (see branch ③) and production tools required for the operations have been made available, the production process can begin. To simplify execution, you can specify the default values for operations and suboperations which are transferred when a work center is assigned. Standard values include wage type, wage group, control key (see previous page for a description of the control key). The personnel calculation rules of incentive wages assign different wage types in the results table depending on the pay procedure. For example, you may have specified a piecework wage per wage group or wages for average pay times, etc.

- *Wage group*: specifies which wage group is to be taken into consideration (short-term training, several weeks training, etc.). The wage group is a classification criterion for valuation of the work. The value is proposed from the work center in routing.

- *Wage type*: specifies the wage type (e.g. piecework wage or premium wage). The wage type is a criterion for calculating an employee's wage or salary. The value is proposed from the work center in routing. Wage type valuation is based on basic valuations. The five steps to valuation are shown in Figure 7.4-5.

Step 1:	Determine work center and basic pay data	Description: The workplace basic pay function places the work center and basic pay data of an employee in the personnel calculation schema.
Step 2:	Form valuation basis for alternative pay	Description: The personnel calculation schema (determination of valuation basis for alternative pay) is run.
Step 3:	Form person-related valuation basis	Description: The personnel calculation schema (determination of valuation basis) reads the processing class (01) for the basic pay type. The pay type is then passed to one of the secondary wage types which form the valuation basis.
Step 4:	Determine wage type based on the valuation basis of Steps 2 and 3	Description: The personnel calculation schema (determination of time wage types) checks whether the time wage types to be valuated with the valuation basis are included.
Step 5:	Valuation	Description: The valuation is also carried out on the basis of the personnel calculation schema (valuation of time wage types), but dependent on the employee subgroup grouping. Employee groups can be formed, e.g. for hourly wage earners, monthly wage earners, salary earners, etc.).

Figure 7.4-5:   Steps to wage type valuation (integration with human resources (HR))

Branch ④ has a sub-branch outlining the **detailed information** available while released operations are being carried out. Operation detail screens can be accessed during execution. Only the most important data of the detail screen is displayed so that you can decide which you require and want to maintain in the future.

The capacity requirement assignment and the process module work center processing are mutually dependent. You can only assign capacities in the production order if you have already defined individual capacities in the relevant work center. Individual capacities are required at the time of capacity planning to achieve more detailed planning of resources and commitments (e.g. machine capacity can be subdivided into several individual machines and you can maintain the available capacity of each machine). If you have not maintained the available capacity for an individual capacity, it is calculated during utilization of the corresponding capacity. Individual capacities have the same **capacity category** as the capacity to which they are assigned. On a further detail screen for the capacity category you can see the qualifications a person is required to have to carry out the operation. The necessary qualifications are determined by jobs, positions, or the requirements profile.

Planned values for performing an operation in the production order are known as **standard values** and are listed in the knowledge map as costs, execution times, and capacity requirements. This overview of the three most important production parameters gives you optimum control of production. You can enter the standard values manually, or the system can determine them automatically. The system can calculate the standard values by means of standard value codes that you have determined (e.g. planning tables).

Apart from the operation scheduling mentioned in the knowledge map, additional detailed data regarding scheduling which is available includes the **interoperation times**. These interoperation times are not included in the execution times and are dependent on the control key. (Operation scheduling is permitted.)

If, during the scheduling of an order (see branch ④ Production order opening, scheduling SAP Process Library, Book 3, Figure 6.5.6-1), it becomes evident that the execution time is longer than the available basic dates, you can implement reduction measures, such as **splitting** or **overlapping** operations. You can maintain data on a detail screen to control when an operation is allowed to be split. Make sure that during scheduling you pay attention to how often an operation can or must be split.

Different types of splits are available; you can split the **quantity** or the **standard values** of the capacity requirements. Quantity splits are useful if partial quantities can be produced by different individual capacities at the same or at different times. Standard value splits are useful if an operation can be subdivided into two or more steps which can be executed at the same time by different individual capacities. To overlap two operations, you must maintain the overlapping data on the operation detail screen of the preceding operation in the production order.

While processing operations, lack of capacity or competence may require that you take advantage of external processing, i.e. operations are processed by external vendors. You can enable this option using a parameter in the control key. In real life, the material components required for the operation are generally provided. The purchasing order (in referring to the purchase requisition) marks components assigned

User Fields	Description
General fields	This refers to texts relevant to the operation (e.g. internal telephone numbers, substitutions, etc.)
Quantity fields	Quantities and units
Value fields	Information with values and units
Date fields	Dates which were not included in the standard (e.g. internal start dates)
Checkboxes	User-defined checkboxes which will later be used for an evaluation

Figure 7.4-6:   User fields for the operation

to external operations as ordered parts. For this processing form, the **subcontractor indicator** must be set on the external processing detail screen. When goods from a subcontractor order are received, consumption posting is carried out for the ordered goods and the costs are assigned to the production order.

The user fields mentioned in the knowledge map are included in the operation detail data for completeness and can be individually defined. You can enter data for the types of user fields shown in Figure 7.4-6.

7.5   Procurement – example: purchase order processing

The purchase order document places an order with the vendor and this is considered to be a contract between the business partners. The price conditions for the ordered quantity (services) are contractually binding and monitored following order processing. If goods have not been received by the agreed deadline, a reminder is sent to the vendor. If some order items are delivered before others, or if there is a partial delivery, the purchase order is monitored by open item management until the final delivery indicator is set in goods receipt processing. The subsequent processes, goods receipt processing, and invoice verification are always carried out with reference to the purchase order. If goods are received without reference to the order, they are generally rejected.

Figure 7.5-2 shows the knowledge map for purchase order processing. Its main branches are discussed in the following sections.

1. *What **data** is transferred **from** which processes, and what manual data input options are available?*
   Purchase orders can be generated automatically from purchase requisition assignments if automation is not hindered by a release strategy (see process module release purchase requisitions SAP Process Library, Book 3, Chapter 7.5.12). If a purchase requisition exists,

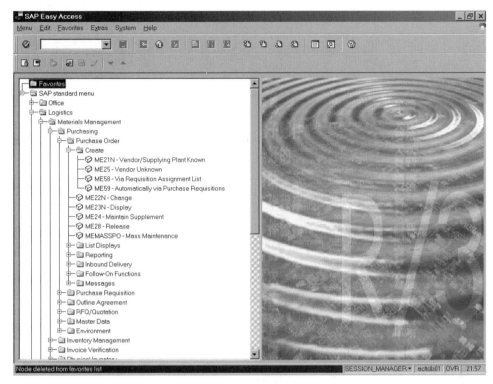

Figure 7.5-1:   EnjoySAP screen – purchase order processing

data can be input indirectly with reference to this purchase document. Several purchase requisitions can be converted automatically in one process step by means of a report (automatic order generation from purchase requisition). The majority of orders can be automated via purchase requisitions, but the direct generation of orders cannot be avoided altogether. The purchaser must still be able to generate an order manually. However, the target must be to plan the procurement of materials by means of purchase requisitions as exactly as possible and thus enable automatic order processing.

The purchaser has two options for generating orders manually.

- *Vendor known*: you generate an order and enter the required vendor directly. A match code search is available to assist selection.

- *Vendor unknown*: you generate an order, but the system automatically determines the source of supply (refer to process module source determination SAP Process Library, Book 3, Chapter 7.5.13).

For orders similar to others generated in the past you can enter the existing order numbers and use these as templates. This reduces time and effort.

2. *How is the purchase **order header** structured?*
The data in the order header is relevant to all following order items, such as the payment and delivery conditions, and certain purchasing texts. The order number,

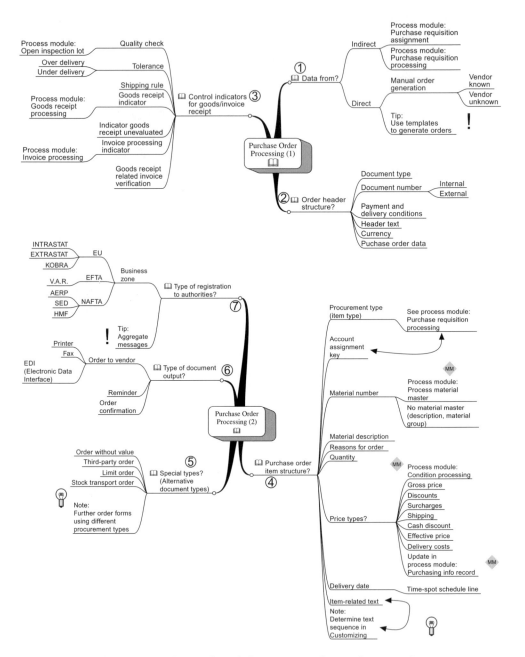

Figure 7.5-2:   Process knowledge map – purchase order processing

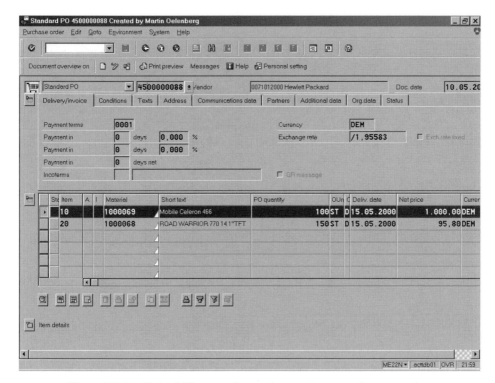

Figure 7.5-3:   EnjoySAP screen for purchase order processing – overview

determined either internally by the system or externally by the user, can be found as a key in the order header and is used as a reference number for the vendor. You can parameterize different order variants in customizing, which are selected as the document type in the order header. The document type determines the type of number assignment, the field selection of the order, the different item types (see branch ④ in the knowledge map), and the links to different purchase requisitions.

3. *Which **control indicators** can you determine for goods/invoice receipt at the time of placing the order?*
   Important control indicators are available on the order form for each order item. These have a decisive influence on the subsequent processes of goods receipt processing and invoice processing. The indicators are as follows.

   • *Tolerance*
   In goods receipt, the correct quantity is not always delivered (e.g. 100 pieces ordered, but 102 pieces delivered). By entering tolerance limits, over- and under- deliveries may be permitted so as not to block a subsequent goods receipt. The goods receipt is posted with reference to the order and tolerance limits are checked.

   • *Quality check*
   This controls the opening of an inspection lot at goods receipt. An inspection lot is generated for a purchase order item if a quality check should be run on that item.

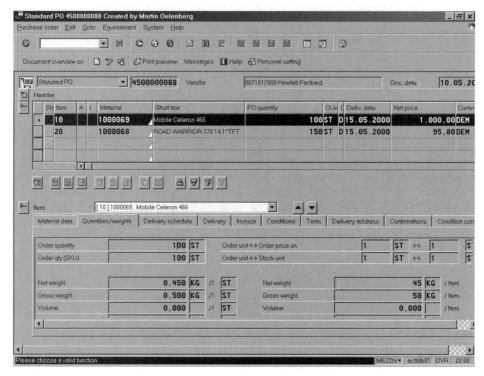

Figure 7.5-4:   EnjoySAP screen for purchase order processing – item

- *Shipping rule*
  This is a key indicating the packing and shipping conditions with which the vendor has to comply.

- *Goods receipt indicator*
  This activates the goods receipt processing process module and updates the purchase order monitor data (open item management, etc.) regarding the extent to which the order has been completed.

- *Indicator goods receipt unevaluated*
  This is set if materials should be evaluated not when goods are received but during invoice verification.

- *Invoice processing indicator*
  This activates the invoice processing process module, thus enabling invoice verification (alternative prices, etc.) with reference to the order.

- *Goods receipt-related invoice verification*
  This activates a goods receipt-related invoice verification. The invoice verification is generally carried out with reference to the order. However, the quantities and prices may not be the same in the purchase document of the order and the goods receipt document, which makes it useful to carry out a goods receipt-related invoice verification.

4. *How is a **purchase order item structured** and what price types are possible and permitted per item?*

For our selected scenario storage material procurement (see Figure 7.5–2, SAP Process Library, Book 3), an order item with a material number is required with a procurement type (item type) **in stock**.

Other procurement types, such as consignment, subcontracting, etc., are possible in the same way as in the purchase requisition process module (see Branch ③ of Figure 7.5.10-1, SAP Process Library, Book 3). If you enter a material in the purchase order which goes directly to consumption, you should specify the necessary account assignment key.

You will find a description of account assignment keys in the purchase requisition process module. They have the same importance when used in the purchase order. An account assignment key determines the type of account assignment (cost center, project, etc.) and specifies which accounts are debited when the invoice is posted, or when goods are received.

If the order item type is determined by the item type and the account assignment type, the quantity and price are determined with the delivery date. You can either determine the net price yourself, or have the system calculate it by means of condition types in the calculation procedure (see condition technique in the sales logistics process module condition processing) (Chapter 7.6). Figure 7.5-5 shows how a calculation procedure is carried out with different price types (condition types) in a purchase order.

You can enter additional information per order item, such as an exact schedule for the delivery date, reasons for the order (e.g. trade fair sales activity), or additional texts which you can differentiate by means of different text types. The location in which a certain text appears on the order document depends on the text type – if you enter a text, the system determines where and in which sequence the text will be output, based on the corresponding text type. Text types are configured in customizing and

Condition Type	Description	Amount	Currency	Per	Unit of Measure
PBXX	Gross price	760.00	US$	1	Piece
	Net value	760.00	US$	1	Piece
NAVS	Non-deductible input tax	0.00	US$		
	Net value incl. input tax	760.00	US$	1	Piece
FRA1	Shipping [%]	3.000	%		
SKTO	Discount	–2.000	%		
	Effective price	767.60	US$	1	Piece

Figure 7.5-5:   Example of conditions in a purchase order

can refer to order header level and item level. Usually, certain requirements are described for an order item and stored as text. Item texts are printed on the form following the order item data (material number, short text, quantity, price, etc.). The following item text types are available in the standard system.

- *Item text*: description of the ordered material. This text can also be imported from the purchase info record process module or from material master processing.

- *Material order text*: you can store special purchase data texts in the purchasing view of the material master process module which can later be transferred to the purchase order.

- *Info order text*: from the purchase info record process module which supplements the material order text.

- *Delivery text*: useful if the delivery instructions for individual material items are different from the overall delivery instructions in the purchase order document. For example, you can indicate that certain goods are to be delivered elsewhere, not with the other materials to the usual location.

- *Supplement texts*: can be added, e.g. on a separate page, for the order items. This is useful if the texts are longer than one page.

5. *What **special types** of purchase orders can you configure with the document type and which do you use?*
One special form is the **stock transport order**. This enables you to transport stock from one plant to another. A prerequisite for this is the transparency of the individual warehouse structures within the enterprise. You can thus see what materials are in stock and which can be procured with a stock transport order.

Another special form of purchase order can occur in the case of sample parts, free gifts, etc. which are entered without a value. For this order, as for other orders, the delivery date is monitored. However, the materials are not represented by values – you create an order with a value of zero.

The **third-party order** is used if you want to procure materials for a third party and have the goods sent to your customer. You place an order with the vendor and pay the invoice when your customer receives the goods from your vendor. Additional control parameters for this special form refer to the item type third party (see branch ④).

Another document type is the control of a **limit order**. This enables you to procure different materials or services up to a certain value (value limit) from a vendor for which the effort involved in processing individual orders is considered too great. For example, you order office materials with a value of $1,000 and enter a validity period instead of a delivery date. The invoices are posted directly with reference to the order, provided that the value limit of $1,000 is not exceeded. The account assignment can be entered at a later stage (see Chapter 7.5-17, SAP Process Library, Book 3).

6. *Which type of **document output (messages)** do you use?*
The document output can be carried out either automatically or manually in purchase order processing, however the individual documents are first sorted in a **transfer queue**. Depending on the transfer procedure, the order can then be printed or transferred via EDI/fax.

In the SAP system, there is a **message determination** in customizing for the individual types of document output. Individual messages are considered as condition records and configured according to the same logic as for the price calculation procedure (see branch ④ **conditions**). The aim of message determination is to manage messages according to previously defined criteria. The output can be controlled differently for each vendor (e.g. vendor 4711 receives the order per fax, vendor 4712 receives a printout). Message determination criteria are:

- message type first printout of order, later printouts as reminder and order confirmation
- purchase document type (purchase order, inquiry, etc.)
- purchase organization
- vendor.

7. *What **type of registration** do you have to send to the **authorities** when working with international vendors?*
   The type of registration required by the authorities depends on the business zone. In Europe, INTRASTAT registration is necessary, and this can be done by means of diskette or magnetic tape (except in Japan where registration must be in paper form). In SAP, the registration data has to be selected from the purchase documents which are entered in a sequential file. Only purchase data posted in financial accounting, and thus declared to be complete, is included. Following registration, this interim file can be updated and overwritten at any time. It is possible to collate messages. With a flexible setting in customizing via the completeness table you can decide, according to your national registration laws, which fields to import as collation criteria. If you do not fill in this completeness table later, the default entries are imported. As a result, the number of lines to be registered is drastically reduced.

7.6   Sales and distribution – example: condition processing

Data for pricing is stored and accessed in the system with the help of conditions. All price elements you wish to use on a daily basis (such as prices, discounts, surcharges for shipment, and taxes) can be stored in the system as condition records (Figure 7.6-1).

1. *What **method** do you use to determine a sales price and of which components does your sales pricing consist?*
   Pricing in SAP offers a wide variety of methods to determine a final price. Here are two examples.

   - A net price is calculated based on a fixed list price per period with discounts for customers and/or promotional discounts.
   - A net price is calculated by adding customer-specific surcharges, based on the goods usage (cost of production or cost price).

   The net price plus value added tax will be the sales price (end price) for the customer in both cases. The method for determining the sales price can be defined by means of

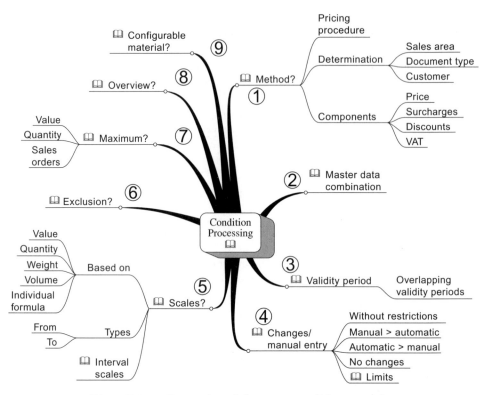

Figure 7.6-1:   Process knowledge map – condition processing

individual pricing procedures in customizing. Different procedures can be defined depending on the sales area, document type, and customer. For example, if a sales department processes sales orders for various foreign customers, these customers can be grouped by country or region. A pricing procedure can then be defined for each customer group. A pricing procedure can contain condition types which define country-specific taxes. You can specify procedures for certain customers and sales document types in sales order processing. The system automatically determines the procedure to be used.

The components of the end price can be divided roughly into four groups: price, surcharges, discounts, and value added taxes. You can combine price elements (known as condition types) from these four groups, thus implementing your method for determining the sales price.

2. *Which **master data combination** do you use to define your price elements (e.g. prices, surcharges, discounts, value added taxes, etc.)?*
   The different price elements (known in SAP R/3 as condition types) of a pricing procedure can be stipulated at different levels. A list price does not have to be specified at material level only, it could also, for example, be different per price list. This means that there is more than one price per material, as prices are specified at material and

price list level. In this case, two price lists can be defined, wholesale and retail. Each customer is assigned one of these price lists and therefore receives the corresponding price for a material. Any number of master data combinations are possible. The most common are available in standard SAP.

- Prices at the levels of:
  sales organization/distribution channel/material
  sales organization/distribution channel/price list/material
  sales organization/distribution channel/customer/material.

- Surcharges/discounts at the levels of:
  sales organization/distribution channel/division/customer
  sales organization/distribution channel/customer/material
  sales organization/distribution channel/customer group/material group.

You can add your own individual master data combinations in customizing as required (Figure 7.6-2).

3. *Do you maintain **validity periods** for your prices, surcharges, and discounts?*
   Condition records for prices, surcharges, and discounts always contain a validity period defined by a start and end date. If you do not enter a validity period, the system

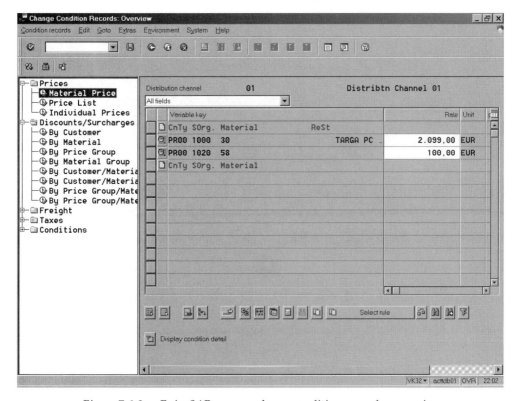

Figure 7.6-2:   EnjoySAP screen – change conditions records – overview

automatically proposes a time period. The validity period proposed is controlled in customizing. You can create different condition records that are the same except for their validity periods. For example, you could create a condition record for a material price which is valid for the entire year. At the same time, you can create a second condition record for the same material with a validity period overlapping that of the first. The second condition record could be, for example, a special sales price for one month during the course of the year.

4. *Do you allow* **changes** *to conditions or* **manual entry** *of conditions in the sales document?*
   During sales order processing, you can make changes to pricing manually. The options available for manual processing depend on the individual condition types. The degree to which each condition type can be manipulated is defined exactly in customizing. The following options are possible.

   • There are no restrictions for manually processing a condition type (this could be the case, for example, for shipment costs).

   • Manual entries have priority over automatically determined pricing results.

   • Automatically determined pricing has priority over manual entries.

   • As a rule, a condition type may not be changed manually (this is the case, for example, for automatically determined sales taxes).

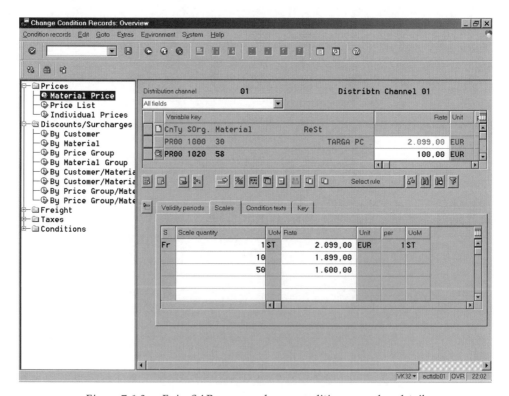

Figure 7.6-3:   EnjoySAP screen – change conditions records – detail

With regards to defining **limits** for condition type changes – if changes are allowed, you can define limits regarding the degree of change permitted. You can specify a price range in the upper and lower limit fields of a condition record, thus restricting the possibilities of manually changing the price in a sales document. If the price is not within the defined price range when the document is entered, the system generates a corresponding error message.

5. *Do you use **scales** for your price elements?*
   When you create a condition record, you can also define scales. For example, you can define a quantity-dependent scale which grants a customer a lower price for a certain product depending on the quantity ordered. The criteria which could form the basis of a scale are: value, quantity, weight, and volume. If these criteria are not sufficient, you can specify individual criteria by means of defining formulas. You must always enter the type of scale. This specifies whether the scale is a "from scale" or a "to scale." In the case of a "from scale" based on quantity, the scale is defined starting from a certain quantity.

   With regards to stipulating prices at each scale level, interval scales enable you to define prices at each level of the price scale for order items. In a normal scale, a price is determined based on the item quantity; the same price applies to each unit of the item. With the interval scale, more than one price can appear on the pricing screen for a single item. In this way, the customer is billed a certain price for the first quantity of items purchased. For items exceeding this quantity a lower price is charged.

   For example:

   - Condition record: material 0815
     Up to 10 pieces $20
     Up to 20 pieces $19
     Up to 30 pieces $18

   - Conditions in sales document (item) with 25 pieces
     $20 per piece = $200 for 10 pieces
     $19 per piece = $190 for 10 pieces
     $18 per piece = $90 for 5 pieces

   - Total $380.

6. *Do your conditions mutually **exclude** each other?*
   The system can mutually exclude conditions so that they are not taken into consideration for pricing in the sales documents. For example, material 0815 costs $150. Some customers receive a discount of $10 per 100 pieces. One customer has been granted the price of $100 per piece. As this is already a special price, this customer should not also be offered the additional $10 per 100 pieces discount. This means that this discount should be excluded from pricing for that customer.

7. *Do you offer certain conditions (e.g. discounts) only up to a **maximum** value over several orders?*
   Customer discounts often are based on cumulative sales order data within the framework of an advertising campaign. If, for example, a customer orders a new product, you could offer an introductory discount up to a certain amount (e.g. $5,000).

When the customer orders the new product, the system must be able to update the cumulated total discount value. The following options are available:

- *maximum value*
- *maximum quantity*
- *maximum number of orders.*

For example, you can specify that a customer should receive a discount of 2 percent for a certain product up to a maximum cumulative discount value of $1,000. When the customer orders the product, the system revalues the cumulative discount value and stores this data at condition record level. As soon as the cumulative discount level reaches $1,000 the discount is automatically deactivated.

8. *Do you create **overviews** (e.g. price lists) of the conditions in the system?*
   If you want to get an overview of the condition records which exist in the system, you can generate condition lists. Condition lists group information from condition records according to different criteria. You create condition lists based on the following types of questions:

   - What customer-specific price agreements were made within a certain time period?

   - What condition records for freight exist in the system?

9. *Do you work with **configurable materials** and does the sales price have to be determined on the basis of characteristic evaluation?*
   The system also offers you the option of determining the price for configurable materials in sales order processing. To determine the relevant surcharges or discounts, complex automatic pricing rules can be set. If you enter a configurable standard material in a sales order and specify values for certain characteristics, the system automatically calculates the prices for the specified values. If, for example, you configure an automobile in a sales order and enter ABS as an optional extra, the system automatically determines the correct surcharge and adds it to the sales order price.

7.7   Customer service – example: service contract

A service contract is an agreement covering the content and scope of services to be performed for a customer. It describes which services are to be performed, for which objects, and under which conditions. Thus you determine, for instance, which customer service tasks are covered by the contract for the specified objects, at what intervals the work is to be performed (response and availability times), what prices apply to the work, on what dates periodic invoicing is to take place, and what cancellation regulations apply. As a service provider you mainly use service contracts to:

- verify customer entitlements regarding service requests;
- agree on prices for service orders;
- send invoices on a regular basis;
- determine service notification tasks automatically.

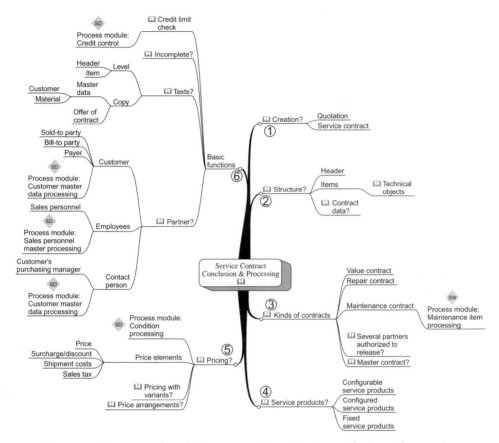

Figure 7.7-1:   Process knowledge map: service contract – conclusion and processing

Figure 7.7-1 shows the knowledge map for a service contract.

1. *Can service contracts be **created** in your enterprise with reference to existing quotations?*
   It is possible to create a new service contract for an existing document. If, for example, a customer accepts one of your quotations, the system can transfer all relevant master data from the quotation when creating the service contract. When a service contract is created with reference to a document, a dialog box appears in which you can choose between the following options:

   • copy (transfer) all items to the new document;

   • transfer some items to the new document (select items).

   In the standard system you can create a service contract with reference to a quotation or service contract, e.g. as part of the service contract follow-up activities (Figure 7.7-2).

2. *How is your service contract **structured**?*
   The service contract is a special type of sales order. It consists of a header and one or more items. The header contains the sold-to party. Contract data, a billing plan, and

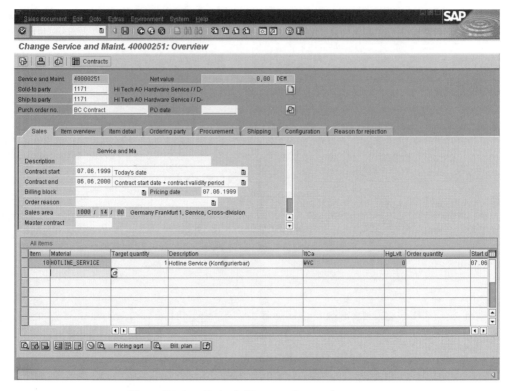

Figure 7.7-2:   EnjoySAP screen for service contract

price agreements may also be stored in the header. This data applies to all items unless you have entered different data for individual items. Order items consist of services, service products, and conditions. Moreover, contract data, a billing plan, and price agreements may also be stored at item level as well as the technical objects on which the services in question will be performed.

Each contract item can be allocated one or several **technical objects**. The contract item is valid for the technical objects allocated to it. Based on the object allocation, a contract can be selected in the service notification, the service contract, or the maintenance item for the reference object entered. A service contract may thus comprise all customer equipment or, at the other end of the spectrum, a separate service contract may be created for each individual piece of equipment.

If you use service contract-relevant agreements for validity periods you will need to enter contract validity data. This includes the contract start, contract end, and other contract-relevant dates (contract conclusion, installation, service acceptance, dismantling date). Contract start and end dates can be determined via date determination rules. Like business data, contract-specific data is stored both in the header and in the individual contract items. The header data applies to all contract items, provided that you do not define different data for individual items.

3. *What kinds of **service contracts** do you conclude with customers?*
   In a contract, you agree with your customer to deliver a certain quantity of products and services within a specified period. Such a contract may, for example, contain additional agreements on special prices. By basing their business relations on a contract, both partners are in a better position to plan their business processes. In the SAP system, contracts are represented in the form of sales document types. The SAP standard system provides a range of different document types, which you can use either directly or as a template for your own processes.

   - *Value contract*
     An outline agreement between your enterprise and a customer, in which the customer agrees to purchase goods and services up to a certain total value (target value) within a specified period.

   - *Repair contract*
     This kind of contract can be concluded for general price agreements, for example. When a service notification is received for a technical object, a repair contract is assigned to the object and the individual price agreement is applied in resource-related billing.

   - *Maintenance contract*
     This type of contract is concluded for products that require ongoing maintenance over a long period of time. If the contract contains an obligation to perform periodic services (e.g. regular inspections), it is linked to a maintenance plan (the maintenance plan automatically creates service orders). This ensures integration of contract agreements and service procedure.

   In addition to the actual contact person, **other business partners** will frequently require authorizations to release against a contract. The headquarters of a group may determine which companies or branches should be authorized to release against an agreed contract.
   In enterprises with complex contract structures, several contracts are often controlled by the same business function. These requirements can be stored in **master contracts**, which are linked with lower level contracts. The master contract contains general framework conditions applying to all referenced lower level contracts. This ensures consistency of all general data throughout lower level contracts. The master contract contains only header data – it does not contain items. In the master contract, you find a list of all lower level contracts linked to it. From this list, you can access the individual lower level contracts. The lower level contract is a standard document, e.g. a service contract containing a reference to a master contract. If you have made settings in customizing to update lower level contracts, changes in the master contract are automatically transferred to all lower level contracts in the workflow.

4. *What types of **service products** do you offer in long-term service agreements?*
   An enterprise can offer its customers different kinds of service products in the framework of contracts and agreements. Depending on your customizing settings, you can choose from the following options.

   - *Configurable service product*
     Service contracts may contain different variants. The product "inspection service" provides different options for the service interval, service radius, and service

location. The service product can be configured via characteristic valuation in the contract. Concrete examples of customizing settings are:
  service interval → monthly
  service location → at customer site
  service radius → less than five hours.
The conditions for the service product usually depend on the characteristic values.

- *Configured service product*
  Characteristic values for configured service products are taken from the evaluation in the material master. They cannot be changed in the contract. For inspection services, for example, two concrete variants can be stored with service materials:

	Inspection service 1	**Inspection service 2**
Service interval	monthly	quarterly
Service location	customer site	customer site
Service radius	less than five hours	less than 24 hours

Frequently used variants can thus be stored in the system. The conditions that apply to the service product also depend on the characteristic values.

- *Fixed service product*
  Defined product without variants and with a price which refers to an activity quantity and a period.

5. *How do you determine **prices**, surcharges, and discounts in the service contract?*
   The net price of a service, i.e. a material, can consist of several price elements. Usually, the net price is calculated by applying discounts or surcharges to a material based on its gross price. In addition, sales taxes are taken into account. The different price elements that you use in your regular pricing procedure are stored in the SAP system as condition types. When entering or maintaining condition types, you create condition records in the system. For further information on creating and maintaining condition records and the basics of the condition technique see process module condition processing (Chapter 7.6). Pricing elements are divided into three main categories for the SAP standard system.

   - *Prices*
     In the SAP standard system, pricing within sales order processing is based on the gross price of a material. The following competing levels (condition tables) are provided. The priority of an individual level is determined by the access sequence.
     - *Material price*
       General price (list price) of the materials within the sales organization and distribution channel.
     - *Price list type*
       Based on the pricing policy of your enterprise you can define your personal price list types to suit your business requirements. For example, you may define price list types for customer groups (wholesale, retail, etc.). Condition records are

created for each price list type. You use the same organizational data as for material prices (sales organization, distribution channel).

– *Customer-specific price*
Special price agreements with customers can be stored in customer-specific condition records in the system. Condition records are assigned to a specific customer/material combination, and the same organizational data is entered as for material prices (sales organization, distribution channel).

- *Surcharges/discounts*
The SAP standard system contains a range of absolute and percentage discounts at different levels (such as customer, customer/material, customer/material pricing group, customer group) which are used in the sales document.

- *Sales tax*
The standard version of the SAP system provides condition types that determine country-specific taxes. There are, for example, value added tax (VAT) condition types for several European countries. For US tax determination the standard version contains sales tax condition types at state, county, and city levels, as well as taxes based on tax jurisdiction codes. For automatic VAT calculation, the following factors are taken into consideration:
  – type of business case (domestic or foreign business);
  – tax classification of the goods recipient (e.g. charity organizations are exempt from value added tax);
  – tax classification of the material (some products are exempt from taxation, others are subject to lower tax rates).

By applying these criteria, the tax rate for each item in the sales order is determined.

Prices, or surcharges and discounts, may have to be determined based on characteristic value assignment for products containing variants. To determine relevant surcharges or discounts for products containing variants, complex automatic pricing rules can be applied. When you enter a configurable standard material in an order and specify values for certain characteristics, the prices for the values entered are calculated automatically. If, for example, you configure a service within a service contract and enter "24 hours" as availability time, the system automatically finds the correct surcharge and adds it to the contract price.

Regarding ⑤: *Do you agree on contract-specific **price arrangements** with customers?*
You can use price agreements to define contract-specific price arrangements. For example, you may want to offer some customers a special discount on spare parts that are required for a service in the framework of the service contract. Condition records for price agreements can be created for:
- all activities of a specific contract;
- a specific material or a material pricing group that is required as a spare part for a service in the framework of a service contract.

If you perform a **credit limit check** at the time of service contract processing, in the framework of credit management, this can be performed at the time of service contract entry or modification. For details on this functionality see the process module credit control, SAP Process Library, Book 4, Chapter 5.5.13.

Some information in the service contract might be regarded as obligatory, i.e. if it were not provided, follow-up activities would be impaired or prevented. The incompletion log will notify you if any important data is still missing in your service contract. When you create a service contract, defaults are proposed from customer and material master data. You can manually enter any additional data or change defaults, as required. The service contract is the basis for various follow-up activities such as billing. However, these downstream functions can often only be performed if the data entered in the service contract is complete. To ensure data completeness, the system logs all missing data in an incompleteness log and informs you of the fact that it still needs to be entered. For a complete sales document, for example, the following data must be entered: purchase order number, conditions of payment, material, order quantity, price. If you do not enter this data, the corresponding fields are included in the incompleteness log and all further processing may be blocked.

If you need **texts** for your service contracts, they may be used internally or externally (e.g. print contract confirmation). You can define any number of texts (general contract requirements, sales texts, cancellation notice, etc.) for service contracts (header and item level). Individual text settings can be made in customizing. Moreover, the following processing and control functions are supported:

- master record texts (customer master, material master, and customer material information record) are proposed as default values in sales documents if set;
- texts can be copied from a reference sales document to another sales document (e.g. from a service contract quotation to a service contract);
- copying of texts may be language-dependent;
- copied texts may be changed;
- standard texts can be integrated into sales documents.

In the SAP standard system, not all document texts are activated for sales form output. Many are for internal information only and will not appear on sales form printouts. Thus, you can maintain data for the contact person in service contract headers which provides important information for sales employees but does not appear on the customer's contract confirmation. You can define which texts should not just be used internally but also appear on sales forms.

Business **partners** for a sales order are identified via different partner roles. The type of partner is defined for each partner role, i.e. is the partner a customer, contact person, or employee? The most important partner roles with customer accounts are sold-to party, bill-to party, and payer. These roles are marked as obligatory in the standard system, as a sales order cannot be processed without them. The different partners in a sales order are transferred from the sold-to party's customer master. This default can be changed manually by the user at any time. Further important partners include the contact person (e.g. the customer's purchasing manager) and employees (e.g. the sales representative in your enterprise). For more details about creating master data for different partners see process module processing customer master data, SAP Process Library, Book 4, Chapter 5.5.1.

Authors

Jürgen Röhricht

Jürgen Röhricht began working as a consultant in the area of financial accounting for SAP in 1994. In this position, he was able to gain considerable experience dealing with the implementation and functionality of the R/3 system working on several national and international projects for large and medium-sized companies. As co-project manager and in charge of rolling out, he was also able to put the process-oriented procedure and methodology into practice in business process optimization and organization modeling projects. Between August 1998 and November 1999 he was marketing manager in the area of corporate marketing, responsible for SAP's implementation solutions. He is currently marketing manager for the marketing department of the SAP internet solutions subsidiary e-SAP.de.

Thomas Teufel

Thomas Teufel has been with SAP since 1993 and has put the process-oriented approach into practice in a number of consultancy projects. He focusses on process organization and the development of creative methodology in the area of knowledge management. He is currently working on an industry template based on the "Mapping the Maps" principle. He also lectures at the technical college in Mannheim.

Birgit Teufel-Weiss

Birgit Teufel-Weiss has been a consultant in the area of financial accounting since 1994. She works for an SAP logo partner, SFO, in Constance and is working on a medium-sized company solution (R/3 ready-to-work) with a team of consultants. She is a believer in simple and pragmatic ways of implementing R/3 which is of particular importance to the medium-sized companies that form their target group.

Peter Willems

Peter Willems has been working with SAP as a consultant for logistics since 1994. He spent three years as an application and integration consultant in the areas of sales and distribution and service management. He has been working primarily as a project manager for process-oriented SAP R/3 implementations since the end of 1997.

References

As SAP is a German company much of the relevant material is only available in German. We have included details here for interested parties.

Albrecht, F., Strategisches Management der Unternehmensressource Wissen – Inhaltliche Ansatzpunkte und Überlegungen zu einem konzeptionellen Gestaltungsrahmen, Frankfurt a.M., 1993.

Allweyer, T., Wissensmanagement mit ARIS-Modellen, in: Scheer, A.-W., ARIS – Vom Geschäftsprozeß zum Anwendungssystem, Berlin, Heidelberg, New York, 1998, pp. 162–168.

Antal, A. B., Lerntransfer vom Individuum zur Organisation – Wie kann Organisationslernen gefördert werden?, in: Krebsbach-Gnath, C. (Hrsg.), Den Wandel in Unternehmen steuern – Faktoren für ein erfolgreiches Change Management, Frankfurt a.M., 1992, pp. 85–102.

Bach, V., Vogler, P., Österle, H. (Hrsg.), Business Knowledge Management, Praxiserfahrung mit Intranet-basierten Lösungen, Springer Verlag, 1999, pp. 20–23.

Balzert, H., CASE Auswahl, Einführung, Erfahrungen, Mannheim, 1993.

Bancroft, N. H. et al., Implementing SAP R/3 – How to introduce a large system into a large organization, Greenwich, CT, 1998.

Baßeler, U. et al., Grundlagen und Probleme der Volkswirtschaft, Köln, 1990.

Bell, D., Die nachindustrielle Gesellschaft, Frankfurt a.M., 1975.

Boll, M., Prozeßorientierte Implementation des SAP Softwarepaketes, in: Wirtschaftsinformatik Nr. 35, 1993, p. 5.

Brenner, W., Hamm, V., Prinzipien des Business Re-engineering, in: Brenner, W., Keller, G. (Hrsg.), Business Re-engineering mit Standardsoftware, Frankfurt a.M., New York, 1995, pp. 24–27.

Buck-Emden R., Galimow, J., Die Client/Server-Technologie des SAP-systems R/3, 2, Auflage, Bonn et al., 1995.

Bullinger, H.-J., Groh, G., Graß, G., Bartenschlager, F., Praxisorientierte TCO-Untersuchung: Ein Vorgehensmodell, in: IM Fachzeitschrift für Information Management & Consulting, Ausgabe 2/98, Saarbrücken, 1998, pp. 13–18.

Bürkle, U., Rascher Return on Investment, in: SAPInfo Nr. 57, Walldorf, July, 1998, pp. 12–13.

Buzan, T., Buzan, B., Das Mind-map-Buch, Landsberg am Lech, 1997.

Champy, J., Re-engineering Management – The Mandate for New Leadership: Managing the Change to the Re-engineered Corporation, New York, 1996.

Cohen, D. et al., Managing Knowledge for Business Success, in: The Conference Board, Report Number: 1194–97-CH, New York, 1997.

Davenport, T., Process Innovation – Re-engineering Work Through Information Technology, Boston, 1993.

Davenport, T., Knowledge Management – Some Principles of Knowledge Management, Texas, 1996.

Davenport, T., Paßt Ihr Unternehmen zur Software?, in: Harvard Business Manager Nr. 1, 1999, pp. 89–99.

Davenport, T., Working Knowledge: How Organizations Manage What They Know, Boston, 1997.

Drucker, P. F., Wissen – die Trumpfkarte der entwickelten Länder, in: Harvard Business Manager, 20, Jahrgang, Book 4, 1998.

Falterbaum, H., Beckmann, H., Buchführung und Bilanz. Grüne Reihe für Studium und Praxis, Book 10, 15. Auflage, Achim bei Bremen, 1993.

Franz, K.-P., Die Prozeßkostenrechnung. Darstellung und Vergleich mit der Plankosten- und Deckungsbeitragsrechnung, in: Ahlert, D. et al., (Hrsg.), Finanz- und Rechnungswesen als Führungsinstrument, Wiesbaden, 1990, pp. 109–136.

Freimuth, J. et al., Auf dem Weg zum Wissensmanagement: Personalentwicklung in lernenden Organisationen, Göttingen, 1997.

Gaarder, J., Sofies Welt. Roman über die Geschichte der Philosophie, München, 1993.

Gabler Wirtschaftslexikon, Books L – P. 12 Auflage, Wiesbaden, 1988.

Gaitanides, M., Prozeßorganisation – Entwicklung, Anstze und Programme proßurientrerter Organisationsgestaltung, München, 1983.

Gartner Group, Die Industrie hat übertrieben Erwartungen, in: Handelsblatt Nr. 221 vom Montag, 15.11.1999, Ohne Seite.

Gfaller, H., SAP lehnt sich weit aus dem Internet-Fenster, in: Computer Woche Nr. 38/99.

Gibbons, M. et al., The New Production of Knowledge – The Dynamics of Science and Research in Contemporary Societies, London, 1994.

Groh, G., Fähnrich K.-P., Total Cost of Ownership in der Praxis. Ein nützliches Instrument zur Evaluation der Informationstechnologie, in: Neue Zürcher Zeitung, ORBIT Sonderausgabe, Zürich, 22.09.1998.

Grupp, B., Anwenderorientierte Istanalyse und Sollkonzeption, Köln, 1993.

Gutenberg, E., Grundlagen der Betriebswirtschaftslehre, Erster Band: Die Produktion, 18, Auflage, Berlin, Heidelberg, New York, 1971.

Haberstock, L., Kostenrechnung I. Einführung, 8, Auflage, Hamburg, 1994.

Haberstock, L., Kostenrechnung II. (Grenz-) Plankostenrechnung, 7, Auflage, Hamburg, 1993.

Hackett, B., The Value of Training in the Era of Intellectual Capital, in: The Conference Board, Report Number 1199–97-RR, New York, 1997.

Hagel III, J., Armstrong, A. G., Net Gain – Profit im Netz: Märkte erobern mit virtuellen Communities, Wiesbaden, 1997.

Hammer, M., Champy, J., Re-engineering the Corporation – A Manifesto for Business Revolution, London, 1994.

Hammer, M., Das prozeßorientierte Unternehmen – Die Arbeitswelt nach dem Re-engineering, Frankfurt a.M., 1996.

Harrington, J., Computer Integrated Manufacturing, New York, 1973.

Heinrich, J., Burgholzer, P., Systemplanung II, 4, Auflage, München, Wien, 1990.

Herzog, E., Jurasek, W., Vertriebscontrolling im System der Grenzplankostenrechnung, in: Männel, W., Müller, H. (Hrsg.), Modernes Kostenmanagement – Grenzplankostenrechnung als Controllinginstrument: Beiträge der Plaut Gruppe, Wiesbaden, 1995, pp. 131–136.

Hess, O., Internet, Electronic Data Interchange (EDI) und SAP R/3, in: Hermanns A., Sauter, M., Management-Handbuch Electronic Commerce, München, 1999, pp. 185–196.

Horvath, P., Prozeßkostenrechnung: Ein Ausweg aus der Krise des Rechnungswesen, in: Script zum Vortrag auf dem IMT-Kongress 'Prozeßkostenrechnung', in Berlin, 1990, Ohne Seite.

Hüsken, W., TCO-basierte SAP R/3 Betriebsführung, in: IM Fachzeitschrift für Information Management & Consulting, Ausgabe 2/98, pp. 19–23.

Information Week, 'Schöne neue digitale Welt', August 1999.

IWI-HSG Institut für Wirtschaftsinformatik der Universität St. Gallen, AcceleratedSAP – 4 Case Studies, St. Gallen, 1998.

Kagermann, H., Perspektiven der Weiterentwicklung integrierter Standardsoftware für das innerbetriebliche Rechnungswesen, in: Horvath, P. (Hrsg.), Strategieunterstützung duch das Controlling – Revolution im Rechnungswesen? Stuttgart, 1990, pp. 277–306.

Keller, G., Nüttgens, M., Scheer, A.-W., Semantische Prozeßmodellierung auf der Grundlage 'Ereignisgesteuerter Prozessketten (EPK)', in: Veröffentlichung des Instituts für Wirtschaftsinformatik, Heft 89, Saarbrücken, 1992.

Keller, G., Teufel, T., SAP R/3 prozeßorientiert anwenden – Iteratives Prozeß-Prototyping zur Bildung von Wertschöpfungsketten, Bonn, 1997.

Kidler, B., Lowest Cost of Ownership, in: SAPInfo, Heft 57, pp. 20.

Kilger, W., Einführung in die Kostenrechnung, 3, Auflage, Wiesbaden, 1992.

Kilger, W., Flexible Plankosten und Deckungsbeitragsrechnung, 10, Auflage, Wiesbaden, 1993.

Kirchmer, M., Business Process-oriented Implementation of Standard Software, Berlin, Heidelberg, 1998.

Krebsbach-Gnath, C., Wandel und Widerstand, in: Krebsbach-Gnath, C. (Hrsg.), Den Wandel in Unternehmen steuern – Faktoren für ein erfolgreiches Change Management, Frankfurt a.M., 1992, pp. 37–56.

Krebsbach-Gnath, C., Den Wandel im Unternehmen steuern, in: Krebsbach-Gnath, C. (Hrsg.), Den Wandel in Unternehmen steuern – Faktoren für ein erfolgreiches Change Management, Frankfurt a.M., 1992, pp. 7–18.

Meinhardt, S., Teufel, T., Business Re-engineering im Rahmen einer prozeßorientierten Einführung der SAP-Standardsoftware, in: Brenner, W., Keller, G. (Hrsg.), Business Re-engineering mit Standardsoftware, Frankfurt a.M., New York, 1995, pp. 69–94.

Mellerowicz, K., Kosten und Kostenrechnung – Verfahren. Book II, Teil 2: Kalkulation und Auswertung der Kostenrechnung und Betriebsabrechnung, Berlin, 1968.

Mezger, T., Wegbereiter: SAP Solution Maps für umfassende Branchenlösungen, in: SAPInfo, Nr. 58, October, 1998.

Möhrlen, R., Kokot, F., SAP R/3 Kompendium, München, 1998, p. 22.

Moore, G. A., Inside The Tornado – Marketing Strategies from Silicon Valley's Cutting Edge, New York, 1995.

Müller, A., Vom Geschäftsprozeßdesign zum prozeßorientierten Managementsystem, in: Scheer, A.-W. (Hrsg.), Neue Märkte, neue Medien, neue Methoden – Roadmap zur agilen Organisation, 19, Saarbrücker, Arbeitstagung 1998 für Industrie, Dienstleistung und Verwaltung, Heidelberg, 1998, pp. 179–192.

Nachreiner, B., Balance braucht Weile – Faktoren der Führung in lernfähigen Unternehmen, in: Krebsbach-Gnath, C. (Hrsg.), Den Wandel in Unternehmen steuern – Faktoren für ein erfolgreiches Change Management, Frankfurt a.M., 1992, pp. 57–84.

Neumann, S. et al., Knowledge Management Systems – optimaler Einsatz des 'Produktionsfaktors Wissen', in: Scheer, A.-W. (Hrsg.), Neue Märkte, neue Medien, neue Methoden – Roadmap zur agilen Organisation, 19, Saarbrücker Arbeitstagung 1998 für Industrie, Dienstleistung und Verwaltung, Heidelberg, 1998, pp. 193–224.

Nuppeney, W., Raps, A., Produktkostencontrolling im System der Grenzplankostenrechnung, in: Männel, W., Müller, H. (Hrsg.), Modernes Kostenmanagement, Grenzplankostenrechnung als Controllinginstrument, Beiträge der Plaut Gruppe, Wiesbaden, 1995, pp. 110–120.

Ohne Autor, Eine runde Sache, Industry Business Solutions schaffen noch mehr Kundennähe, in: SAPInfo, Nr. 57, July, 1998.

Ohne Autor, Schöne neue digitale Welt, in: Themenheft E-Commerce, Information Week, August, 1999.

Olfert, K., Kostenrechnung. Kompendium der Praktischen Betriebswirtschaft, 8, Auflage, Ludwigshafen (Rhein), 1991.

Österle, H., Business Engineering – Prozeß- und Systementwicklung, Book 1: Entwurfstechniken, 2, Auflage, Berlin et al., 1995.

Pawlowsky, P. (Hrsg.), Wissensmanagement: Erfahrungen und Perspektiven, Wiesbaden, 1998.

Perez, Mario, Hildenbrand, A., Matzke, B., Zencke, P., Geschäftsprozesse im internet mit SAP R/3: Chance zur Neugestaltung betriebswirtschaftlicher Informationswege, Bonn, 1998.

Pfohl, H.-C., Stölzle, W., Anwendungsbedingungen, Verfahren und Beurteilung der Prozeßkostenrechnung in industriellen Unternehmen, in: Zeitschrift für Betriebswirtschaft, Ausgabe 61/1991, pp. 1281–1305.

Plattner, H., Neue Wege für das Controlling in einem hochintegrierten Anwendungssystem, in: Scheer, A.-W. (Hrsg.), Rechnungswesen und EDV, 8, Saarbrücker, Arbeitstagung 1987, Heidelberg, 1987, pp. 58–81.

Plaut, H.-G., Die Grenzplankostenrechnung, Zweiter Teil: Grundlagen der Grenz-Plankostenrechnung, in: Männel, W., Müller, H. (Hrsg.), Modernes Kostenmanagement – Grenzplankostenrechnung als Controllinginstrument, Beiträge der Plaut Gruppe, Wiesbaden, 1995, pp. 20–31.

Popp, K., Business Process Re-engineering mit dem R/3-Referenzmodell, in: SAPInfo, Thema: Business Re-engineering, Heft März, 1995.

Preiser, S., Buchholz, N., Kreativitätstraining – Das 7-Stufen-Programm für Alltag, Studium und Beruf, Augsburg, 1997.

Probst, G. et al., Wissen managen: Wie Unternehmer ihre wertvollste Ressource optimal nutzen, Wiesbaden, 1997.

Raps, A., Reinhardt, D., Projekt-Controlling im System der Grenzplankostenrechnung, in: Männel, W., Müller, H. (Hrsg.), Modernes Kostenmanagement – Grenzplankostenrechnung als Controllinginstrument, Beiträge der Plaut Gruppe, Wiesbaden, 1995, pp. 121–130.

Reiß, M., Wandel im Management des Wandels, in: Scheer, A.-W. (Hrsg.), Neue Märkte, neue Medien, neue Methoden – Roadmap zur agilen Organisation, 19, Saarbrücker Arbeitstagung 1998 für Industrie, Dienstleistung und Verwaltung, Heidelberg, 1998. pp. 264–276.

Reiß, M., Change Management als Herausforderung, in: Reiß et al., (Hrsg.), Change Management: Programme, Projekte und Prozesse, Stuttgart, 1997, pp. 6 ff.

Riepl, L., TCO versus ROI, in: IM Fachzeitschrift für Information Management & Consulting, Ausgabe 2/98, 1998, pp. 7–12.

Rißmann, M. et al., Electronic Commerce – Der Kampf um den Konsumenten auf der neuen Agorà, in: Hermanns A., Sauter, M., Management-Handbuch Electronic Comerce, München, 1999, pp. 141–156.

SAP AG (Hrsg.), Funktionen im Detail – Ergebnis- und Vertriebs-Controlling, Walldorf, 1996.

SAP AG (Hrsg.), Funktionen im Detail – Gemeinkosten-Controlling, Walldorf, 1996.

SAP AG (Hrsg.), Funktionen im Detail – Hauptbuchhaltung, Walldorf, 1996.

SAP AG (Hrsg.), Funktionen im Detail – Materialwirtschaft, Walldorf, 1998.

SAP AG (Hrsg.), Funktionen im Detail – Integrierte Produktionsplanung und – steuerung, Walldorf, 1997.

SAP AG (Hrsg.), Funktionen im Detail – Produktkosten-Controlling, Walldorf, 1996.

SAP AG (Hrsg.), Funktionen im Detail – Prozeßkosten-Controlling, Walldorf, 1996.

Scheer, A.-W., Architektur integrierter Informationssysteme, Berlin, et al., 1991.

Scheer, A.-W., Wirtschaftsinformatik – Informationssysteme im Industriebetrieb, 3, Auflage Berlin et al., 1990.

Scheer, A.-W., ARIS – Vom Geschäftsprozeß zum Anwendungssystem, 3, völlig neubearbeitete und erweiterte Auflage, Saarbrücken, 1998a.

Scheer, A.-W., ARIS – Modellierungsmethoden – Metamodelle, Anwendungen, 3, völlig neubearbeitete und erweiterte Auflage, Saarbrücken, 1998b.

Schmalenbach, E., Die fixen Kosten und ihre Wirkungen, in: Saar-Wirtschaftszeitung, 33, Jg, Völklingen, 1982.

Schneider, U. (Hrsg.), Wissensmanagement: Die Aktivierung des intellektuellen Kapitals, Frankfurt a.M., 1996.

Schöning, U., Logik für Informatiker, Mannheim, 1989.

Schüppel, J., Wissensmanagement – Organisatorisches Lernen im Spannungsfeld von Wissens- und Lernbarrieren, Wiesbaden, 1996.

Servatius, H.-G., Re-engineering Programme umsetzen – Von erstarrten Strukturen zu fließenden Prozessen, Stuttgart, 1994.

Servatius, H.-G., Vom Re-engineering zum Wissensmanagement, in: Scheer, A.-W. (Hrsg.), Neue Märkte, neue Medien, neue Methoden – Roadmap zur agilen Organisation, 19, Saarbrücker Arbeitstagung 1998 für Industrie, Dienstleistung und Verwaltung, Heidelberg, 1998, pp. 323–351.

Seubert, M., Entwicklungsstand und Konzeption des SAP-Datenmodells, in: Scheer, A.-W.

(Hrsg.), Datenbanken 1991 – Praxis relationaler Datenbanken, Fachtagung, Saarbrücken, 1991, pp. 87–109.

Seubert, M., Schäfer, T., Schorr, M., Wagner, J., Praxisorientierte Datenmodellierung mit der SAP-SERM-Methode, in: Informatik – Zeitschrift der schweizerischen Informatikorganisationen, 2 (1995) 1, pp. 15–23.

Sinz, E. J., Das Entity Relationship Model (ERM) und seine Erweiterungen, in: Handbuch der modernen Datenverarbeitung – Theorie und Praxis der Wirtschaftsinformatik, 27 (1990) 152, pp. 17–29.

Spek, R.v.d., de Hoog, R., Towards a methodology for knowledge management, Technical Note Knowledge Management Network, 23, November 1994, http://ceres.cibit.nl/web/kmn/pospaper.nsf.

Stocker, T., Die Kreativität und das Schöpferische, Frankfurt a.M., 1988.

Striening, H.-D., Rationalisierungsanalysen und -maßnahmen im Gemeinkostenbereich, in: Witt, F.-J. (Hrsg.), Aktivitätscontrolling und Prozeßkostenmanagement, Stuttgart, 1991, pp. 131–149.

Striening, H.-D., Prozeß-Management, Frankfurt a.M., 1988, pp. 20–50.

Sveiby, K. E., Lloyd T., Das Management des Know-how, Führung von Beratungs-, Kreativ- und Wissensunternehmen, Frankfurt, 1990.

Taylor, D. A., Business Engineering with Object Technology, New York et al., 1995.

Teufel, T., Ertl, F., Prozeßorientierte Einführung mit dem R/3-Analyzer, in: SAPInfo – Business Re-engineering, 1995, pp. 22–24.

Teufel, T., Wertschöpfung pur, Der Business Engineer hilft Michehls auf die Sprünge, in: SAPInfo – Erfolg durch IT-Management, Mittelstand, November 1997, pp. 50–52.

Thome, R., Hufgard, A., Continuous System Engineering – Entdeckung der Standardsoftware als Organisator, Würzburg, 1996.

Tushman, M. L., O'Reilly, C. A., Unternehmen müssen auch den sprunghaften Wandel meistern, in: Harvard Business Manager, 20, Jahrgang, Book 1, 1998.

Uhle, M., Die LEGO Story – Der Stein der Weisen, Frankfurt, 1998.

Vester, F., Standpunkt – Die totale Information, in: Bild der Wissenschaft, July 1995, pp. 14–15.

Vikas, K., Beinhauer, M., Gemeinkostencontrolling im System der Grenzplankostenrechnung, in: Männel, W., Müller, H. (Hrsg.), Modernes Kostenmanagement – Grenzplankostenrechnung als Controllinginstrument, Beiträge der Plaut Gruppe, Wiesbaden, 1995, pp. 99–109.

Warnecke, H. J., Die Fraktale Fabrik – Revolution der Unternehmensstruktur, Reinbek bei, Hamburg, 1996.

Weisberg, R., Kreativität und Begabung – Was wir mit Mozart, Einstein und Picasso gemeinsam haben, Heidelberg, 1989.

Wildemann, H., Virtuelle Markplätze: die Zukunft des industriellen Einkaufs, in: Frankfurt Allgemeine Zeitung, vom 11, October, 1999, p. 34.

Wöhe, G., Einführung in die Allgemeine Betriebswirtschaftslehre, 19, Auflage, München, 1996.

Wolf, K., Holm, Ch., Total Cost of Ownership – Kennzahl oder Konzept, in: IM Fachzeitschrift für Information Management & Consulting, Ausgabe 2/98, pp. 19–23.

Wüthrich, H. A., Philipp, A. F., Virtuelle Unternehmen – Leitbild digitaler

Geschäftsabwicklung, in: Hermanns A., Sauter, M., Management-Handbuch Electronic Comerce, München, 1999, pp. 49–60.

Zencke, P., Modellgestützte R/3-Systemkonfiguration für eine Betriebswirtschaft des Wandels, in: SAPInfo – Continuous Business Engineering, pp. 6–9.

Zerdick, A. et al., Die internet–Ökonimie – Strategien für die digitale Wirtschaft, European Communication Council Report, Berlin/Heidelberg/New York, 1990.

Index

Page numbers in italics refer to diagrams; page numbers in bold represent core sections on the subject